Praise for *RESTful Web Clients*

"An accessible, sensible book on the importance of hypermedia APIs that anyone working with APIs should read, whether you are a business stakeholder all the way up to an existing hypermedia skeptic—a must read."

—*Kin Lane, The API Evangelist*

"*RESTful Web Clients* is a timely, much needed deep dive on a very important part of the API landscape."

—*John Musser, CEO, API Science*

"This book does a great job of explaining the basics and benefits of hypermedia and clearly articulates how client apps can make use of them. A must read for both API producers and consumers."

—*Lorinda Brandon, API Strategist and Evangelist*

"A must read for API practitioners who want to discover a way to design web applications with more resilience, agility, and reusability for both the short and the long term."

—*Mehdi Medjaoui, Founder of APIdays conferences/OAuth.io*

"A great resource on what to consider and implement when building RESTful web APIs and clients. I highly recommend it for anyone trying to build reusable APIs."

—*Jeremy Wilken, Software Architect*

"Whether you are a frontend or backend developer, reading this book will help you shift your understanding of designing and consuming APIs into higher gear."

—*Mark W. Foster, Enterprise Architect, Distributed Systems*

"This book is a must have for anyone building hypermedia based systems. It broaches one of the toughest and least understood topics head on, how to build hypermedia clients."

—*Glenn Block, Director of Product Management for Auth0*

"Mike's delightful writing and technical excellence tells an easy-to-understand and relatable story that takes you from an RPC-style rookie to a hypermedia connoisseur in just a few pages. Impressive and highly recommended reading!"

—*Asbjørn Ulsberg, Business Architect, PayEx*

"This book delivers on the piece developers have been missing about hypermedia: Learn to stop worrying and love responding to what the server sends."

—*Brian Sletten, President of Bosatsu Consulting, Inc.*

"*RESTful Web Clients* shows how applying hypermedia correctly results in a smaller, generic codebase that can adapt and evolve as the server's capabilities change."

—*Erik Mogensen, Chief Architect, Escenic*

"APIs change, clients break. But does it have to be this way? What if they could not only survive, but adapt to change? This book is your guide through this adventure."

—*Carles Jove i Buxeda, Full-stack Developer and OS Contributor*

RESTful Web Clients
Enabling Reuse Through Hypermedia

Mike Amundsen

Beijing · Boston · Farnham · Sebastopol · Tokyo

RESTful Web Clients

by Mike Amundsen

Published by O'Reilly Media, Inc., 1005 Gravenstein Highway North, Sebastopol, CA 95472.

O'Reilly books may be purchased for educational, business, or sales promotional use. Online editions are also available for most titles (*http://www.oreilly.com/safari*). For more information, contact our corporate/institutional sales department: 800-998-9938 or *corporate@oreilly.com*.

Editor: Meg Foley	**Indexer:** WordCo Indexing Services
Production Editor: Colleen Lobner	**Interior Designer:** David Futato
Copyeditor: Gillian McGarvey	**Cover Designer:** Randy Comer
Proofreader: Jasmine Kwityn	**Illustrator:** Rebecca Demarest

February 2017:   First Edition

Revision History for the First Edition

2017-02-06:   First Release

See *http://oreilly.com/catalog/errata.csp?isbn=9781491921906* for release details.

978-1-491-92190-6

[LSI]

This book is dedicated to all those who have had to endure my repeated promises to write it. My apologies to you all—for all my promises and for the modest results that appear within these pages.

Table of Contents

Foreword

In the foreword to this book's precursor, *RESTful Web APIs* (O'Reilly), Sam Ruby says:

> Hopefully the pebbles that [*RESTful Web APIs*] kicks loose will have the same effect as its predecessor [*RESTful Web Services*] did. Who knows, perhaps in another seven years it will be time to do this all over again, and highlight some other facet of Representational State Transfer that continues to be under-appreciated.

Well, it hasn't quite been seven years, but this is exactly where *RESTful Web Clients* comes in. Mike has quite the pedigree in the API space and, with this text, has brought his usual style of clarity, both in writing and in thought, to this oft-ignored part of web APIs.

Roy Fielding's dissertation, *Architectural Styles and the Design of Network-based Software Architectures*, is the definitional text of REST. In the very first section, Fielding describes the seven essential architectural constraints that describe REST. The first one is called *client–server*, and is described like this:

> Separation of concerns is the principle behind the client–server constraints. By separating the user interface concerns from the data storage concerns, we improve the portability of the user interface across multiple platforms and improve scalability by simplifying the server components. Perhaps most significant to the Web, however, is that the separation allows the components to evolve independently, thus supporting the Internet-scale requirement of multiple organizational domains.

Clearly, servers and clients are both incredibly important to this way of designing systems. However, there's been a bias in the works done that build on top of Fielding: almost all of them focus on the servers, and rarely discuss the clients. But doing so leaves out an incredibly important part of the picture: many of the benefits of a RESTful architecture can only be realized with a properly designed client. There are many systems which have a client-server style, but aren't driven by the same principles as the Web. If we must adapt the way that we code servers to make them more web-like, so must we change the way we code clients.

And indeed, this is a difficult part of moving to a "web way of thinking" when it comes to building APIs. I have had many, many discussions with organizations interested in deploying hypermedia techniques who then struggle when it comes to putting them into practice. I believe that a lot of the difficulty here comes from this focus on the *production* of hypermedia, without also considering the changes to the way that you *consume* it. An API designer who expects to build a client for a web API using the same principles as other APIs is going to be frustrated with the results. Yet this is completely understandable, as those of us who advocate this architectural style have often focused almost entirely on production.

In hindsight, this deficiency seems quite obvious: how can we design systems properly if we only focus on half of the equation! I actually believe that this situation is a second-order effect of the way that the majority of people consider APIs today: my organization focuses on how to have an API for my product, but since it's your organization that consumes it, it's your job to deal with it. This underlying sentiment has been magnified by the trends of the last five to ten years with APIs: a move toward "simple APIs that don't require a complex SDK to get useful work done." An organization that provides an API client is often viewed with skepticism. We're now starting to see this turned around, as developers grow tired of re-implementing new API clients for every API they wish to use. First-party SDKs are now being viewed in a positive light, as consumers of these APIs can focus more on their application, and worry less about integration.

Furthermore, the Web is increasingly being viewed as an application platform, rather than as a way to easily share text documents. With the rise of proprietary platforms, especially in the mobile space, those who love the free and open nature of the Web are mobilizing to significantly expand the Web platform's capabilities. To take advantage of this, applications are sprouting more and more JavaScript code as their products grow more ambitious. These applications are yet another kind of client, and one that's becoming more and more important by the day.

As the gestalt shifts, organizations are in a position to once again consider both sides of the equation. In a broad sense, I think this will lead to even better APIs, but it's not all roses. As I mentioned before, there are no end to the books you can purchase to help you understand the server side of the equation. But there's a complete dearth of similar manuals for the client side—until now.

I have been eagerly awaiting this book since Mike first told me he was starting to work on it, and he has not disappointed. It is a fantastic guide to this underserved part of the web API equation, and I am confident that its impact and influence will be noted for years to come. I would tell you that I hope you'll enjoy reading this book as much as I did, but I don't need hope—I know you will.

— Steve Klabnik, July 2016

Preface

"The beginning is the most important part of the work."

  —Plato

Web-based REST and hypermedia services are getting more common every day but there are very few client libraries that take advantage of these powerful API features. This is mostly because the techniques and patterns needed to create successful hypermedia *clients* have been ignored. Yet, when done right, hypermedia-based client applications exhibit more stability and flexibility than typical one-off custom client code.

The aim of this book is to give developers both a solid background and a source of working examples that provide clear recommendations for dealing with hypermedia-style APIs. One of the key ideas in this book is that client applications should rely on something I call the *Request, Parse, Wait* loop or RPW. This is the way all computer games are implemented and it is the way all event-driven interfaces work from windowing-style workstations to reactive machine interfaces.

I've been told that some frontend developers might find the RPW model unusual; one person even characterized my recommendations as "radical." I can understand that viewpoint. So many of the client libraries and practices today focus on designing specially built one-off user interfaces that are difficult to modify and have a hard time reacting to new information provided by services at runtime. However, after reviewing the examples in this book, I hope that frontend developers—most all of whom are much more skilled than I—will be able to build on this initial work and help create a rich collection of best practices, tooling, and reusable libraries for creating high quality user experiences for the growing number of hypermedia APIs, which meet both the desire for high-quality user experience and the need for adaptive clients that can keep up with evolving service interfaces without the need for constant upgrades.

What's in This Book

This book takes the reader on a journey from custom bespoke implementations to powerful general-purpose client applications and, along the way, shows how you can harness many of the basic principles that underpin the World Wide Web. The outline is a mix of code-centric chapters and ones that explore important related topics like the representor pattern, human–computer interaction (HCI) modeling, and the challenge of versioning web APIs. Along the way, there is quite a bit of code (over 20 GitHub repos were created for this book). I'll use small snippets of code within the text of the book, but sometimes those snippets will be hard to understand by themselves. For that reason, I'll always point the reader to the full code repository online where you'll find fully functional examples of the ideas covered in the book.

The Chapters

This book explores the world of generic hypermedia-style clients—what they look like, how they differ from typical JSON-object style clients, and how both client and server developers can leverage this style to build systems that are easier to support and adapt over time. The book contains chapters targeting a small set of selected formats (HTML, plain JSON, HAL, Siren, and Collection+JSON) as well as chapters that go into the background on the theories and practices familiar to all web developers, including (1) server-side support for message formats, (2) human–computer interaction modeling, (3) versioning, and (4) implementing a single solution that supports multiple hypermedia formats while interacting with several independent back-end services.

Most chapters can stand on their own and could be consumed in any order. But I encourage you to treat the book as a single journey and read it from start to finish in order to get the most out of it. Here is a brief look at how that journey will unfold:

Chapter 1, Our HTML Roots and Simple Web APIs
> This chapter introduces us to a classic HTML-only client. We'll use this to quickly review how browsers work and how they've affected some people's view of what's possible with hypermedia formats on the Web. This chapter also covers the process of converting an HTML-only service output into an initial JSON-only API service. This service will be the basis for all the other client apps we build for this book.

Chapter 2, JSON Clients
> Most client-side web developers have learned to build "JSON clients." They memorize URLs, consume static objects, and navigate over fixed workflow paths. This is a great way to *start* but turns out to be a terrible way to work over time. In this chapter we'll explore ways to overcome the challenges of maintaining plain JSON-style client apps.

Chapter 3, The Representor Pattern

The representor pattern is a simple—and vital—way to deal with web API server output. It is the process of converting internal object models into external message models. We'll review the pattern (including its roots) and cover how we'll apply it for providers using the Web Service Transition Language (WeSTL) on the server and the HTML DOM on browser clients.

Chapter 4, HAL Clients

The HAL media type is currently one of the more popular hypermedia formats. It is used, for example, by the Amazon Web Services team for at least two of their APIs. HAL handles one of the three important elements all web clients deal with: ADDRESSES. We'll see what it's like to build a generic client using HAL as the message format and introduce the HAL-FORMS extension for improving its action-handling capabilities.

Chapter 5, The Challenge of Reusable Client Apps

You'll notice that most of the client applications we'll build here look similar. Essentially, we're building "explorers" that can—in some limited way—fend for themselves as they explore the world around them. These clients follow a pattern called the Request, Parse, Wait loop, or RPW. This pattern is based on several classic notions of how we interact with our world, and we'll explore them here.

Chapter 6, Siren Clients

Another powerful hypermedia type is the Siren content type. Currently used as part of the Zetta IoT platform, Siren is designed to handle two of the three key tasks of a web client: ADDRESSES and ACTIONS. We'll see what it's like to build a generic client using Siren as the message format and we'll explore a Siren extension (Profile for Object Display, or POD) that enhances its ability to handle metadata for UI displays.

Chapter 7, Versioning and the Web

What happens to the notion of API versions when you start using hypermedia types as the basis for client-side web applications? This chapter looks at the various attempts to manage change over time and how relying on message-based hypermedia-style APIs reduces the need to change the interface *contract* when you change the interface *features*.

Chapter 8, Collection+JSON Clients

In this chapter we'll explore another hypermedia format—Collection+JSON, or Cj. Cj is able to handle all three of the key elements of web clients: OBJECTS, ADDRESSES, and ACTIONS. We'll see what it's like to build a generic client using Collection+JSON as the message format and learn how to extend Cj's data display and validation routines.

Chapter 9, Hypermedia and Microservices

What would it take to create a single generic hypermedia client that could seamlessly consume multiple services? And what if those services each emitted different hypermedia media types? What would it take to craft a single client application that is "multilingual" when it comes to message format? We'll see how that looks in our final chapter.

The Dialogues

All of the chapters in this book start and end with short vignettes or dialogues. These are fictional conversations offered as a way to illustrate some of the challenges and thought processes that happen in any organization working to implement scalable, robust projects on the WWW. These dialogues also act as stage settings and summaries for the primary theme of each chapter.

The dialogues are also meant to act as prompts to give you a chance to start thinking about the challenge as presented and how *you* would approach it and come up with a solution. It may be helpful to start by reading through the dialogues and then take a few minutes to map out (maybe even write down) your ideas about how to solve the problem. Taking the time to interact with the material in this way can result in some additional insight into both the solution that is provided and your own skills in problem solving.

Finally, I've added these dialogues so that those who are interested in only skimming the book can still get quite a bit out of the experience. Hopefully, you can read through the dialogues alone and glean the basics of the material. The chapters are then the place where the details and subtleties of the material is explored in depth. You may find that, for at least some of the chapters, reading the dialogues gives you all the information you are looking for on a particular topic or challenge—and that's fine, too.

The Artwork

The book includes diagrams and artwork by some very talented people. Dana Amundsen, an accomplished artist based in Louisville, KY, worked with me to create the characters Carol and Bob who appear throughout the book. She also designed the BigCo logo you see in the sample apps. It turns out Dana created much more material than I could include in this book and I hope I can share that art via other means in the near future.

The diagrams you see in this book were created by my good friend, Diogo Lucas; a very skilled software developer, architect, speaker, and teacher. I first met Diogo while on a trip to Brazil (where he lives) when he showed me his amazing dashed-off sketches of some of the ideas I'd been working on for this book. I jumped at the chance to invite him to create the illustrations and, luckily, Diogo agreed to lend his considerable artistic talents to this project.

Licensing

All the artwork in this book created by Dana and Diogo is licensed under Creative Commons - Attribution-NoDerivatives 4.0 International (CC BY-ND 4.0).

Both Dana and Diogo have added something special to the book and I thank them both very much.

What's Not in This Book

This book covers quite a bit of ground in a relatively short number of pages. In order to do that, I needed to leave out quite a bit of helpful material. Here's a quick run-down of what I decided to *not* include in this book.

User Interface Design

While I refer to some material on user interface design in the book, those references are cursory. I also do not spend any time on the details of human–computer interaction (HCI) or design methodology in general.

I should also give the reader a heads-up that this book provides a basic UI look-and-feel in the examples. My primary focus is on the network- and message-level techniques that allow services to provide recognizable and useful hypermedia hints to client applications. I also spend time on client-level coding best practices for parsing and activating these hypermedia signals. I leave the work of decorating these interfaces with improved visual appeal to others who are more skilled in this art.

Special thanks to Benjamin Young

I need to give special recognition to my long-time friend and skilled web developer, Benjamin Young. He took the time to extensively review my rudimentary UI designs and provided a coherent look-and-feel to all the client applications. Truth be told, I gave Benjamin limited room to be creative and he still produced a solid, consistent style guide for all of the apps. If they look at all pleasing, that's a reflection of Benjamin's talent and persistence. If they fall short in any way, that's because I didn't allow him the freedom he needed.

Basics of Hypermedia

This book also does not spend much time on the value of hypermedia as an implementation style or go very far to make the case for using hypermedia in your own projects. My work on previous books, *RESTful Web APIs* (with Leonard Richardson) and *Building Hypermedia APIs with HTML5 and Node* (both from O'Reilly), are better sources for the history and value of using hypermedia for web APIs, and I encourage the reader to look there and to other sources for this kind of information.

Programming with HTML, CSS, and JavaScript

Finally, I don't devote any pages to the basics of programming on the Web in general, such as the topics of HTTP protocol, HTML5, JavaScript, and CSS. These are all very important subjects and well beyond the scope of this small book. There are many books on these subjects and I am confident the reader can find what they are looking for elsewhere.

Source Code

There is quite a bit of related source code for this book. Almost every chapter has at least one relevant project and some have two or more. Including *all* the source code in the pages of this book would make it tedious to read and difficult to navigate. For that reason, only short snippets of important code blocks appear in the text.

The entire set of source code is available in a public Git repo (*https://github.com/rwcbook*). The repos will be updated from time to time and should be considered the most accurate source for any code that appears in the pages of this book. Readers are encouraged to clone/fork the code in the repos and create pull requests for any needed changes.

External References

Throughout the book, I make references to external source material including other books, published papers, articles, public standards, and blog posts. In the text, I will mention the reference but not include a direct citation or footnote as that tends to interrupt the flow of the material. Instead, I will add a section at the end of each chapter that includes the name of the source and, where appropriate, online links to the cited material.

Conventions Used in This Book

The following typographical conventions are used in this book:

Italic
> Indicates new terms, URLs, email addresses, filenames, and file extensions.

`Constant width`
> Used for program listings, as well as within paragraphs to refer to program elements such as variable or function names, databases, data types, environment variables, statements, and keywords.

`Constant width bold`
> Shows commands or other text that should be typed literally by the user.

`Constant width italic`
> Shows text that should be replaced with user-supplied values or by values determined by context.

 This element signifies a tip or suggestion.

 This element signifies a general note.

 This element indicates a warning or caution.

O'Reilly Safari

 *Safari* (formerly Safari Books Online) is a membership-based training and reference platform for enterprise, government, educators, and individuals.

Members have access to thousands of books, training videos, Learning Paths, interactive tutorials, and curated playlists from over 250 publishers, including O'Reilly Media, Harvard Business Review, Prentice Hall Professional, Addison-Wesley Professional, Microsoft Press, Sams, Que, Peachpit Press, Adobe, Focal Press, Cisco Press, John Wiley & Sons, Syngress, Morgan Kaufmann, IBM Redbooks, Packt, Adobe Press, FT Press, Apress, Manning, New Riders, McGraw-Hill, Jones & Bartlett, and Course Technology, among others.

For more information, please visit *http://oreilly.com/safari*.

How to Contact Us

Please address comments and questions concerning this book to the publisher:

O'Reilly Media, Inc.
1005 Gravenstein Highway North
Sebastopol, CA 95472
800-998-9938 (in the United States or Canada)
707-829-0515 (international or local)
707-829-0104 (fax)

We have a web page for this book, where we list errata, examples, and any additional information. You can access this page at *http://bit.ly/restful-web-clients*.

To comment or ask technical questions about this book, send email to *bookquestions@oreilly.com*.

For more information about our books, courses, conferences, and news, see our website at *http://www.oreilly.com*.

Find us on Facebook: *http://facebook.com/oreilly*

Follow us on Twitter: *http://twitter.com/oreillymedia*

Watch us on YouTube: *http://www.youtube.com/oreillymedia*

Acknowledgments

A book like this does not happen without lots of input and assistance from several people. I am especially grateful to all those who volunteered to read and comment on early drafts of the book. In particular, I'd like to thank Todd Brackley, Carles Jove i Buxeda, Pedro Felix, Mark Foster, Toru Kawamura, Mike Kelly, Steve Klablnik, Ronnie Mitra, Erik Mogensen, Irakli Nadareishvili, Leonard Richardson, Kevin Swiber, Stefan Tilkov, Ruben Verborgh, and Jeremy Wilken for all their feedback and advice in shaping the book.

I'd also like to thank the team at O'Reilly for all their support and trust. Especially Meg Foley and Simon St.Laurent, who had the unenviable task of constantly prodding me and encouraging me through the long process of making this book a reality. Also, a big thanks to my production editor Colleen Lobner, who had to endure my endless picking at minor layout and font details while she worked to make my material presentable. And I'd especially like to thank my colleagues in the API Academy and CA Technologies for all their help and support throughout the project.

Finally, thanks to my family for once again having to deal with me as I worked through my ideas, hunkered down with headphones for long stretches, and as I stared off into space pondering details and testing scenarios in my head. They dealt with my temporary malady as best they could—with patience and humor. Thanks.

Prologue: Well, That Was a Fun Trip, Eh?

"Experience is the best way to learn."

—Shannon Kaiser, "50 Things My Future Self Wants Me To Know"

Bob and Carol

 "OK, Bob. I think that wraps it up, right?"

"Right, Carol. Amazing how much we've covered in the twelve weeks since we took on our new roles here at BigCo."

 "Yep. I was skeptical when I agreed to pass you my seasoned server-side team and start out the new client-side development group. But it has been quite an enjoyable experience."

"It *has* been interesting. I learned quite a bit converting your initial HTML-only backend to a web API service. And I learned more as I watched you and your team first build the basic JSON-object client and then the HAL, Collection +JSON, and Siren hypermedia apps—and all in the last month or so."

 "Well, we both learned quite a bit in a short time. Your research into the representor implementation and the API versioning stuff was great."

"As was your work on human–computer interaction (HCI) design. And I especially liked when we teamed up to coordinate my team's microservice-style backend release with your team's adaptable client that can automatically switch between hypermedia formats at runtime."

 "Yep, that really brought it all full circle, didn't it, Bob?"

"Sure did. Makes me almost forget where we started three months ago…"

 "Hm… You know, I can hardly remember either, Bob…"

References

1. Shannon Kaiser's quote is from a September 2014 article (*http://g.mamund.com/ewvgz*) she wrote for MindBodyGreen (*http://mindbodygreen.com*).

Bob, Carol, and BigCo, Inc.

All the chapters in this book start and end with short dialogues between two IT-department colleagues at BigCo, Inc.—a successful multinational enterprise. The two players in these dialogues are Bob and Carol. Both are experienced and well-trained software professionals. Here is a bit of background on each of them and on their employer, BigCo, Inc. to help you get acquainted.

BigCo, Inc.

 The Bayesian International Group of Companies (BigCo) is an organization with a long history of both prosperity and generosity. Founded in 1827 in Scotland, BigCo's motto is "The principle end of the company is the happiness of its customers and employees." Originally focused on demography and finance based on the work of Richard Price, by the 1900s BigCo was a manufacturer of important turn-of-the-century technologies including mobile x-ray machines and hydrophones by working with inventors Frederick Jones and Reginal Fessenden, respectively. BigCo was also one of the few non-US contractors attached to the Manhattan project, providing parts for the first nuclear reactors designed by Dr. Leona Wood.

During the postwar boom, BigCo opened offices in the United States and played an instrumental role in helping establish fields of study in the modern computer era, including predictive algorithms and robotics controls. Currently, BigCo products focus on "inverse probability" problems and how they can be used to help improve decisions and policy-making in both the private and public sectors.

Carol

Carol has been leading successful teams at BigCo for several years and, before that, spent over five years writing code for both desktop and web systems. She has degrees in computer science and information systems and is active in several high-profile open source communities. Carol is also an accomplished visual artist and is a member of a local art society. When she is not working on OSS projects or relaxing at home with her two cats, Carol attends area comics conventions where she sells her artwork and catches up with colleagues in the comics community.

Bob

Bob recently joined the company from a Silicon Valley startup merger. He's built several successful web-based companies (one while still attending college) and tells people he has "the startup bug." After selling his first company for a handsome profit, Bob took time off to complete his bachelor's degree in computer science and then immediately went back to creating new startups. He spends what little spare time he has rock climbing and trail bike riding at nearby state parks and national forests. A couple of times a year, he heads off to the Rocky Mountains or the Cascades to do some serious Alpine-style climbing with friends.

Credits

- Images and logo design by Dana Amundsen (@DanaAmundsen).
- While BigCo is an imaginary company, all the people mentioned in its description (Price, Jones, Fessenden, and Woods) are real historical figures. If BigCo *did* exist, it is possible they would have been part of its history, too.

CHAPTER 1

Our HTML Roots and Simple Web APIs

"What's so fascinating and frustrating and great about life is that you're constantly starting over, all the time, and I love that."

—Billy Crystal

Bob and Carol

 "Hello, Carol. I'm Bob. I wanted to stop by to talk."

"Right, Bob. I remember you from the acquisition party last month. Good to see you again. What's up?"

 "Well, remember at the party you and I talked about working on a new project together? I was thinking about teaming up to work on taking the TPS project to the next level."

"Right, the Task Processing System. That's a great idea, Bob. I think the current TPS HTML app has lots of potential and can help people all over the company better manage their time and resources."

 "I agree. So, as a first step, let's set up two teams. How about you form a new team to focus on the client side while I take on the existing group to work exclusively on the server side."

"So, I guess you'll be in charge of the switch from HTML-only to a web service API, right?"

 "Yep. We'll start work on a standalone web API while you and your new team focus on the client side that consumes the API."

 "There will be some challenges adapting the HTML app into an API but you'll have a good team behind you, Bob."

 "I hope it's not too challenging. We've got a window of about twelve weeks to pull this all together."

 "Well, I guess we should get started then."

Before jumping right into the process of creating hypermedia client applications, let's back up a bit and join the quest at the early end of the web application's history. Many web applications began as websites—as HTML-based pages that were little more than just a list of static documents. In some cases, the initial web app was a pure HTML app. It had tables of data, forms for filtering and adding data, and lots of links to allow the user to transition from one screen to the next (Figure 1-1).

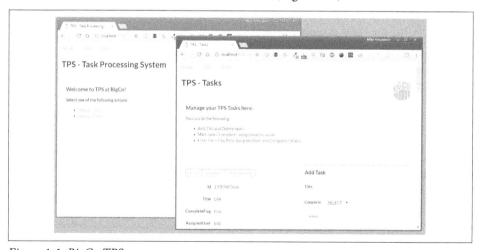

Figure 1-1. BigCo TPS screens

One of the things that make pure HTML applications interesting is that they are written in a very *declarative* style. They work without the need for imperative programming code within the client application. In fact, even the visual styling of HTML applications is handled declaratively—via Cascading Style Sheets (CSS).

It may seem unusual to attempt to create user experiences using only declarative markup. But it should be noted that many users in the early days of the Web were already familiar with this interaction style from the mainframe world (see Figure 1-2). In many ways, early web applications looked and behaved much like the typical monochrome experiences users had with mainframe, minicomputers, and the early personal computers (see Figure 1-3). And this was seen as a "good thing."

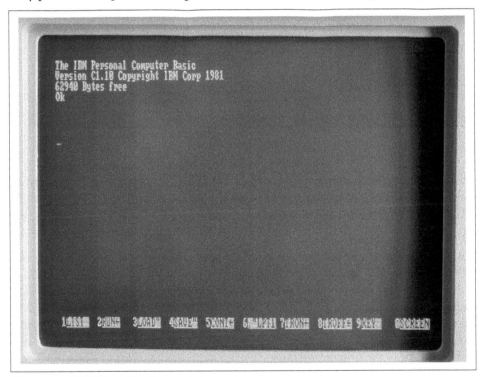

Figure 1-2. IBM Portable Personal Computer

Typically, at some point in the life of successful HTML-based web app, someone gets the idea to convert it into a *web API*. There are lots of reasons this happens. Some want to "unleash the value" locked inside a single application to make the underlying functionality available to a wider audience. There might be new opportunities in other UI platforms (e.g., mobile devices, rich desktop apps, etc.) that don't support the HTML+CSS experience. Maybe someone has a new creative idea and wants to try it out. Whatever the reasons, a web API is born.

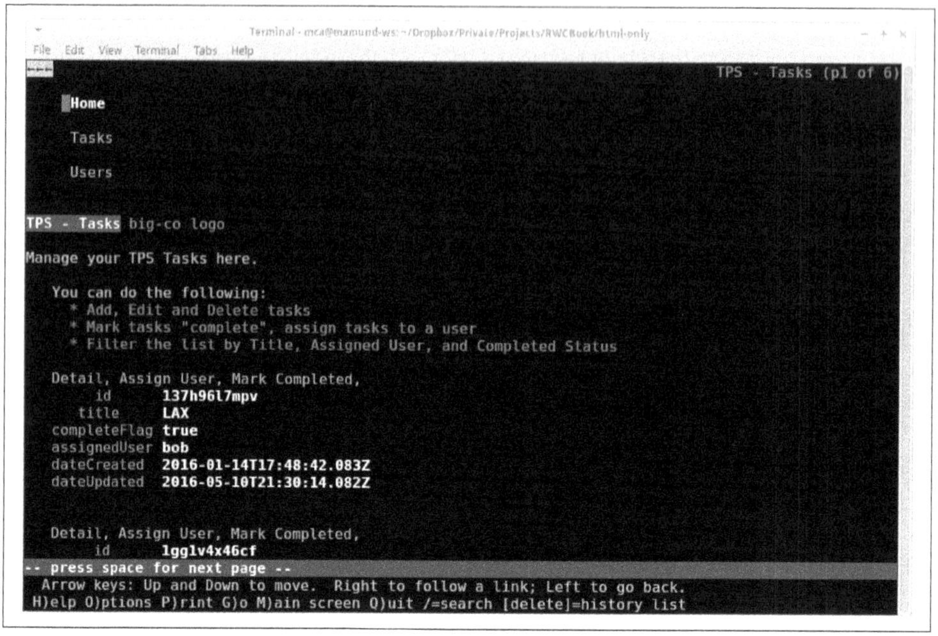

Figure 1-3. Early Lynx HTML browser

Usually, the process is seen as a straightforward effort to expose an API that covers the internal workings of the existing web app but without the baggage of the existing HTML UI. And often the initial work is just that—taking away the UI (HTML) and exposing the data model or object model within the web server code as *the* web API.

Next, it is assumed, a new team can build a better user interface by consuming the server-side web API directly from a client application. Often the goal is to build a native app for smartphones or an advanced web app using one of the latest client-side frameworks. The first pass at the API is usually pretty easy to understand, and building a set of client apps can go smoothly—especially if both the client- and server-side imperative code are built by the same team or by teams that share the same deep understanding of the original web app.

And that's the part of the journey we'll take in this chapter—from HTML to API. That will lay the groundwork for the remainder of the book as we work through the process of building increasingly robust and adaptable client applications powered by the principles and practices of hypermedia.

The Task Processing System (TPS) Web App

For quick review, Carol's team built a web app that delivers HTML (and CSS) from the web server directly to common web browsers. This app works in any brand and version of browser (there are no CSS tricks, all HTML is standard, and there is no

JavaScript at all). It also runs quickly and gets the job done by focusing on the key use cases originally defined when the app was first designed and implemented.

As you can see from Figure 1-4, the UI, while not likely to win any awards, is usable, practical, and reliable—all things we wish for in any application.

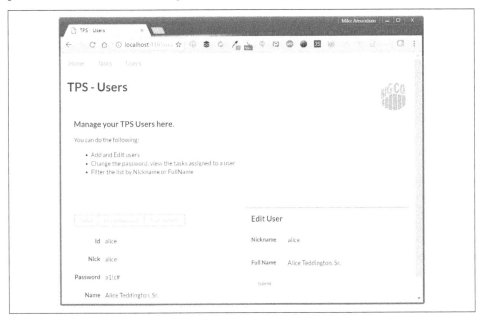

Figure 1-4. TPS user screen

 The source code for this version of the TPS can be found in the associated GitHub repo (*https://github.com/RWCBook/html-only*). A running version of the app described in this chapter can be found online (*http://rwcbook01.herokuapp.com*).

HTML from the Server

Part of the success of the TPS app is that it is very simple. The web server delivers clean HTML that contains all the links and forms needed to accomplish the required use cases:

```
<ul>
  <li class="item">
    <a href="https://rwcbook01.herokuapp.com/home/" rel="home">Home</a>
  </li>
  <li class="item">
    <a href="https://rwcbook01.herokuapp.com/task/" rel="collection">Tasks</a>
  </li>
  <li class="item">
```

```
      <a href="https://rwcbook01.herokuapp.com/user/" rel="collection">Users</a>
    </li>
  </ul>
```

For example, in the preceding code listing, you can see the HTML anchor tags (<a>…
</a>) that point to related content for the current page. This set of "menu links"
appear at the top of each page delivered by the TPS app:

```
<div id="items">
  <div>
    <a href="https://rwcbook01.herokuapp.com/user/alice"
      rel="item" title="Detail">Detail</a> ❶
    <a href="https://rwcbook01.herokuapp.com/user/pass/alice"
      rel="edit" title="Change Password">Change Password</a> ❷
    <a href="https://rwcbook01.herokuapp.com/task/?assignedUser=alice"
      rel="collection" title="Assigned Tasks">Assigned Tasks</a> ❸
  </div>

  <table> ❹
    <tr>
      <th>id</th><td>alice</td>
    </tr>
    <tr>
      <th>nick</th><td>alice</td>
    </tr>
    <tr>
      <th>password</th>
      <td>a1!c#</td>
    </tr>
    <tr>
      <th>name</th><td>Alice Teddington, Sr.</td>
    </tr>
  </table>
</div>
```

Each user rendered in the list by the server contains a link pointing to a single user
item, and that item consists of a pointer (❶), a handful of data fields (❹), and some
links that point to other actions that can be performed for this user (❷ and ❸). The
links allow anyone viewing the page to initiate updates or password changes (assuming they have the rights to perform these actions):

```
<!-- add user form -->
<form method="post" action="https://rwcbook01.herokuapp.com/user/">
  <div>Add User</div>
  <p>
    <label>Nickname</label>
    <input type="text" name="nick" value=""
      required="true" pattern="[a-zA-Z0-9]+" />
  </p>
  <p>
    <label>Full Name</label>
    <input type="text" name="name" value="" required="true" />
```

```
    </p>
    <p>
      <label>Password</label>
      <input type="text" name="password" value=""
        required="true" pattern="[a-zA-Z0-9!@#$%^&*-]+" />
    </p>
    <input type="submit"/>
  </form>
```

The HTML for adding a user is also very simple (see the preceding HTML). It is a clean HTML <form> with associated <label> and <input> elements. In fact, all the input forms in this web app look about the same. Each <form> used for queries (*safe* operations) has the method property set to get, and each <form> used for writes (*unsafe* operations) has the method property set to post. That is the only important difference in the <form> settings for this implementation.

A Note About HTML and POST

In HTTP, the POST method defines a nonidempotent, unsafe operation (RFC7231). Some of the actions in the TPS web app could be handled by an idempotent, unsafe operation, but HTML (still) does not support PUT or DELETE (the two idempotent, unsafe operations in HTTP). As Roy Fielding has pointed out in a 2009 blog post (*http://g.mamund.com/sstuc*), it is certainly possible to get everything done on the Web with only GET and POST. But it would be a bit easier if some operations were idempotent since that makes replaying failed requests much easier to deal with. As of this writing, the several attempts to bring PUT and DELETE to HTML have been given a chilly reception.

Along with the typical list, read, add, edit, and remove actions, the TPS web app includes actions like Change Password for users and Assign User for tasks. The following HTML is what drives the Assign User screen (Figure 1-5 shows the screen itself):

```
<!-- assign user form -->
<form method="post" action="//rwcbook01.herokuapp.com/task/assign/137h96l7mpv">
  <div>Assign User</div>
  <p>
    <label>ID</label>
    <input type="text" name="id" value="137h96l7mpv" readonly="readonly" />
  </p>
  <p>
    <label>User Nickname</label>
    <select name="assignedUser">
      <option value="">SELECT</option>
      <option value="alice">alice</option>
      <option value="bob" selected="selected">bob</option>
```

```
        <option value="carol">carol</option>
        <option value="mamund">mamund</option>
        <option value="ted">ted</option>
      </select>
    </p>
    <input type="submit" />
  </form>
```

Note that this form uses the HTTP POST method. Since HTML only provides GET and POST, all unsafe actions (create, update, remove) are enabled using a POST form. We'll have to deal with this later when we convert this HTML-only web app into a web API.

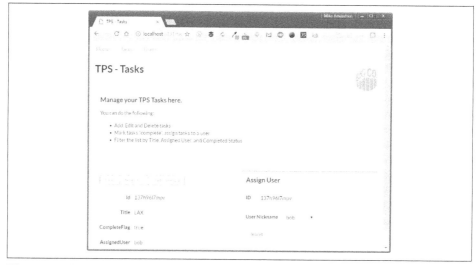

Figure 1-5. Assign user screen

Common Web Browser as the Client

The client side of common web browser applications like this one is pretty uninteresting. First, this app has no client-side JavaScript dependencies. It runs fine without any JavaScript running locally. The app does take advantage of a handful of HTML5 user experience features such as:

- HTML pattern to perform local input validations
- HTML required to guide the user in filling out important fields
- HTML readonly to prevent users from changing important FORM data

These, along with the use of a SELECT input control to supply users with valid input options, do a pretty good job of providing client-side interaction—all without relying on custom JavaScript. The CSS styling here is handled by a library called *Semantic UI*. It supports lots of UI design elements while still supporting reasonable HTML markup. Semantic UI libraries also support JavaScript-driven enhancements that may be used in future updates for this app.

Observations

It turns out that, at least for this web app, the client-side experience is pretty boring to talk about. There just isn't much here to cover! That's actually good news. The common web browser is designed to accept HTML markup and—based on the response links and forms—provide a solid user experience *without* the requirement of writing imperative JavaScript code.

Here are a few other observations:

Very few "bugs"
> Because there is no custom JavaScript code for this client, there are almost no bugs. It is possible that the server will emit broken HTML, of course. And a poorly implemented CSS rule can cause the UI to become unusable. But the fewer lines of code involved, the less likelihood a bug will be encountered. And this app has *no* imperative client code.

POST-only updates
> Because the app is limited to HTML-only responses, all data updates such as create, update, and delete, along with the domain-specific actions like `assign-user` and `change-password`, are handled using HTML `POST` requests. This is, strictly speaking, not a *bug*, but it does run counter to the way most web developers think about actions on the Web. The use of the nonidempotent `POST` action does introduce a slight complication in edge cases where users are not sure if a `POST` was successful and will attempt the action a second time. In this case, it is up to the server to prevent double-posting of adds, etc.

Links and forms
> One of the nice things about using HTML as a response format is that it contains support for a wide range of hypermedia controls: links and forms. The TPS responses include the `<a>...</a>` tag to handle simple immutable links, `<form method="get">` elements to handle safe searches and queries, and `<form method="post">` controls to handle all the unsafe write operations. Each response contains all the details for passing arguments to the server. The `<input>` elements even include simple client-side validation rules to validate user inputs before the data is sent to the server. Having all this descriptive information in the server responses makes it easy for the browser to enforce specific input rules without having any custom client-side code.

Limited user experience

Despite the reality of a "bug-free" app and fully functional write operations via POST, the user experience for this web app is still limited. This might be acceptable within a single team or small company, but if BigCo plans to release this app to a wider public—even to other teams within the company—a more responsive UX would be a good idea.

So, now that we have a baseline web app to start from, let's take a look at how BigCo's Bob and Carol can take this app to the next level by creating a server-side web API that can be used to power a standalone web client application.

The Task Services Web API

Often the next logical step in the life of an HTML-based web application is to publish a standalone web API—or *application programming interface*—that can be used by client applications directly. In the dialogue at the start of this chapter, Bob has taken on the task of leading the server-side team that will design, implement, and publish the Task Processing System API while Carol's team will build the client applications that consume that API.

 The source code for the JSON-based RPC-CRUD web API version of the TPS can be found in the associated GitHub repo (*https://github.com/RWCBook/json-crud*). A running version of the app described in this chapter can be found online (*http://rwcbook02.herokuapp.com*).

Let's first do a quick rundown on the design process for a typical web API server followed by a review of the changes needed to convert our existing TPS HTML-only web app into a proper JSON-based RPC-CRUD web API.

Web API Common Practice

The common practice for creating web APIs is to publish a fixed set of Remote Procedure Call (RPC) *endpoints* expressed as URLs that allow access to the important functionality of the original application. This common practice also covers the design of those URLs, the serialized objects that are passed between server and client, and a set of guidelines on how to use HTTP methods, status codes, and headers in a consistent manner. For most web developers today, this is the state of the art for HTTP.

HTTP, REST, and Parkinson's Law

At this point in many discussions, someone mentions the word "REST," and a fight (literally or *actually*) may break out between people who want to argue about the proper way to design URLs, which HTTP headers you should *not* use, why it is acceptable to ignore some HTTP status codes, and so forth. Disputes about the content and meaning of IETF documents specifying the HTTP protocol, and disagreements about the shape of URLs are all subplots to the main adventure: building solid web applications. Arguing about URLs instead of discussing which interactions are needed to solve a use case is missing the point. HTTP is just tech, and REST is just a style (like punk rock or impressionist painting, etc.). Disagreeing on what is true REST or proper HTTP is a classic cases of Parkinson's Law of Triviality—debating the trivial points while ignoring the important issues.

It turns out that designing and implementing reliable and flexible applications that live on the Web *is* nontrivial. It takes a clear head, an eye for the future, and a willingness to spend time engaged in systems-level thinking. Instead of focusing on those hard problems, some get caught up in disagreements on the characters in a URL or other silliness. I plan to avoid those pitfalls and just focus on the functionality.

What follows in this section is a retelling of the common practice for HTTP-based web APIs. It is not, as I will illustrate in the ensuing chapters, the *only* way to implement services on the Web. Once we get beyond this particular design and implementation detail we can move on to explore additional approaches.

Designing the TPS Web API

Essentially, we need to *design* the web API. Typically this means (1) defining a set of *objects* that will be manipulated via the API, and (2) applying a fixed set of *actions* on those objects. The actions are *Create, Read, Update, and Delete*—the *CRUD* operations. In the case of the TPS example, the list of published objects and actions would look something like that shown in Table 1-1.

Table 1-1. TPS API endpoints

URL	Method	Returns Object	Accepts Object
/task/	GET, POST	TaskList	Task(POST)
/task/{id}	GET,PUT,DELETE	Task	Task(PUT)
/user/	GET,POST	UserList	User(POST)
/user/{id}	GET,PUT	User	User(PUT)

This looks fairly simple: four endpoints and about ten operations (we'll handle the missing one in a minute).

As you can see from the table, there are essentially two forms of the object URL: *list* and *item*. The *list* form of the URL contains the object name (Task or User) and supports (1) HTTP GET to return a list of objects, and (2) HTTP POST to create a new object and add it to the list. The *item* form of the URL contains both the object name (Task or User) and the object's unique id value. This URL supports (1) HTTP GET to return a single object, (2) HTTP PUT to support updating the single object, and (3) HTTP DELETE to support removing that object from the collection.

However, there are some exceptions to this simple CRUD approach. Looking at the table, you'll notice that the TPS User object does not support the DELETE operation. This is a variant to the common CRUD model, but not a big problem. We'd need to document that exception and make sure the API service rejects any DELETE request for User objects.

Also, the TPS web app offers a few specialized operations that allow clients to modify server data. These are:

TaskMarkCompleted

    Allow client apps to mark a single Task object with the completeFlag="true"

TaskAssignUser

    Allow client apps to assign a User.nick to a single Task object

UserChangePassword

    Allow client apps to change the password value of User object

None of the operations just listed falls neatly into the CRUD pattern, which happens quite often when implementing web APIs. This complicates the API design a bit. Typically, these special operations are handled by creating a unique URL (e.g., /task/assign-user or /user/change-pw/) and executing an HTTP POST request with a set of arguments to pass to the server.

Finally, the TPS web API supports a handful of filter operations that need to be handled. They are:

TaskFilterByTitle

    Return a list of Task objects whose title property contains the passed-in string value

TaskFilterByStatus

    Return a list of Task objects whose completeFlag property is set to true (or set to false)

TaskFilterByUser

> Return a list of Task objects whose assignedUser property is set to the passed-in User.nick value

UserFilterByNick

> Return a list of User objects whose nick property contains the passed-in string value

UserFilterByName

> Return a list of User objects whose name property contains the passed-in string value

The common design approach here is to make an HTTP GET request to the object's *list* URL (/task/ or /user/) and pass query arguments in the URL directly. For example, to return a list of Task objects that have their completeFlag set to true, you could use the following HTTP request: GET /task/?completeFlag=true.

So, we have the standard CRUD operations (nine in our case), plus the special operations (three), and then the filter options (five). That's a fixed set of 17 operations to define, document, and implement.

A more complete set of API Design URLs—one that includes the arguments to pass for the write operations (POST and PUT)—would look like the one in Table 1-2.

Table 1-2. Complete set of TPS API endpoints

Operation	URL	Method	Returns	Inputs
TaskList	/task/	GET	TaskList	none
TaskAdd	/task/	POST	TaskList	title, completeFlag
TaskItem	/task/{id}	GET	Task	none
TaskUpdate	/task/{id}	PUT	TaskList	id, title, completeFlag
TaskDelete	/task/{id}	DELETE	TaskList	none
TaskMarkComplete	/task/completed/{id}	POST	Task	none
TaskAssignUser	/task/assign/{id}	POST	Task	id, nick
TaskFilterByTitle	/task/?Title={title}	GET	TaskList	none
TaskFilterByStatus	/task/?CompleteFlag={status}	GET	TaskList	none
TaskFilterByUser	/task/?AssignedUser={nick}	GET	TaskList	none
UserList	/user/	GET	UserList	none

Operation	URL	Method	Returns	Inputs
UserAdd	/user/	POST	UserList	nick, password, name
UserItem	/user/{nick}	GET	User	none
UserUpdate	/user/{nick}	PUT	UserList	nick, name
UserChangePassword	/user/changepw/{nick}	POST	User	nick, oldPass, newPass, checkPass
UserFilterByNick	/user/?nick={nick}	GET	UserList	none
UserFilterByName	/user/?name={name}	GET	UserList	none

A Note about URL Design

The URLs in the Task System API example are just one of a number of ways to design URLs for a web API. There are several books (Allamaraju, Masse) that devote pages to the proper way to design a URL for human use. In truth, *machines* don't care about the shape of the URL—they only care that it follows the standards for valid URLs (RFC3986) and that each URL contains enough information for the service to route the request to the right place for processing. In this book, you'll find a wide range of URL designs, none of which are meant to be the single right way to design URLs.

Documenting data-passing

By now, you've probably noticed that what we have done here is document a set of Remote Procedure Calls (RPCs). We've identified the actions using URLs and listed the arguments to pass for each of them. The arguments are listed in the table but it is worth calling them out separately, too. We'll need to share these with API developers so that they know which data element to pass for each request.

Table 1-3. Arguments to pass for the TPS web API

Agument Name	Operation(s)
id	TaskItem, TaskUpdate, TaskDelete
title	TaskAdd, TaskUpdate, TaskFilterByTitle
completeFlag	TaskAdd, TaskUpdate, TaskMarkComplete, TaskFilterByStatus
assignedUser	TaskAssignUser, TaskFilterByUser
nick	UserAdd, UserChangePassword, UserFilterByNick
name	UserAdd, UserUpdate, UserFilterByName
password	TaskAdd, TaskChangePassword

Agument Name	Operation(s)
oldPass	TaskChangePassword
newPass	TaskChangePassword
checkPass	TaskChangePassword

Notice that the last three arguments in the table (oldPass, newPass, and checkPass) do not belong to any TPS *objects* (e.g., Task or User). They only exist in order to complete the UserChangePassword operation. Usually, RPC-CRUD-style APIs restrict data-passing to arguments that belong to some defined object. But, as we've seen already, there are exceptions to this general rule. This is another challenge you'll encounter when attempting to implement web APIs in the RPC-CRUD style.

 Some RPC-CRUD API designs will document an additional set of objects just for passing arguments. I'll not be covering that here, but it *is* an option you may encounter when working with other RPC-CRUD APIs.

It is not enough to just document *which* data arguments are passed with each HTTP request. It is also important to document the *format* used to pass arguments from the client to the service when passing HTTP bodies. There is no set standard for data-passing with JSON-based APIs, but the typical option is to pass arguments as JSON dictionary objects. For example, the TaskAdd operation in Table 1-2 lists two inputs: title and completeFlag. Using a JSON dictionary to pass this data would look like this:

```
POST /task/ HTTP/1.1
content-type: application/json
...

{
  "title" : "This is my job",
  "completeFlag" : "false"
}
```

Even though the most common way to pass data from client to server on the WWW is using the common HTML FORM media type (application/x-www-form-urlencoded), it is limited to sending simple name–value pairs from client to server. JSON is a bit more flexible than FORM data since it is possible to pass arbitrarily nested trees of data in a single request. However, for this implementation, we'll use the typical JSON dictionary approach.

That covers the endpoints, arguments, and format details for sending data from client to server. But there is another important interface detail missing here—the format of the responses. We'll pick that up in the next section.

Serialized JSON objects

Another important element of the RPC-CRUD style of web API practice is to identity the format and *shape* of the serialized objects passed from server to client and back again. In the case of the TPS web API, Bob has decided to use simple JSON-serialized objects to pass state back and forth. Some implementations will use nested object trees to pass between parties, but BigCo's serialized objects are rather simple for the moment.

Scanning the Returns column of Table 1-2, you'll notice there are four different return elements defined:

- TaskList
- Task
- UserList
- User

These are the return collections/objects that need to be explicitly defined for API developers. Lucky for us, the TPS web API has only two key objects as that will make our definition list rather short.

Tables 1-4 and 1-5 define the properties for the Task and User objects in our TPS web API.

Table 1-4. Task object properties

Property	Type	Status	Default
id	string	required	none
title	string	required	none
completeFlag	"true" or "false"	optional	"false"
assignedUser	MUST match User.nick	optional	""

Table 1-5. User object properties

Property	Type	Status	Default
nick	[a-zA-Z0-9]	required	none
password	[a-zA-Z0-9!@#$%^&*-]	required	none
name	string	required	none

All fields are defined as "string" types. This is just to simplify the implementation of the TPS API for the book. While some APIs employ schemas or other means of "strong-typing" data passed between client and server, these add another level of complication to the implementation. We'll talk more about this in Chapter 7. Also, the stored record layout includes dateCreated and dateUpda ted fields that are not listed in our design here. These were left out of the tables for clarity.

For our TPS app, we'll make things easy and define the TaskList and UserList return objects as simply JSON arrays of the Task and User objects respectively. Following are examples of each object:

```
/* TaskList */
{
  "task": [
    {
      "id": "dr8ar791pk",
      "title": "compost",
      "completeFlag": false,
      "assignedUser": "mamund"
    }
    ... more tasks appear here ...
  ]
}

/* UserList */
{
  "user": [
    {
      "nick": "lee",
      "name": "Lee Amundsen",
      "password": "p@ss"
    }
    ... more user records appear here ...
  ]
}
```

So we've defined the following for our TPS web API:

- URLs and HTTP methods for each RPC endpoint
- Arguments and format for passing data to the service
- JSON objects returned to the clients

There are a few other implementation details that we'll skip over here (handling errors, HTTP return codes, etc.). These would all appear in a complete documentation set for RPC-CRUD APIs. For now, we'll make some assumptions and move on to some implementation details for creating the running TPS web API.

Implementing the TPS Web API

We need to make some changes to the existing TPS website/app in order to implement our JSON web API. We don't need to start from scratch (although in some real-life cases that might be the way to go). For our example, we'll just fork the existing HTML web implementation to create a new standalone codebase that we can alter and turn into a functioning JSON-based RPC-CRUD web API.

> The source code for the JSON-based RPC-CRUD web API version of the TPS can be found in the associated GitHub repo (*https://github.com/RWCBook/json-crud*). A running version of the app described in this chapter can be found online (*http://rwcbook02.herokuapp.com*).

We have two important things to do here. First, we need to modify the TPS website to get it to stop emitting HTML and start emitting valid JSON responses. That won't be too tough since the TPS server has some smart tech built in to make *representing* stored data in various media types relatively easy.

> We'll dig into the tech for *representing* responses in Chapter 3.

The second job is to add support for all the HTTP requests documented in Table 1-2. The good news is *most* of those operations are already supported by the TPS website app. We just need to add a few of them (three, actually) and clean up some of the server-side code to make sure we have all the operations working properly.

So, let's get started.

Defaulting to JSON responses

The TPS website/app emits HTML for all responses. Instead of HTML (`text/html`), our TPS web API will emit JSON (`application/json`) for all responses. Another important change we'll make is to limit the service responses to only send the actual stored `Task` and `User` objects and properties. This will follow along with the information documented in Table 1-2 and the details in Tables 1-4 (Task Object Properties) and 1-5 (User Object Properties).

Based on that information, here is an example of the JSON output from a request to the `/task/` URL:

```
{
  "task": [
```

```
{
    "id": "137h96l7mpv",
    "title": "Update TPS Web API",
    "completeFlag": "true",
    "assignedUser": "bob"
  },
  {
    "id": "1gg1v4x46rf",
    "title": "Review Client API",
    "completeFlag": "false",
    "assignedUser": "carol"
  },
  {
    "id": "1hs5sl6bdv1",
    "title": "Carry Water",
    "completeFlag": "false",
    "assignedUser": "mamund"
  }
  ... more task records here
  ]
}
```

Note that there are no links or forms in the JSON responses. This is typical for RPC-CRUD style API responses. The URLs and action details are included in the human-readable documentation for this project (in GitHub (*https://github.com/RWCBook/json-crud-docs*)) and will be hardcoded into the client application calling this API.

 The human-readable documentation for this RPC-CRUD API can be found in the GitHub (*https://github.com/RWCBook/json-crud-docs*) repository and we'll cover the details of creating a JSON-based RPC-CRUD client based on those docs in Chapter 2, *JSON Clients*.

As you would expect, the responses for calls to the /user/ endpoint look similar to those from the /task/ URL:

```
{
  "user": [
    {
      "id": "alice",
      "nick": "alice",
      "password": "a1!c#",
      "name": "Alice Teddington, Sr."
    },
    {
      "id": "bob",
      "nick": "bob",
      "password": "b0b",
      "name": "Bob Carrolton"
    },
```

```
        .... more user records here
    ]
}
```

So, that covers the service responses. Next, we need to make sure all the actions documented in Table 1-2 are covered in the code.

Updating the TPS web API operations

The TPS HTML web app supported edit and remove operations via the HTML POST method. While this is perfectly fine from an HTML and HTTP point of view, it runs counter to the common practice that has grown up around the JSON-based RPC-CRUD pattern. In CRUD-style APIs, *Edit* operations are handled by the HTTP PUT method and *Remove* operations are handled by the HTTP DELETE operations.

To make our TPS web API compliant, we need to add two things:

- Support for PUT and DELETE on /task/{id} URLs
- Support for PUT on the /user/{nick} URLs

Since the TPS service already supports the actions of *Update* and *Remove* for Tasks (and *Update* for Users), the only thing we need to add to the server-side code is support for executing those actions via HTTP PUT and DELETE. A quick look at the code from our TPS server (with the functionality updated) is provided in Example 1-1.

Example 1-1. Modifying TPS Service to support PUT and DELETE for Tasks

```
...
case 'POST':
  if(parts[1] && parts[1].indexOf('?')===-1) {
    switch(parts[1].toLowerCase()) {
      /* Web API no longer supports update and remove via POST ❶
      case "update":
        updateTask(req, res, respond, parts[2]);
        break;
      case "remove":
        removeTask(req, res, respond, parts[2]);
        break;
      */
      case "completed":
        markCompleted(req, res, respond, parts[2]);
        break;
      case "assign":
        assignUser(req, res, respond, parts[2]);
        break;
      default:
        respond(req, res,
          utils.errorResponse(req, res, 'Method Not Allowed', 405)
        );
```

```
    }
  }
  else {
    addTask(req, res, respond);
  }
break;
/* add support for update via PUT */ ❷
case 'PUT':
  if(parts[1] && parts[1].indexOf('?')===-1) {
    updateTask(req, res, respond, parts[1]);
  }
  else {
    respond(req, res,
      utils.errorResponse(req, res, 'Method Not Allowed', 405)
    );
  }
break;
/* add support for remove via DELETE */ ❸
case 'DELETE':
  if(parts[1] && parts[1].indexOf('?')===-1) {
    removeTask(req, res, respond, parts[1]);
  }
  else {
    respond(req, res,
      utils.errorResponse(req, res, 'Method Not Allowed', 405)
    );
  }
break;
...
```

 Don't worry if this isolated code snippet is hard to parse in your head. The complete source code for the JSON-based RPC-CRUD web API version of the TPS can be found in the associated GitHub repo (*https://github.com/RWCBook/json-crud*).

As you can see from the preceding code snippet, the HTTP handler for Task data no longer supports the *Update* and *Remove* actions via POST (❶). They are now accessed via HTTP PUT (❷) and DELETE (❸). A similar change was made to support *Update* for User data, too.

To be complete, the web API service should also be updated to no longer serve up the assignUser, markCompleted, and changePassword pages. These were provided by the TPS website/app to allow users to enter data via HTML standalone <form> responses. Because our web API doesn't support <form>, we don't need these pages anymore.

Here is the TPS web API Task handler with the assignUser and markCompleted <form> pages turned off:

```
....
case 'GET':
  /* Web API no longer serves up assign and completed forms
  if(flag===false && parts[1]==="assign" && parts[2]) {
    flag=true;
    sendAssignPage(req, res, respond, parts[2]);
  }
  if(flag===false && parts[1]==="completed" && parts[2]) {
    flag=true;
    sendCompletedPage(req, res, respond, parts[2]);
  }
  */
  if(flag===false && parts[1] && parts[1].indexOf('?')===-1) {
    flag = true;
    sendItemPage(req, res, respond, parts[1]);
  }
  if(flag===false) {
    sendListPage(req, res, respond);
  }
break;
....
```

Testing the TPS web API with cURL

Even though we need a fully functioning JSON CRUD client (or test runner) to test
all of the TPS web API, we can still do some basic testing using the curl command-
line utility. This will confirm that we have set up the TPS web API correctly (per the
API design just shown) and allow us to do some simple interactions with the running
API service.

The following is a short curl session that shows running all the CRUD operations on
the Task endpoint as well as the TaskMarkCompleted special operation:

```
// create a new task record
curl -X POST -H "content-type:application/json" -d '{"title":"testing"}'
  http://localhost:8181/task/

// fetch the newly created task record
curl http://localhost:8181/task/1z4yb9wjwi1

// update the existing task record
curl -X PUT -H "content-type:application/json" -d '{"title":"testing again"}'
  http://localhost:8181/task/1z4yb9wjwi1

// mark the record completed
curl -X POST -H "content-type:application/json"
  http://localhost:8181/task/completed/1z4yb9wjwi1

// delete the task record
curl -X DELETE -H "content-type:application/json"
  http://localhost:8181/task/1z4yb9wjwi1
```

To save space and stay within the page layout, some of the command lines are printed on *two* lines. If you are running these commands yourself, you'll need to place each command on a single line.

To review, we've made all the implementation changes needed to get the TPS web API up and running:

- Set the API responses to all emit simple JSON (`application/json`) arrays
- Added support for `PUT` (Update) and `DELETE` (Remove) for `Task` objects
- Removed support for `POST` (Update) and `POST` (Remove) for `Task` objects
- Removed support for `GET` (assignUser) and `GET` (markCompleted) FORMS for `Task` objects
- Added support for `PUT` (Update) for `User` objects
- Removed support for `POST` (Update) for `User` objects
- Removed support for `GET` (changePassword) FORMS for `User` objects

As you can see from the list, we actually did more to *remove* support in the web API than anything else. Remember that we also removed all the links and forms from all the web API responses. The description of what it takes to filter and modify data on the TPS service will now need to be documented in human-readable form and *that* will need to be coded into the JSON client application. We'll see how that works in Chapter 2.

Observations

Now that we have a working TPS web API service up and running, it's worth making a few observations on the experience.

Plain JSON responses
A hallmark of web APIs today is to emit plain JSON responses—no more HTML, just JSON. The advantage is that supporting JSON in JavaScript-based browser clients is easier than dealing with XML or parsing HTML responses. Although we didn't get to see it in our simple example, JSON responses can carry a large nested graph of data more efficiently than HTML, too.

API design is all about URLs and CRUD
When we were designing our web API, we spent most of the time and effort crafting URLs and deciding which methods and arguments to pass for each request. We also needed to make sure the exposed URLs map the Create-Read-Update-Delete (CRUD) semantics against important JSON objects. There were a

few actions that didn't map well to CRUD (three for our use case) and we had to create special URLs for them.

No more links and forms

Another common feature of web APIs is the lack of links and forms in responses. Common web browsers use the links and forms in HTML responses to render a user interface for humans to scan and activate. This works because the browser already *understands* links and forms in HTML. Since JSON doesn't have things like <a>...</a> and <form method="get"> or <form method="post">, the information needed to execute actions from the UI will need to be baked into the API client code.

API servers are rather easy

Since most of what we did to make our TPS web app into a web API is *remove* features, it seems building API servers is relatively easy to do. There are certainly challenges to it—our TPS web API is pretty simple—but for the most part, we have less things to decide when creating these RPC-CRUD style APIs than when we are creating both the data responses *and* the connections (LINKS) and data-passing instructions (FORMS) from the standard website/app.

Completing the API is only part of the story

We found out that once you have the web API up and running, you still need to test it with some kind of client. We can't just point a web browser at the API because browsers don't know about our CRUD and special operations. For now, we used the curl command-line utility to execute HTTP-level requests against the API to make sure it was behaving as expected.

Summary

In this chapter, we started our journey toward hypermedia clients by first stepping back a bit and reviewing a kind of early history of typical web APIs—especially their roots in simple HTML-only websites/apps. We were introduced to BigCo's Task Processing System (TPS) web app and learned that the HTML5 app worked just fine without any JavaScript code at all.

But we're interested in API services and API clients. So the first task was to convert this simple HTML-only web app into a pure JSON web API service. And it was not too hard. We adopted the common RPC-CRUD design model by establishing a key URL for each API object (Task and User) and implementing the Create-Read-Update-Delete (CRUD) pattern against these objects and their URLs. We had to create a few other special URLs to support unique operations (using POST), and documented a set of filter routines against the web API's collection URLs (/task/ and /user/). We then documented the JSON objects that were returned and established that all payloads sent from client to server should be formatted as JSON dictionary objects.

With the design completed, we needed to actually implement the API. We were able to fork the existing website app and spent most of our efforts *removing* functionality, simplifying the format (we dropped all the links and forms in the JSON responses), and cleaning up the web API code. Finally, we used the curl command-line utility to confirm that our API was functioning as expected.

This gives us a great start on our TPS API service. The next challenge is building a fully functional JSON CRUD client that understands the TPS web API documentation. Since we spent a lot of our time eliminating descriptive information in the web API responses, we'll need to add that information to the API client instead. We'll take on that challenge next.

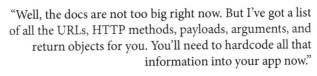

"So, Bob. Do you have the TPS web API up and running yet?"

"Actually, Carol, I do. Implementing it was not as hard as I thought but did take a bit more designing than I'd planned."

"Right, with the links and forms no longer in the responses, you needed to redesign the API to support the CRUD pattern, right?"

"Yep. The Create-Read-Update-Delete pattern is what most JSON API developers expect. But we still had to support some other non-CRUD actions like our *Assign User*, *Mark Completed*, and *Change Password* use cases."

"Yeah, not all actions will fit into the pattern. So, I assume you've got some serious documentation for me now, too."

"Well, the docs are not too big right now. But I've got a list of all the URLs, HTTP methods, payloads, arguments, and return objects for you. You'll need to hardcode all that information into your app now."

"Oh, now I see what you meant when you said the implementation was not so hard. Your team took a bunch of stuff out of the server-side API and *my* team needs to spend time putting it all back in on the client side."

"Well, that's one way to look at it, I guess. Hadn't thought about it like that before."

 "No worries, Bob. So, you set for my team to start working on the JSON API client for the TPS API?"

"Yep, and the sooner the better. I can't use a browser to test this API anymore and I need a fully functional client to help me figure out if there is anything we missed."

 "OK, Bob. We'll get right on it and meet you back here in a few days."

References

1. The monochrome computer screen image is a photo of an IBM Portable PC from Hubert Berberich (HubiB) (Own work) [CC BY-SA 3.0], via Wikimedia Commons (*http://creativecommons.org/licenses/by-sa/3.0*).

2. The Lynx browser screenshot is taken from a modern implementation of the Lynx specification (*http://lynx.browser.org*). The data displayed is our own TPS web app, too.

3. Roy Fielding's 2009 blog post "It is okay to use POST" (*http://g.mamund.com/sstuc*) points out that his dissertation never mentions CRUD and that it is fine to use GET and POST for web apps.

4. Two books I recommend when looking for guides in URL design are *RESTful Web Services Cookbook* by Subbu Allamaraju (O'Reilly, 2010) and *REST API Design Rulebook* by Mark Masse (O'Reilly, 2011). There are quite a few more, but these are the books I find I use often.

5. Parkinson's Law of Triviality is sometimes referred to as *bikeshedding* and was first described by C. Northcote Parkinson in his book *Parkinson's Law and Other Studies in Administration* (Houghton Mifflin Company, 1957). When referring to the case of committees working through a busy agenda, Parkinson observed, "The time spent on any item of the agenda will be in inverse proportion to the sum [of money] involved."

CHAPTER 2

JSON Clients

"All my books started out as extravagant and ended up pure and plain."

—Annie Dillard

Bob and Carol

 "OK, Carol. The TPS web API is up and running and ready for your team to create a client."

"Sounds good, Bob. I see your team provided the API documentation, too. Wow, that seems like a lot of documentation for such a small API!"

 "Well, when you get down to it, there are lots of details to work out when writing your client app. The objects, the URLs, all the parameters for adding and updating records —it adds up."

"Right. No problem. I just thought the whole Create-Read-Update-Delete pattern would make most of this easy."

 "Even though we used CRUD where we could, not all the API actions fit neatly into those four actions. You'll see a couple things where we just use HTTP POST with arguments."

"That's fine. I'll discuss this with the team and hopefully we can get our first client app into production by the end of next week."

"OK, Carol. Keep me posted and we'll get together next week."

Now that we have a fully functional JSON web API (covered in Chapter 1), we're ready to build the client app. Since the web API we're targeting is an RPC-CRUD API, we'll need to consult the documentation and be sure to build into the app all the rules for constructing URLs, handling unique response objects and collections, and knowing the full details on how to execute all the operations for filtering, displaying, and modifying service data (almost 20 of them in our TPS app).

Also, after building and releasing our API client, we'll simulate some real-life scenarios and update the backend service to see how that affects our client in production. Ideally, we'd like that client to support any new features of the updated backend. But anyone who has built these RPC-CRUD clients knows that's not very likely. At least we'd like the app to *not crash* when the backend changes and even that is an iffy proposition depending on how we implement the client. We'll work through the changes needed to keep our web API client up-to-date and close the chapter with some observations before we move on to our next project.

So, let's get started.

The JSON Web API Client

For many readers, the typical JSON web API client is nothing new—it's the style that most web APIs are designed to support right now. We'll review some of the basic elements of this client and then, after a short detour into the service code to explore JSON API output, we'll work through the coding needed to create a fully functional JSON web API client. Along the way, we'll learn how the JSON client needs to handle important elements such as:

- Recognizing the OBJECTS in responses
- Constructing ADDRESSES (the URLs) for interacting with the service
- Handling ACTIONS such as filtering, editing, or deleting data

Let's take a minute to review each of these three elements before starting to look at the way client apps deal with them.

The OAA Challenge

Throughout the book, I'll refer to this as the OAA Challenge (as in OBJECTS, ADDRESSES, and ACTIONS). We'll see that every web API client app needs to deal with them and, especially when we start looking at the hypermedia-style clients, that there are varying ways to handle this challenge.

Objects

One of the most important things that JSON web API clients need to deal with are the JSON objects that appear in responses. Most JSON web APIs expose a unique object model via the responses. Before you can even *start* using the API in any meaningful way, your client app needs to understand the object model.

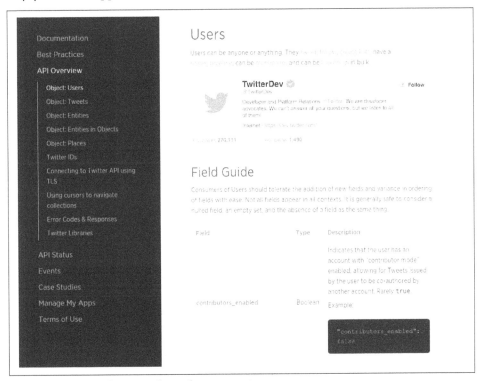

Figure 2-1. Twitter's JSON object documentation

For example, as of this writing, the Twitter API Overview page lists five baseline objects:

- Users
- Tweets

- Entities
- Entities in Objects
- Places

Many of these objects contain nested dictionary and array objects, too. And there are several complete sets of JSON objects in addition to these for related Twitter APIs such as streaming services, ad services, and others.

Recognizing objects

Lucky for us, the TPS web API has only two main objects (`Task` and `User`) and each of them are just a set of name–value pairs. This simple design makes our sample apps easy to work with and explore. However, most non-trivial production apps are likely to have several objects and tens (possibly hundreds) of properties.

As we saw in Chapter 1, the TPS web API responses are simple arrays:

```
{
  "task": [
    {
      "id": "137h96l7mpv",
      "title": "LAX",
      "completeFlag": "true",
      "assignedUser": "bob",
      "dateCreated": "2016-01-14T17:48:42.083Z",
      "dateUpdated": "2016-01-27T22:03:02.850Z"
    },
    {
      "id": "1gg1v4x46cf",
      "title": "YVR",
      "completeFlag": "false",
      "assignedUser": "carol",
      "dateCreated": "2016-01-14T18:03:18.804Z",
      "dateUpdated": "2016-01-27T17:45:46.597Z"
    },
    .... more TASK objects here
  ]
}
```

Our client app will need to recognize the `"task"` array name and act accordingly at runtime. One good way to do this is to use the object identifier as a *context switch*. When our app sees `"task":[...]` in the response, it will switch to "task-mode" and display the data (and possible actions) related to tasks. When the server response contains `"user":[...]`, the app can switch to "user-mode." Of course, our app won't know what to do if a service response contains `"note ":[...]` or some other unknown context value. For now, we'll need to ignore anything we don't recognize.

"Ignore anything you don't recognize" is a valuable implementation pattern for writing robust client apps. I'll cover this and other patterns for creating resilient client apps in Chapter 7.

Displaying data

Just knowing the objects and their properties is not enough. Client applications also need to know how to deal with them when they show up in an API response. For example, whether to show the data item at all, and if so, which properties to display, the human prompts associated with the properties, and so on.

For example, the `Task` object emitted by the TPS web API looks like this:

```
{
  "id": "137h96l7mpv",
  "title": "Review API Design",
  "completeFlag": "false",
  "assignedUser": "bob",
  "dateCreated": "2016-05-14T17:48:42.083Z",
  "dateUpdated": "2016-05-27T22:03:02.850Z"
},
```

For our client app, we've decided to *not* display the `dateCreated` and `dateUpdated` fields. In fact, we'll need to keep track of which fields to hide and which to show for *all* the TPS objects.

We also need to decide which prompts to display for each property in the TPS `Task` and `User` objects. Most of the time, client-side developers need to keep an internal set of prompts (possibly even tagged for more than one language) and map those prompts to the property names at runtime. For our simple app, we'll just use a CSS trick to capitalize the property names when displaying them as prompts (see ❶ in the code provided in Example 2-1).

Example 2-1. Using CSS to generate UI prompts

```
span.prompt {
  display:block;
  width:125px;
  font-weight:bold;
  text-align:right;
  text-transform:capitalize; ❶
}
```

This works because we only need to support a single language and we're just working with a simple demo app. Production apps will need more attention to detail on this point. We'll see a more robust way to handle onscreen displays in Chapter 6, *Siren Clients*.

So, our client app will keep track of all the important JSON objects coming from the server, know how to handle each of them, and know which properties to display and what prompts are associated with them.

The next thing to deal with is the object's ADDRESSES—their URLs.

Addresses

Most JSON RPC-CRUD API responses don't include URLs—the addresses of the objects and arrays the client application is processing. Instead, the URL information is written up in human-readable documentation and it is up to the developer to work out the details. Often this involves hardcoding URLs (or URL templates) into the app, associating those addresses with objects and collections at runtime, and resolving any parameters in the URL templates before actually *using* them in the app.

The number of URLs and templates in an API can be very large. For example, using the Twitter API (mentioned previously) as an example, there are close to 100 URL endpoints displayed on just one page of the Twitter API documentation (see Figure 2-2). While it is likely that a single API client will not need to handle *all* 97 of the URLs listed on that page, any useful Twitter client app will likely need to deal with dozens of them.

For the TPS web API, there are 17 URLs and templates to deal with. They're listed in Table 1-2. We'll need to sort out which addresses belong to each context object (Task or User) and which of them are more than simple read actions (e.g., HTTP POST, PUT, and DELETE actions).

There are many different ways of handling URLs and templates for JSON web APIs. The approach I'll use in our sample app is to create a JSON dictionary of all the URLs for each object. For example, Example 2-2 shows how I'll "memorize" some of the Task operations (Note that I included a prompt element for use when displaying these URLs as links in the client UI).

Example 2-2. Coding URLs into the JSON Web API Client

```
actions.task = {
  tasks:   {href:"/task/", prompt:"All Tasks"},
  active:  {href:"/task/?completeFlag=false", prompt:"Active Tasks"},
  closed:  {href:"/task/?completeFlag=true", prompt:"Completed Tasks"},
}
```

I'll also need to keep some information on *when* to display links. Should they appear on every page? Just on the pages associated with tasks? Only when a *single* task is displayed? Various client-side JavaScript frameworks deal with these details in different ways. Since I'm not tying my client or server to any single framework, my solution is to use an additional property of my address list, called `target`, which is set to values such as "`all`" or "`list`" or "`single-item`", etc. We'll see that later in this chapter.

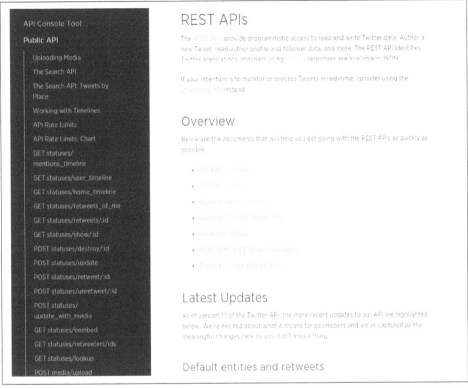

Figure 2-2. Twitter's JSON endpoint documentation

So, OBJECTS and ADDRESSES. That's pretty good, but it's not enough. We also need to know the details on ACTIONS that involve query parameters and actions that require construction of request bodies (e.g., `POST` and `PUT`).

Actions

The third important element that web API clients need to deal with are filters and write operations of a web API. Just like the URL construction rules, this information is typically written up in human-readable documentation and then translated into client-side code by a developer. For example, Twitter's API for updating existing lists takes up to seven parameters and looks like Figure 2-3 in the documentation.

The documentation for our TPS web API appears in Table 1-2. Similar to the Twitter API documentation, the TPS docs show the URL, the method, and the set of parameters. This all needs to be "baked" into the web API client app, too.

Figure 2-3. Twitter's update list API documentation

You can find the complete TPS web API docs in the associated repository on GitHub (*https://github.com/RWCBook/json-crud-docs*).

There are many different ways to encode action information into client apps—from hardcoding it into the app, keeping it as metadata in a separate local file, or even as a remote configuration file sent with the JSON response. For our TPS client, I'll use an approach similar to the one I used when handling simple URLs (see Example 2-2).

For example, Table 2-1 shows what the UserAdd action looks like in the TPS documentation.

Table 2-1. TPS UserAdd action

Operation	URL	Method	Returns	Inputs
UserAdd	/user/	POST	UserList	nick, password, name

And the web API client app will store that information in the actions element (see the following code). Note that the pattern property information comes from another part of the TPS documentation (provided earlier in Table 1-5).

```
actions.user = {
  add:  {
    href:"/user/",
    prompt:"Add User",
    method:"POST",
    args:{
      nick: {
        value:"",
        prompt:"Nickname",
        required:true,
        pattern:"[a-zA-Z0-9]+"
      },
      password: {
        value:"",
        prompt:"Password",
        required:true,
        pattern:"[a-zA-Z0-9!@#$%^&*-]+"
      },
      name: {
        value:"",
        prompt:"Full Name",
        required:true
      }
    }
  }
}
```

And this kind of information needs to be handled for *all* the actions your client app needs to perform. In the TPS web API, that is 17 actions. A nontrivial app will need to handle quite a few more.

I'll show a more robust way to handle describing these kinds of interactions in Chapter 4.

Quick Summary

So now we have a good sense of what a web API client for a JSON RPC-CRUD style API will need to deal with. Along with the usual code for requests, parsing, and rendering responses, every JSON API client will also need to know how to handle:

- OBJECTS unique to each API
- ADDRESSES (URLs and URL templates) for all the actions of the API
- ACTION details including HTTP methods and arguments for all non-trivial actions including HTTP POST, PUT, and DELETE requests.

With this in mind, we can now dig into the actual code for the JSON web API client.

The JSON SPA Client

Now we're ready to walk through the JSON web API client app code. We'll look at the HTML container for the single-page app (SPA), the top-level request, parse, render loop, and check out how this client app handles the three things we reviewed earlier: OBJECTS, ADDRESSES, and ACTIONS. Along the way, we'll see the JSON client in action and look ahead to see how it will deal with backend API changes.

The source code for the TPS JSON web API client can be found in the associated GitHub repo (*https://github.com/RWCBook/json-client*). A running version of the app described in this chapter can be found online (*http://rwcbook03.herokuapp.com/files/json-client.html*).

Throughout the book, I'll be showing examples of single-page apps, or SPAs, hosted within a browser. Also, I chose to build all the apps for this book without using one of the many JavaScript frameworks in order to make it easier for you to see the code that matters. So, the code here is not production-ready because I wrote it for this book. But making it production-ready is just a matter of making it bulletproof, and you don't need any fancy frameworks for that.

The HTML Container

The SPA client created for the TPS web API starts with a single HTML document. This document acts as the *container* for the entire API client application. Once the initial HTML is loaded, all other requests and responses will be handled by the running JavaScript code parsing and rendering the JSON objects returned from the TPS web API service.

The HTML container looks like this:

```
<!DOCTYPE html>
<html>
  <head>
    <title>JSON</title>
    <link href="json-client.css" rel="stylesheet" /> ❶
  </head>
  <body>
    <h1 id="title"></h1> ❷
    <div id="toplinks"></div>
    <div id="content"></div>
    <div id="actions"></div>
    <div id="form"></div>
    <div id="items"></div>
    <div>
      <pre id="dump"></pre>
    </div>
  </body>
  <script src="dom-help.js">//na </script> ❸
  <script src="json-client.js">//na </script> ❹
  <script>
    window.onload = function() {
      var pg = json();
      pg.init("/home/", "TPS - Task Processing System"); ❺
    }
  </script>
</html>
```

As you can see from the preceding HTML listing, there is not much to talk about in this document. The part that all the *code* will be paying attention to starts at ❷—the seven DIV elements. Each of them has a unique identifier and purpose at runtime. You can figure most of that out just by reading the names. The last DIV actually encloses a <pre> tag that will hold the full "dump" of the JSON responses at runtime. This is a handy kind of debug display and isn't needed for production.

Along with the HTML, there is a single CSS file (❶) and two JavaScript references; a simple DOM library (❸) and the complete client-side code (❹). We'll inspect the json-client.js library throughout this section of the chapter.

I'm using a small helper library (dom-help.js) to reduce tedious HTML DOM manipulation in the client code. This is usually handled by other JS frameworks like JQuery, etc. I used this one just to get rid of library dependency and make it easy to see that there is no 'magic' going on in some library.

Finally, once the page is loaded, a single function is executed (see ❺). This initializes the client with a starting URL and (optionally) a title string. The URL shown here works fine when the client app is hosted in the same web domain as the TPS web API. If you want to run the client app from a separate domain, all you need to do is update this initial URL and the app will work just fine.

So, let's look inside the `json-client.js` library and see how it works.

The Top-Level Parse Loop

The client app is designed to act in a simple, repeating loop that looks like this:

1. Execute an HTTP request.
2. Store the JSON response in memory.
3. Inspect the response for *context*.
4. Walk through the response and render the context-related information on screen.

We talked about *context* earlier in the chapter. This client is expecting multiple custom object models from the TPS web API (`Task`, `User`, and `Home`) and uses the returned object model as *context* in deciding how to parse and render the response.

```
// init library and start ❶
function init(url, title) {
  if(!url || url==='') {
    alert('*** ERROR:\n\nMUST pass starting URL to the library');
  }
  else {
    global.title = title||"JSON Client";
    global.url = url;
    req(global.url,"get"); ❷
  }
}

// process loop ❸
function parseMsg() {
  setContext();
  toplinks();
  content();
  items();
  actions();
}
```

When the app first loads, the `init` function is called (❶). That validates the initial URL, stores it, and eventually makes the first HTTP request to that URL (❷). Once the response returns (not shown here) the `parseMsg` function is called (❸) and that starts the parse/render loop.

The `parseMsg` function does a handful of things. First, it calls `setContext` to inspect the response and set the app's current *context* so that it knows how to interpret the response. For our app, a global `context` variable is set to `"task"`, `"user"`, or `"home"`. Next, the page's top links are located and rendered (`toplinks`), and any HTML content is displayed (`content`). The `items` function finds all the objects in the response (`Task` or `User`) and renders them on the screen, and the `actions` function constructs all the links and forms appropriate for the current *context*.

That's quite a bit in a single function and we'll get into some details of that in just a bit. But first, let's look at how the JSON client keeps track of the TPS objects, addresses, and actions that were written up in the human documentation.

Objects, Addresses, and Actions

Since the TPS web API is just returning custom JSON objects and arrays, our client app needs to know what those objects are, how to address them, and what actions are possible with them.

TPS objects

The TPS objects (`Task` and `User`) are simple name–value pairs. So, all our client app needs to know are the properties of each object that need to be rendered on screen. For example, all TPS objects have `dateCreated` and `dateUpdated` properties, but our client doesn't need to deal with them.

This app uses a simple array to contain all the object properties it needs to know about:

```
global.fields.task = ["id","title","completeFlag","assignedUser"];
global.fields.user = ["nick","name","password"];
```

Now, whenever parsing incoming objects, the client app will compare the property on the object with its own list of properties and ignore any incoming property it doesn't already know about.

An example of how this works can be seen in the code that handles on-screen rendering of objects in the response:

```
// g = global storage
// d = domHelper library

// handle item collection
function items() {
  var rsp, flds, elm, coll;
  var ul, li, dl, dt, dd, p;

  rsp = g.rsp[g.context]; ❶
  flds = g.fields[g.context];
```

```
elm = d.find("items");
d.clear(elm);
ul = d.node("ul");

coll = rsp;
for(var item of coll) {
  li = d.node("li");
  dl = d.node("dl");
  dt = d.node("dt");

  // emit the data elements
  dd = d.node("dd");
  for(var f of flds) { ❷
    p = d.data({text:f, value:item[f]});
    d.push(p,dd);
  }
  d.push(dt, dl, dd, li, lu);
}
d.push(ul,elm);
}
```

Note (in ❶) the first step in the routine is to use the shared context value to locate the data in the response (rsp) and select the internal properties to use when inspecting the data (flds). This information is used (in ❷) to make sure to only render the fields the client decides is appropriate (see Figure 2-4).

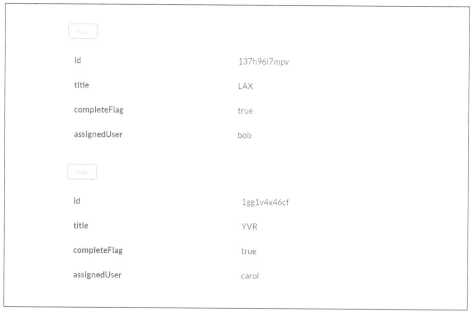

Figure 2-4. Rendering task items in the JSON client

The code examples for this book use the ES6 for..of iterator. When this book first went to press for..of was supported in *some* browsers, but not all. I used the Chrome browser (both the Google release and the Chromium open source release) while writing the examples and they all ran fine. Be sure to check your browser's support for the for..of iterator.

Addresses and actions

This client app stores both the addresses (URLs) and actions (HTTP method and parameter information) in a single internal collection called actions. There is additional metadata about each action that indicates *when* it should be rendered (based on context information) and *how* it should be executed (e.g., as a simple link, form, or direct HTTP method call).

The list of actions for the TPS web API is rather long (17 separate actions), but the following code snippet gives you a good idea of how they are stored in the client app:

```
// task context actions
global.actions.task = {
    tasks:   {target:"app", func:httpGet, href:"/task/", prompt:"Tasks"}, ❶
    active:  {target:"list", func:httpGet, href:"/task/?completeFlag=false",
                prompt:"Active Tasks"
             },
    byTitle: {target:"list", func:jsonForm, href:"/task", ❷
                prompt:"By Title", method:"GET",
                args:{
                  title: {value:"", prompt:"Title", required:true}
                }
             },
    add:     {target:"list", func:jsonForm, href:"/task/", ❸
                prompt:"Add Task", method:"POST",
                args:{
                  title: {value:"", prompt:"Title", required:true},
                  completeFlag: {value:"", prompt:"completeFlag"}
                }
             },
    item:    {target:"item", func:httpGet, href:"/task/{id}", prompt:"Item"},
    edit:    {target:"single", func:jsonForm, href:"/task/{id}", ❹
                prompt:"Edit", method:"PUT",
                args:{
                  id: {value:"{id}", prompt:"Id", readOnly:true},
                  title: {value:"{title}", prompt:"Title", required:true},
                  completeFlag: {value:"{completeFlag}", prompt:"completeFlag"}
                }
             },
    del:     {target:"single", func:httpDelete, href:"/task/{id}", ❺
                prompt:"Delete", method:"DELETE", args:{}
             },
};
```

In the preceding code snippet, you can see a simple, safe, read-only action (❶) as well as a safe action that requires user input (❷). There are also the classic CRUD actions (❸, ❹, and ❺) with the expected HTTP method names, prompts, and (where appropriate) argument lists. These action definitions are selected based on runtime context information. For example, the `target` property indicates which actions are appropriate for app-level, list-level, item-level, and even single-item level context.

Here's an example of the code that uses context information and scans the list of actions to render list-level links:

```
// d = domHelper library

// handle list-level actions
function actions() {
  var actions;
  var elm, coll;
  var ul, li, a;

  elm = d.find("actions");
  d.clear(elm);
  ul = d.node("ul");

  actions = g.actions[g.context]; ❶
  for(var act in actions) {
    link = actions[act];
    if(link.target==="list") { ❷
      li = d.node("li");
      a = d.anchor({
        href:link.href,
        rel:"collection",
        className:"action",
        text:link.prompt
      });
      a.onclick = link.func;
      a.setAttribute("method",(link.method||"GET"));
      a.setAttribute("args",(link.args?JSON.stringify(link.args):"{}"));
      d.push(a,li);
      d.push(li, ul);
    }
  }
  d.push(ul, elm);
}
```

You can see in this code that both the object context (❶) and the internal render context (❷) are used to select only the links appropriate for display at the moment.

The actions that contain argument details will be rendered at runtime using HTML `<form>` elements (see Figure 2-5). The code that handles this is shown here:

```
// d = domHelper library
```

```
// render inputs
coll = JSON.parse(link.getAttribute("args")); ❶
for(var prop in coll) {
  val = coll[prop].value;
  if(rsp[0][prop]) {
    val = val.replace("{"+prop+"}",rsp[0][prop]); ❷
  }
  p = d.input({ ❸
    prompt:coll[prop].prompt,
    name:prop,
    value:val,
    required:coll[prop].required,
    readOnly:coll[prop].readOnly,
    pattern:coll[prop].pattern
  });
  d.push(p,fs);
}
```

In the small snippet just shown, you can see the collection of args (❶) from the action definition is used to create HTML form inputs. At ❷ you can see that any current object is used to populate the value of the inputs before the actual HTML input element is created (❸). Note the inclusion of the HTML5 properties required, readonly, and pattern in order to improve the client-side user experience, too.

Figure 2-5. JSON client rendering a form

Quick summary

There is more to the json-client.js library that we won't cover here, including all the Ajax-related code to handle HTTP requests and responses. Even with all the low-level HTTP code, the total size of the library is around 500 lines of JavaScript—and that includes extensive comments. In fact, the breakdown of the various parts of the client are worth noting.

HTTP-level handlers

> For example, the Ajax-related low-level HTTP code takes up about 100 lines. This code would typically be handled by jQuery or other framework libraries. Also, this code will not grow or shrink as the number of unique objects, addresses, and actions changes within the web API. The HTTP-handling code is a fixed size.

Parsing and rendering

> The heart of the JSON client code is about 300 lines that handle the parsing and rendering of the user interface. That content is also unlikely to change as the web API objects and functionality changes. However, this part of the codebase *could* grow as more client-side UX features are added to the library.

Web API objects, and actions

> Finally, the other large portion of the code library is the 150 or so lines of Java-Script used to declare the TPS web API objects, address, and action configuration. This is the part of the library that will be directly affected by the web API objects and actions. As the API functionality grows, this code *must* grow, too.

This last item points to an important aspect of JSON API clients: changing the backend API will *force* the client frontend to change, too. I've done my best to isolate those changes to a single section of the library, but I can't eliminate the need for these changes to occur since the client code has all the service's OBJECTS, ADDRESSES, and ACTIONS baked directly into the code.

So, let's make some changes to the backend web API and see how this JSON client handles it.

Dealing with Change

Change is a fundamental part of the Web. Several key design aspects of the HTTP protocol and HTML make change not only easy to do but also easy to support without breaking existing HTTP clients. The content of HTML pages can change without the need to recode and release new HTML browsers. The HTTP protocol has undergone a handful of updates over the last 25 years without crashing existing web servers or requiring them to all be updated at the same time. Change is essentially "designed in" to the WWW. I'll review this topic in more detail in Chapter 7.

Unfortunately, most web APIs today do not share this fundamental ability to support change over time. Changes on the server side of a web API usually require changes on the client side. Sometimes existing production API clients will even crash or operate improperly once the server-side code has been changed. The problem has become so common that most web developers resort to using explicit version numbers on web APIs in order to make it easy for developers to know when something has changed—usually so developers can recode and deploy their production client apps in order to maintain compatibility with the service.

Throughout the book, I'll be introducing backend changes to service APIs *after* the client application has been completed (and presumably released into production). I'm doing this to explore how various API client implementations deal with change and to see what it takes to create API clients that can adapt to selected changes in the API at runtime.

So, let's make some changes to the TPS web API and see how our JSON client reacts.

Adding a Field and Filter

A common change that can occur in a production API is adding a new field to the data storage. For example, the team at BigCo working on the web API might decide to add a `tag` field to the `Task` storage object. This will allow users to tag tasks with common keywords and then recall all the tasks with the same keyword.

 The source code for the updated (v2) TPS JSON web API service can be found in the associated GitHub repo (*https://github.com/ RWCBook/json-crud-v2*). A running version of the service can be found online (*http://rwcbook04.herokuapp.com/task/*).

Adding the `tag` field means we'll probably need a new search option, too: `TaskFilter ByTag`. It would take a single parameter (a string) and use that to search all the task record's `tag` fields, returning all `Task` objects where the search value is contained in the `tag` field.

Changing the TPS web API

The process of changing the TPS web API to support the new `tag` functionality is not too complex. We'll need to:

1. Add the `tag` property to the `Task` storage definition.
2. Introduce a new query for `Task` storage and export that via HTTP.

To add the new `tag` field to the server's storage support, we first need to update a line of code that defines the valid fields for the `Task` object (❶).

```
// task-component.js
// valid fields for this record
props = [
  "id",
  "title",
  "tag", ❶
```

```
      "completeFlag",
      "assignedUser",
      "dateCreated",
      "dateUpdated"
    ];
```

Next, we need to modify the validation rules for adding and updating Task objects on the server. The following code snippet shows the addTask routine with the new tag field (❶). A similar change was made to the updateTask routine, too.

```
function addTask(elm, task, props) {
  var rtn, item;

  item = {}
  item.tags = (task.tags||"");  ❶
  item.title = (task.title||"");
  item.assignedUser = (task.assignedUser||"");
  item.completeFlag = (task.completeFlag||"false");
  if(item.completeFlag!=="false" && item.completeFlag!=="true") {
    item.completeFlag="false";
  }
  if(item.title === "") {
    rtn = utils.exception("Missing Title");
  }
  else {
    storage(elm, 'add', utils.setProps(item, props));
  }

  return rtn;
}
```

Testing the Updated TPS web API

With these changes in place, we can use the curl command-line app to validate our changes. A command to create a record with the tag value set to "test" looks like this:

```
curl -X POST -H "content-type:application/json" -d
  '{"title":"Run remote client tests","tags":"test"}'
  http://localhost:8181/task/
```

and creates a new task record that looks like this:

```
{
  "id": "1sog9t9g1ob",
  "title": "Run server-side tests",
  "tags": "test",
  "completeFlag": "false",
  "assignedUser": "",
  "dateCreated": "2016-01-28T07:16:53.044Z",
  "dateUpdated": "2016-01-28T07:16:53.044Z"
}
```

Assuming several new records were created, executing the filter query would look like this:

```
curl http://localhost:8181/task/?tags=test
```

and would return one or more `task` records with the `tag` value that contains `"test"`:

```
{
  "task": [
    {
      "id": "1m80s2qgsv5",
      "title": "Run client-side tests",
      "tags": "test client",
      "completeFlag": "false",
      "assignedUser": "",
      "dateCreated": "2016-01-28T07:14:07.775Z",
      "dateUpdated": "2016-01-28T07:14:07.775Z"
    },
    {
      "id": "1sog9t9g1ob",
      "title": "Run server-side tests",
      "tags": "test",
      "completeFlag": "false",
      "assignedUser": "",
      "dateCreated": "2016-01-28T07:16:53.044Z",
      "dateUpdated": "2016-01-28T07:16:53.044Z"
    },
    {
      "id": "242hnkcko0f",
      "title": "Run remote client tests",
      "tags": "test remote",
      "completeFlag": "false",
      "assignedUser": "",
      "dateCreated": "2016-01-28T07:19:47.916Z",
      "dateUpdated": "2016-01-28T07:19:47.916Z"
    }
  ]
}
```

With the TPS web API updated and validated, we next need to see how the JSON API client handles the change in production.

 For completeness, we should also update the TPS web API documentation. We'll skip that step right now, though.

Testing the JSON API client

The easiest way to test the JSON API client's support for the new `tag` field and filter option is to simply run the existing client and check the results. Figure 2-6 shows a screenshot from the JSON API client making a request to the new TPS web API server.

Figure 2-6. JSON API client without tag support

As you can see from the screenshot, even though the new `task` records appear in the client, the `tag` field is missing from the display as well as the new filter option. The good news is our JSON client didn't *crash* when the new feature was added. The bad news is our client simply ignored the new functionality.

> The source code for the updated (v2) TPS JSON Web Client can be found in the associated GitHub repo (*https://github.com/RWCBook/ json-client-v2*). A running version of the service can be found online (*http://rwcbook05.herokuapp.com/files/json-client.html*).

The only way our JSON client will be able to take advantage of this new option is to recode and redeploy a new version of the app into production.

Coding a New Client

To get the JSON API client to reflect the new `tag` support, we need to update the client's object and action data. The client needs to know about the tag feature before it can use it. Because our JSON client was designed to keep the object and action data separate from the rest of the library, adding the new feature is relatively easy.

First, we need to update the client's object properties (❶):

```
// task fields
g.fields.task = [
  "id",
  "title",
  "tags", ❶
  "completeFlag",
  "assignedUser"
];
```

Next, we need to add the new filter option to the list of the client's `task.actions`:

```
byTags: {
        target:"list",
        func:jsonForm,
        href:"/task",
        prompt:"By Tag",
        method:"GET",
        args:{
          tags: {value:"", prompt:"Tags", required:true}
        }
      }
```

and update the `addTask` and `updateTask` action definitions (❶ and ❷):

```
add:  {
        target:"list",
        func:jsonForm,
        href:"/task/",
        prompt:"Add Task",
        method:"POST",
        args:{
          title: {value:"", prompt:"Title", required:true},
          tags: {value:"", prompt:"Tags"}, ❶
          completeFlag: {value:"", prompt:"completeFlag"}
        }
      },
edit: {
        target:"single",
        func:jsonForm,
        href:"/task/{id}",
        prompt:"Edit",
        method:"PUT",
        args:{
          id: {value:"{id}", prompt:"Id", readOnly:true},
          title: {value:"{title}", prompt:"Title", required:true},
          tags: {value:"{tags}", prompt:"Tags"}, ❷
          completeFlag: {value:"{completeFlag}", prompt:"completeFlag"}
        }
      }
```

With these changes in place, we can now see that the JSON client supports the new tag features of the TPS web API, as shown in Figure 2-7.

You may have noticed that the changes we made to the client app look similar to the changes we made in the server API. That's not by accident. Typical JSON APIs require that the client app and the server-side code share the same OBJECT/ADDRESS/ACTION profiles in order to keep in step with each other. *That means every new feature on the service requires a new release for the client.*

Figure 2-7. JSON client v2 supports tagging

The original JSON client app we created was able to keep offering the same functionality without an update because the TPS web API didn't introduce breaking changes. If, for example, the service had changed the `addTask` and `updateTask` operations to make the `tag` field *required* when adding/editing `Task` objects, the original client app would no longer be able to save `Tasks`. Since the service made the `tag` field an optional input, the initial client app was still able to function; it just couldn't take advantage of the new feature. Essentially, when API services change, the best client apps can hope for is that services will not make *breaking* changes to the API (e.g., removing fields/functions, changing existing functions, or adding new required fields, etc.).

However, there are ways to design service APIs that allow clients to adapt to changing responses—even have the ability to expose new features (like the `tag` field and filter) without the need for recoding the client. We'll explore that in future chapters.

Summary

In this chapter we reviewed the key aspects of JSON API clients—namely, the need to:

- Handle key OBJECTS in the service model
- Construct and manage service ADDRESSES or URLs
- Know all the ACTIONS metadata, such as parameters, HTTP methods, and input rules

We then did a walk-through of our sample JSON client and saw how it handled the OAA Challenge. We also noted that the client app was written using a simple loop pattern that made a request, parsed the response, and (based on context information) rendered information to the screen for a human to deal with. The fully functional SPA client requires just over 500 lines of JavaScript—even with all the low-level HTTP routines.

JSON Clients and the OAA Challenge

It turns out clients that receive only plain JSON responses don't do well on our OAA Challenge. These clients either break or ignore changes to any of the three elements. They need to be recoded and redeployed any time an OBJECT, ADDRESS, or ACTION is added, removed, or changed.

Finally, we introduced a new feature on the TPS web API service and saw that our JSON client ignored the new feature. Luckily, the service was updated in a backward-compatible way and our client didn't crash or *lose* functionality. But we had to recode and redeploy the client in order to take advantage of the new `tag` feature.

Bob and Carol

"Hey, Bob. Just stopping by to review our experiences with the TPS web API project."

"Hi, Carol. Good to see you. Let's get started."

"First, we certainly learned a lot in the last week. It took some doing, but even with handling close to 20 operations in this API, we were able to get our JSON client SPA implementation down to around 500 lines of JavaScript."

"That's pretty impressive. And testing the functionality of the initial client went really well."

"Right, but that brings up a major problem we encountered. Changes to the backend made our client app obsolete."

"Yeah, sorry about that, Carol. After we released the API into production, we were asked for that tagging feature."

"Well, at least you made sure to add the new feature in a way that didn't *break* our JSON client. But none of the customers could see the new features until we recoded and redeployed our app."

"Yep. Hopefully, that won't happen too often."

"Well, Bob, I'm a bit concerned that it *will* keep happening. I mean, change is inevitable, right?"

"I guess that's right. But we can't stop people asking for new features. I guess this is just they way the Web works. We keep updating and rereleasing from now on."

"I'm not so sure about that, Bob. I think we need to look into another way to build web APIs and client apps. One that does a better job of supporting changes over time."

"Well, Carol, I'd like to hear more about that. But right now, I need to meet with my server-side team to review some more changes we need to make to the API."

"More changes? OK, Bob. Talk to you later."

References

1. You can learn more about Twitter's API by reviewing the online documentation (*https://dev.twitter.com/overview/documentation*).

2. There is a nice ECMAScript compatibility chart hosted on GitHub (*https://kangax.github.io/compat-table/es6/*).

CHAPTER 3

The Representor Pattern

"But it is a pipe."

"No, it's not," I said. "It's a drawing of a pipe. Get it? All representations of a thing are inherently abstract. It's very clever."

—John Green, *The Fault in Our Stars*

Bob and Carol

 "Hi, Carol. I'm just stopping by to talk you about some server-side features. Specifically, about implementing support for multiple output formats. See, we started with HTML and we just recently added support for plain JSON."

"Right, and some of the teams were starting to ask about support for additional registered formats like HAL, Collection+JSON, Siren, and so forth. We were about to dig into that when you and I launched the two teams."

 "Yep, your old colleagues have been bringing me up to speed and I wanted to check back with you and go over your initial notes."

"Well, I don't know how much I can offer since we have just begun our discovery."

"OK, well, I have some solid info on the formats you mentioned, but what I really wanted to review with you is some implementation ideas."

"OK, Bob. Makes sense. What do you have so far?"

"I was in a meeting yesterday where people were getting into heated debates about which of these formats to support. There seems to be a wide consensus on adding support for plain JSON objects and there are also people very adamant about supporting hypermedia formats like HAL, Cj, and Siren. It got me to thinking that this could be a real mess."

"Well, you don't really need to decide *which* format to support. In fact, I think that's a losing strategy."

"Wait, what? I don't need to decide on a format? That doesn't sound right."

"Well, instead of trying to get everyone to agree on a single format, the better approach is to implement the TPS API in a way that makes supporting one or more formats *trivial*."

"Hm. You mean diffuse these format arguments by saying 'yes' to everyone? That sounds even worse to me than picking one."

"One of the things I was exploring before the re-org was the notion of separating the message format from the internal object model of the API—a kind of loose-coupling approach to response formats."

"Oh, I get it. That way, the actual resolution of the format question doesn't adversely affect the rest of the system."

"Right, Bob. I got the idea from an old paper on software modularity. I can't recall which one, but I think that's in the notes you already have."

"Ah, good. So, decoupling the output format from the internal object model means we can make changes to the internal model without adversely affecting the external message model."

"Yep, and I bet you can come up with an implementation pattern that makes it relatively easy to support more than one message format for the same internal model. Now that would be something!"

 "Yes, Carol, that would be something. OK, I need to get back to the team and see what they think about all this. We'll let you know what we find."

"Sounds good, Bob. Talk to you soon."

Almost every team that starts out on the journey of implementing APIs for the Web runs up against the decision of which output format(s) to support. Most often, this decision is a matter of accepting the current norms rather than engaging in a series of experiments and research efforts. Usually, teams don't have the time or energy to go through decades of material on software implementation and systems engineering in order to decide which output format the API will use. Instead, the current custom or fad is the one that wins the day.

And *selecting* a format is only part of the challenge. A more important consideration is just *how* to write services that implement output format support. Sometimes services are implemented in a way that tightly binds the internal object model to the external output format. That means changes in the internal model leak out into the output format and are likely to break client applications which *consume* the service API.

That leads to another important challenge you'll face when dealing with messages passed between API consumer and API provider: protecting against breakage. Long ago, writers on software modularity offered clear advice on how to isolate parts of a system that are likely to change often and implement them in ways that made changes to that part of the system relatively cheap, safe, and easy. Keeping this in mind is essential for building healthy and robust API-based solutions.

So, there are a number of things to cover here. Let's put aside the history of modularity for a bit and first address the challenge most API developers face: "Which message format should we use for our API?"

XML or JSON: Pick a Side!

So you want to implement an API, eh? Well, one of the first decisions you will face is which message format to use. Today, almost everyone decides on JSON—often with little to no discussion. That's the power of current popularity—that the decision is made without much contemplation. But it turns out selecting JSON may not be the best choice or the *only* choice when it comes to your API output format.

All through the late 1990s and early 2000s, the common custom was to rely on message formats based on the XML standard. At that time, XML had a strong history —HTML and XML both had the same progenitor in SGML (ISO 8879:1986)—and there were lots of tools and libraries geared to parsing and manipulating XML documents. Both the SOAP specification and much of what would later be known as the SOA (service-oriented architecture) style started as XML-based efforts for business computing.

XMLHttpRequest

One of the most important API-centric additions to the common web browser—the ability to make direct calls to services *within* a single web page—was called the XMLHttpRequest object *because* it was assumed that these browser-initiated inline requests would be returning XML documents. And they did in the beginning. But by the mid-2000s, the JavaScript Object Notation (JSON) format would overtake XML as the common way to transfer data between services and web browsers. The format has changed, but the JavaScript object name never has.

But, as we all know, selecting XML for passing data between services and clients did not *end* the format debate. Even while the XML-based SOAP document model was being published as a W3C Note in May 2000, there was another effort underway to standardize data-passing documents—the JavaScript Object Notation format, or JSON.

Douglas Crockford is credited with specifying JSON in early 2001. Even though the JSON RFC document (RFC627) was not published until 2006, the format had experienced wide use by that time and was gaining in popularity. As of this writing, JSON is considered the default format for any new API. Recent informal polls and surveys indicate few APIs today are being published using the XML output format and—at least for now—there is no new format likely to undermine JSON's current popularity.

"I did not invent JSON"

In 2011, Douglas Crockford gave a talk he dubbed "The True Story of JSON" in which he said "I do not claim to have invented JSON. …What I did was I found it, I named it, I described how it was useful. …So, the idea's been around there for a while. What I did was I gave it a specification, and a little website." He even states that he saw an early example of JSON-like data-passing as early as 1996 from the team that was working on the Netscape web browser.

Of course, XML and JSON are not the only formats to consider. For example, another valuable format for passing data between parties is the comma-separated values (CSV) format. It was first standardized by the IETF in 2005 (RFC4180) but dates back to the late 1960s as a common interchange format for computers. There are likely going to be cases where an API will need to output CSV, too. For example, almost all spreadsheet software can easily consume CSV documents and place them in columns and rows with a high degree of fidelity.

And there have also been several binary formats created over the years, such as XML-based Fast Infoset from 2007, Google's Protobuf created in 2008, and more recent binary formats such as Apache Avro (2016) and Thrift from Facebook, which also defines extensive RPC protocol details.

Clearly the problem is not just deciding between XML and JSON.

The New Crop of Hypermedia Formats

Starting in the early 2010s, a new crop of text-based formats emerged that offered more than just structure for describing data; they included instructions on how to manipulate the data as well. These are formats I refer to as *hypermedia formats*. These formats represent another trend in APIs and, as we will see later in the book, can be a valuable tool in creating API-based services that support a wide range of service changes without breaking existing client applications. In some cases, they even allow client applications to "auto-magically" acquire new features and behaviors without the need for rewriting and redeploying client-side code.

Atom Syndication and Publishing

Although most of the new hypermedia formats appeared on the scene around 2010 and later, one format (the Atom Syndication Format) was standardized in 2005 as RFC4287. It has similar roots as the SOAP initiative and is an entirely XML-based specification. The Atom Format, along with the Atom Publishing Protocol (RFC5023) in 2007, describe a system of publishing and editing web resources that is based on the common Create-Read-Update-Delete (CRUD) model of simple object manipulation.

Atom documents are mostly used in read-only mode for news feeds and other simple record-style output. However, several blog engines support editing and publishing entries using Atom documents. There are also a number of registered format extensions to handle things like paging and archiving (RFC5005), threads (RFC4685), and licensing content (RFC4946). I don't often see Atom used to support read/write APIs on the WWW but still see it used in enterprise cases for handling outputs from queues and other transaction-style APIs.

Atom is interesting because it is an XML-based format that was designed specifically to add read/write semantics to the format. In other words, like HTML, it describes rules for adding, editing, and deleting server data.

And, since the release of the Atom specifications, a handful of other formats have been published.

Other hypermedia formats

There was a rush of text-based hypermedia-style formats published and registered with the IANA starting around 2011. They all share a similar set of assumptions even though each has unique strengths and focuses on different challenges for API formats. I'll cover some of these at length in the book and wanted to mention them here to provide a solid background for dealing with the challenge of selecting and supporting formats for APIs.

Hypermedia Application Language (HAL)
> The HAL format was registered with the Internet Authority for Names and Addresses (IANA) in 2011 by Mike Kelly. Described as "a simple format that gives a consistent and easy way to hyperlink between resources," HAL's design focus is on standardizing the way links are described and shared within messages. HAL does not describe write semantics but does leverage the URI Templates specification (RFC6570) to describe query details inline. We'll spend an entire chapter exploring (and using) this very popular hypermedia type.

Collection+JSON format (Cj)
> I published the Collection+JSON hypermedia format the same year as Mike Kelly's HAL (we had been sharing ideas back and forth for quite a while before that). Unlike HAL, Cj supports detailed descriptions of the common Create-Read-Update-Delete (CRUD) semantics inline along with a way to describe input metadata and errors. It is essentially a JSON-formatted fork of the Atom Publishing Protocol that is focused on common list-management use cases. We'll spend time coding for Cj formats later in the book.

The Structured Interface for Representing Entities (Siren)
> The Siren format was created by Kevin Swiber and registered at the IANA in 2012. Siren "is a hypermedia format for representing entities with their associated

properties, children, and actions." It has a very rich semantic model that supports a wide range of HTTP verbs and is currently used as the default format for the Zetta Internet of Things platform. We'll get a chance to dig into Siren later in the book.

The Universal Basis for Exchanging Representations (UBER)
I released a working draft of the UBER format in 2014. Unlike the other hypermedia formats listed here, UBER does not have a strong message structure, but instead has just one element (called "data") used for representing all types of content in a document. It also has both a JSON and XML variant. UBER has not yet been registered with the IANA and will not be covered in this book.

Other formats
There are a number of other interesting hypermedia-style formats that have recently appeared that won't be covered in this book. They include Jorn Wildt's Mason (*https://github.com/JornWildt/Mason*), the JSON API (*http://jsonapi.org/*) spec from Yehuda Katz, Cross-Platform Hypertext Language (*https://github.com/ mikestowe/CPHL*) by Mike Stowe, and several others.

Currently none of these new formats are a clear leader in the market and that, I think, is a good thing. In my experience, it is not common that an important universally valuable message format appears "out of the blue" from a single author. It is more likely that many formats from several design teams will be created, published, and tested in real-world scenarios before any possible "winner" will emerge. And the eventual solution will likely take several years to evolve and take several twists and turns along the way.

So, even though many people have said to me "I wish someone would pick *just one* format so I would know what to use," I don't think that will happen any time soon. It may seem like a good thing that you don't have a choice to make, but that's rarely true in the long run.

We need to get used to the idea that there is no "one API format to rule them all."

The Fallacy of *The Right One*

So, despite all the new hypermedia formats out there (and the continued use of XML in enterprises), with the current trend pointing toward JSON as the common output format, it would seem an easy decision, right? Any time you start implementing an API, just use JSON and you're done. Unfortunately, that's almost never the way it goes.

First, some industry verticals still rely on XML and SOAP-based formats. If you want to interact with them, you'll need to support SOAP or some other custom XML-based formats. Examples might be partner APIs that you work with on a regular basis, government or other standards-led efforts that continue to focus on XML as their preferred format, and even third-party APIs that you use to solve important business goals.

Second, many companies invested heavily in XML-based APIs over the last decade and are unwilling to rewrite these APIs *just* to change the output format. Unless there is a clear advantage to changing the messages format (e.g., increased speed, new functionality, or some other business metric), these XML-based services are not likely to change any time soon.

Finally, some data storage systems are XML-native or default to outputting data as XML documents (e.g., dbXML, MarkLogic, etc). While some of these services may offer an option to output the data in a JSON-based format, many continue to focus on XML and the only clear way of converting this data to JSON is to move it to JSON-native data storage systems like MongoDB, CouchDB, and others.

So, deciding on a single format for your team's service may not be feasible. And, as your point of view widens from a single team to multiple teams within your company, multiple products within an enterprise, on up to the entire WWW itself, getting everyone to agree to both produce and consume a single output format is not a reasonable goal.

As frustrating as this may be for team leaders and enterprise-level software architects, there is no single "Right One" when it comes to message formats. It may be possible to control a single team's decision (either through consensus or fiat) but one's ability to exert this control wanes as the scope of the community grows.

And that means the way forward is to rethink the problem, not work harder at implementing the same solution.

Reframing the Problem

One way to face a challenge that seems insurmountable is to apply the technique of *reframing*—to put the problem in a different light or from a new point of view. Instead of working harder to come up with a solution to the perceived problem, reframing encourages us to step outside the frame and change our perspective. Sometimes this allows us to recognize the scenario as a completely different problem—one that may have an easier or simpler solution.

Cognitive Reframing

The current use of the term *reframing* came from the cognitive therapy work of Aaron T. Beck in the 1960s. As he was counseling patients experiencing depression he hit upon the idea that patients could be taught to become aware of negative thoughts as they arose and to "examine and evaluate them," even turning them into positive thoughts. Initially called *cognitive reframing*, now the term is used to describe any technique that helps us reflect on our thoughts and situation and take a new perspective.

In our case (the challenge of selecting a single format for your APIs), it can help to ask "Why do we need to decide on a single format?" or, to put it another way, "Why not support many formats for a single API?" Asking these questions gives us a chance to lay out some of the reasons for and against supporting multiple formats. In this way, we've side-stepped the challenge of picking *one* format. Now we're focused on a new aspect of the same problem. Why not support *multiple* formats?

Why is supporting one format "better"?

The common pattern is to *assume* that selecting a single format is the preferred solution. To that end, there are some typical justifications for this point of view:

One format is easier
Usually people make the case for supporting a single format for API output because it is thought to be easier than supporting multiple formats. It may not be ideal to select just one format, but it is preferable to the cost of supporting more than one. And this is a valid consideration. Often we work with programming tools and libraries that make supporting multiple output formats costly in some way (additional programming time, testing difficulty, runtime support issues, etc.).

Multiple formats is anarchy
There are other times when making the case for supporting more than one format is perceived as making the case for supporting *any* format. In other words, once you open the door for one additional format, you MUST support any format that might be thought of at some point in the future.

The format you prefer is "bad"
Sometimes, even in cases where multiple formats might be possible, some start to offer value judgments for one or more of the suggested formats by saying they are (for any number of reasons) "bad" or in some other way insufficient and should not be included. This can turn into a "war of attrition" that can prompt leadership to just pick one and be done with the squabbling.

We can't know what people will like in the future anyway

Another reason to argue for just one format is that selecting any group of formats is bound to result in *not* selecting one or more formats that, at some future point, will become very popular. If you can't accurately predict which ones to pick for the future, it's a waste of time to pick any of them.

You Aren't Gonna Need It (YAGNI)

Finally, most API projects start with a single client in mind—often a client built by the same group of people building the service API. In these cases, it *seems* to make sense to invoke this famous maxim from the Extreme Programming (XP) community. Another version of this idea is to "Do the simplest thing that could possibly work." And, in cases where your API is unlikely to gain much reach or will have a limited lifetime, this kind of shortcut can make sense. However, if you are creating an API that will last more than a few years (most of them do) or one that will be used in a multichannel (desktop, browser, smartphone, etc.) environment, creating a service that is tightly coupled to a single message format can be costly in the long run. And, when done correctly, you can still abide by the YAGNI rule while keeping your options open for supporting multiple formats in the future.

The list goes on with any number of variations. But the theme is usually the same: you won't be sure to pick the right formats, so just pick a single one and avoid the costly mistakes of adding other formats no one will like or use in the future. The underlying assumptions in these arguments are also generally the same. They look something like this:

- Supporting multiple formats is hard.
- There is no way to safely add formats over time without disrupting production code.
- Selecting the right formats *today* is required (and is impossible).
- Supporting multiple formats is too costly when you don't have guaranteed uptake.

And it turns out, these assumptions are not always true.

What would it take to support multiple formats?

One way of helping a team reframe the message format challenge is to cast it as a "What would it take…?" question. Essentially, you ask the team to describe a scenario under which the suggested alternative (in our case, supporting multiple output formats) would be a reasonable idea. And it turns out that the assumptions listed before are a great starting point for setting out a scenario under which supporting multiple formats for your API is reasonable.

For example, you might make the following statements:

- Supporting multiple formats for the same API needs to be relatively easy to do.
- We need to be able to safely add new format support over time without disrupting production code (or existing clients).
- We need some kind of consistent criteria for selecting which formats to add both now and in the future.
- Adding a format needs to be cheap enough so that even it if turns out to be little-used, it is not a big deal.

Even though most of the statements here are qualitative criteria ("relatively easy," "cheap enough," etc.) we can use the same patterns of judgment and evaluation on the format challenge that we do when resolving other implementation-related challenges such as "What is an API resource?", "Which HTTP method should we use?", and others we face every day.

Luckily, there is a set of well-tested and documented programming patterns that we can use as a test case for implementing multiple format support for our APIs. And they date back to some of the earliest work on software patterns in the 1980s.

The Representor Pattern

To explore what it would take to make supporting multiple output formats for APIs, we need to work on a couple things. For a start, we should try to make it (1) relatively easy initially, and (2) safe to add new formats after production release. I've found that the first task is to clearly separate the work of format support from the actual functionality of the API. Making sure that you can continue to design and implement the basic API functionality (e.g., managing users, editing content, processing purchases, etc.), without tightly binding the code to a single format will go a long way toward making multiple format support safe and easy—even after the initial release of your API into production.

The other challenge for this kind of work is to cast the process of converting internal domain data (e.g., data graphs and action details) into a message format and a consistent algorithm that works well for a wide range of formats. This will require some software pattern implementation as well as an ability to deal with a less than 100% fidelity between the domain model and the output model. We deal with this every day with HTML (HTML doesn't know anything about objects or floating-point types) and we need to adopt a similar approach when dealing with common API message formats, too.

Finally, we'll need a mechanism for *selecting* the proper format for each incoming request. This, too, should be an algorithm we can implement consistently. Preferably this will rely on existing information in HTTP requests and will not introduce some new custom metadata that clients will need to support.

OK—separate format processing, implement a consistent way to convert domain data into an output format, and identify request metadata to help us select the proper format. Let's start with separating the format processing from the domain.

Separating Format from Functionality

All too often, I see service implementations that are bound too tightly to a single format. This is a common problem for SOAP implementations—usually because the developer tooling *leads* programmers into relying on a tight binding between the internal object model and the external output format. It is important to treat all formats (including SOAP XML output) as independent of the internal object model. This allows some changes in the internal model to happen without requiring changes to the external output format.

To manage this separation, we'll need to employ some *modularity* to keep the work of converting the domain model into a message external from the work of manipulating the domain model itself. This is using modularity to split up the assignment of work. Typically modularity is used to collect related functionality in a single place (e.g., all the functionality related to users or customers or shoppingCarts). The notion of using modularity as primarily a work assignment tactic comes from David Parnas's 1972 paper "On the Criteria to be Used in Decomposing Systems into Modules." As Parnas states:

> [M]odule is considered to be a *responsibility assignment* rather than a subprogram. The modularizations include the design decisions which must be made before the work on independent modules can begin. [Emphasis in the original]

Viewing the work of converting internal domain data into external output formats as a *responsibility assignment* leads us to isolate the conversion process into its own module. Now we can manage that module separately from the one(s) that manipulate domain data. A simple example of this clear separation might look like this:

```
var convert = new ConversionModule(HALConverter);
var output = convert.toMessage(domainData);
```

In that imaginary pseudo-code, the conversion process is accessed via an instance of the conversionModule() that accepts a message-specific converter (in this case, HAL Converter) and uses the toMessage function that accepts a domainData instance to produce the desired output. This is all quite vague right now, but at least we have a clear target for implementing safe, cheap, easy support for multiple output formats.

Once the functionality of the internal domain model is cleanly separated from the external format, we need some guidance on how to consistently convert the domain model into the desired output format. But before that, we'll need a pattern for selecting which format is appropriate.

The Selection Algorithm

An important implementation detail when supporting multiple output formats for an API is that of the output *selection* process. There needs to be some consistent algorithmic way to select the correct output format at runtime. The good news is that HTTP—still the most common application-level protocol for web APIs—has this algorithm already defined: content negotiation.

Section 3.4 of the HTTP specification (RFC7231) describes two patterns of content negotiation for "representing information":

Proactive
> The server selects the representation based on the client's preferences.

Reactive
> The server provides a list of possible representations to the client and the client selects the preferred format.

The most common pattern in use on the Web today is the proactive one and that's what we'll implement in our representor. Specifically, clients will send an Accept HTTP header that contains a list of one or more format preferences, and the server will use that list to determine which format will be used in the response (including the selected format identifier in the server's Content-Type HTTP header).

A typical client request might be:

```
GET /users HTTP/1.1
Accept: application/vnd.hal+json, application/vnd.uber+json
...
```

And, for a service that supports HAL but does not support UBER, the response would be:

```
HTTP/1.1 200 OK
Content-Type: application/vnd.hal+json
...
```

It's All About Quality

The content negotiation examples shown in this book are greatly simplified. Client apps may include several media types in their accept list—even the "*/*" entry (which means "I accept everything!"). Also, the HTTP specification for the Accept header includes what is known as the q parameter, which can qualify each entry in the accept list. Valid values for this parameter include a range of numbers from 0.001 (least preferred entry) to 1 (most preferred entry).

For example, this client request shows that, of the two acceptable formats, the HAL format is the most preferred by this client app:

```
GET /users/ HTTP/1.1
application/vnd.uber+json;q=0.3,
application/vnd.hal+json;q=1
```

So, that's what it looks like on the "outside"—the actual HTTP conversation. But what pattern is used *internally* to make this work on the server side? Thankfully, a solution for this kind of selection process was worked out in the 1990s.

Adapting and Translating

Many of the challenges of writing solid internal code can be summed up in a common *pattern*. And one of the most important books on code patterns is the 1994 book *Design Patterns* by Gamma, Helm, Johnson, and Vlissides (Addison-Wesley Professional). Those are rather tough names to remember and, over time, this group of authors has come to be known as the *Gang of Four* (GoF). You'll sometimes even hear people refer to the *Gang of Four book* when discussing this important text.

Patterns in Architecture

The notion that architecture can be expressed as a common set of patterns was first written about by Christopher Alexander. His 1979 book *The Timeless Way of Building* (Oxford University Press) is an easy and thought-provoking read on how patterns play a role in physical architecture. It was his work on patterns that inspired the authors of the *Design Patterns* book and so many other software patterns books.

There are about twenty patterns in the GoF book, categorized into three types:

- Creational patterns
- Structural patterns

- Behavioral patterns

The pattern that will help us in our quest to implement support for multiple output formats for our API that is safe, cheap, and easy is the **Adapter** structural pattern.

The Adapter pattern

As established on OODesign.com, the intent of the **Adapter** pattern is to:

> Convert the interface of a class into another interface clients expect. Adapter lets classes work together that couldn't otherwise because of incompatible interfaces.

And that's essentially what we need to do—convert an internal class (or model) into an external class (or message).

There are four participants to the **Adapter** pattern (Figure 3-1):

Target
Defines the domain-specific interface that client uses. This will be the message model or media type we want to use for output.

Client
Collaborates with objects conforming to the target interface. In our case, this is our API service—the app that is using the **Adapter** pattern.

Adaptee
Defines an existing interface that needs adapting. This is the internal model that needs to be converted into the target message model.

Adapter
Adapts the interface of adaptee to the target interface. This will be the specific media-type plug-in that we write to handle the work of converting the internal model to the message model.

So, we need to write an adapter plug-in for each target media type (HTML, HAL, Siren, Collection+JSON, etc.). That's not too tough. But the challenge is that each internal object model (the adaptee) is going to be different. For example, writing a plug-in to handle Users then writing one to handle Tasks, and on and on. That can mean lots of code is needed to write the adapters and—even more disappointing— these adapters may not be very reusable.

To try to reduce the need for tightly coupled adapter code, I'm going to introduce another pattern—one based on the **Adapter** pattern: the **Message Translator**.

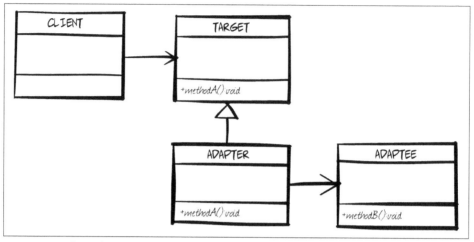

*Figure 3-1. The **Adapter** pattern*

That means we need to spend a few minutes on what the **Message Translator** pattern looks like and how it can be used to standardize the process of converting internal object models into external message models.

The Message Translator pattern

To cut down on lots of custom adapters, I'm going to introduce another pattern—derived from the **Adapter** pattern—called the **Message Translator**. This comes from Gregor Hohpe and his book *Enterprise Integration Patterns* (Addison-Wesley Professional).

Hohpe describes the **Message Translator** as:

> Use a special filter, a *Message Translator*, between other filters or applications to translate one data format into another.

A message translator is a special form of the adapter class in the GoF set of patterns.

To make this all work, I'll introduce a general message format—the Web Service Transition Language (WeSTL)—in the next section of this chapter. That will act as a standardized adaptee and make it possible to generalize the way adapter plug-ins can be coded. Now, the process of translating can be turned into an algorithm that doesn't need to rely on any domain-specific information. As illustrated in Figure 3-2, we can write WeSTL-to-HAL or WeSTL-to-Cj or WeSTL-to-Siren translators and then the only work is to convert the internal model into a WeSTL message. This moves the complexity to a new location, but does so in a way that reduces the amount of custom code needed to support multiple formats.

So, armed with this background, we can now look at a set of concrete implementation details to make it all happen.

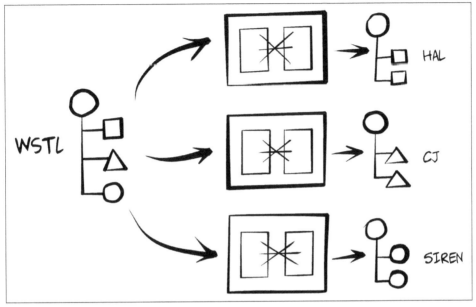

Figure 3-2. The Message Translator pattern

A Server-Side Model

In this section, I'll walk through the high-level details of a working representor implementation: the one that is used in all the services created for this book. Implementing a representor means dealing with the following challenges:

- Inspecting the HTTP request to identify the acceptable output formats for the current request.
- Using that data to determine which output format will be used.
- Converting the domain data into the target output format.

Handling the HTTP Accept Header

The first two items on that list are rather trivial to implement in any WWW-aware codebase. For example, identifying acceptable output formats for a request means reading the Accept HTTP header. Here is a snippet of NodeJS code that does that:

```
// rudimentary accept-header handling
var contentType = '';
var htmlType = 'text/html';
```

```
var contentAccept = req.headers['accept'];
if(!contentAccept || contentAccept==='*/*') {
  contentType = htmlType;
}
else {
  contentType = contentAccept.split(',')[0];
}
```

Note that the preceding code example makes two key assumptions:

1. If no `Accept` header is passed or the `Accept` header is set to "anything", the `Accept` header will be set to `text/html`.

2. If the `Accept` header lists more than one acceptable format, this service will just grab the first one listed.

This implementation is very limited. It does not support the use of q values to help the server better understand client preferences, and this service defaults to the `text/html` type for API responses. Both of these assumptions can be altered and/or improved through additional coding, but I've skipped over that for this book.

Implementing the Message Translator Pattern

Now that we have the requested format value—the output *context* for this request—we can move on to the next step: implementing the Message Translator pattern in NodeJS. For this book, I've created a simple module that uses a `switch ... case` element that matches the request context string (the accepted format) with the appropriate translator implementation.

The code looks like this:

```
// load representors ❶
var html = require('./representors/html.js');
var haljson = require('./representors/haljson.js');
var collectionJson = require('./representors/cj.js');
var siren = require('./representors/siren.js');

function processData(domainData, mimeType) {
  var doc;

  // clueless? assume HTML ❷
  if (!mimeType) {
    mimeType = "text/html";
  }

  // dispatch to requested representor ❸
  switch (mimeType.toLowerCase()) {
    case "application/vnd.hal+json":
      doc = haljson(object);
      break;
```

```
      case "application/vnd.collection+json":
        doc = collectionJson(object);
        break;
      case "application/vnd.siren+json":
        doc = siren(object);
        break;
      case "text/html":
      default: ❶
        doc = html(object);
        break;
    }
    return doc;
  }
```

In the preceding code snippet, you can see that a set of *representors* are loaded at the top (see ❶). The code in these modules will be covered in "Runtime WeSTL" on page 105). Next (❷), if the mimeType value is not passed (or is invalid) it is automatically set to text/html. This is a bit of defensive coding. And then (at ❸) the switch … case block checks the incoming mimeType string with known (and supported) mime type strings in order to select the appropriate format processing module. Finally, in case an unknown/unsupported format is passed in, the default statement (❹) makes sure that the service runs the html() module to produce valid output.

We now have the basics of the representor outlined. The next step is to actually implement each format-specific translator (HTML, HAL, etc.). To solve this challenge, we need to take a side road on our journey that establishes a general format understood by all translators—the WeSTL format.

General Representor Modules

In the Message Translator pattern, each format module (html(), haljson(), etc.) is an instance of a translator. While implementing these modules as domain-specific converters (e.g., userObjectToHTML, userObjectToHAL, etc.) would meet the needs of our implementation, that approach will not scale over time. Instead, what we need is a general-purpose approach to a translator that will *not* have any domain-specific knowledge. For example, the translator module used to handle user domain data will be the same translator module used to handle customer and accounting or any other domain-specific domain data.

To do that, we'll need to create a common interface for passing domain data into format modules that is independent of any single domain model.

The WeSTL Format

For this book, I've worked up a common interface in the form of a standardized object model, one that service developers can quickly load with domain data and pass to format modules. I also took the opportunity to reframe the challenge of defining interfaces for web APIs. Instead of focusing on defining resources, I chose to focus on defining *state transitions*. For this reason, I've named this interface design the *Web Service Transition Language*, or WeSTL (pronounced *wehs'-tul*).

Basically, WeSTL allows API service developers to use a standardized message model for converting internal object models into external message formats. This reduces the cost (in time and effort) to craft new **Translators** and pushes the complexity of converting internal models into messages to a single instance—converting from the internal model to WeSTL.

Figure 3-3 provides a visual representation of the request/response life cycle of services that use the WeSTL format.

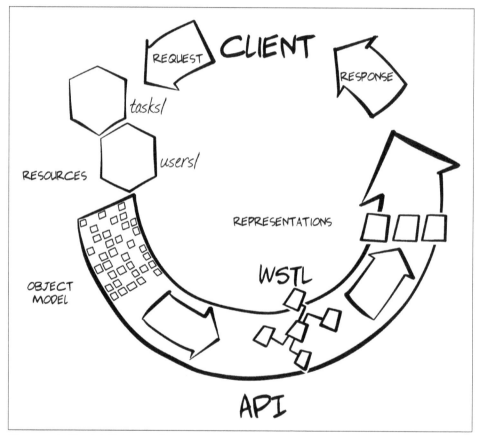

Figure 3-3. The WeSTL transformation cycle

Curious About WeSTL?

I won't be able to go into too much depth on the *design* of the WeSTL format in this chapter. I want to focus instead on how we can use WeSTL to drive our general representation module implementation. If you're curious about the thinking behind the WeSTL, check out the WeSTL Specifications (*http://rwcbook.github.io/wstl-spec/*) page and the associated online GitHub (*http://github.com/RWCBook/wstl-spec*) repo.

When designing and implementing web APIs with WeSTL, the service developer collects all the possible state transitions and describes them in the WeSTL model. By *state transitions*, I mean all the links and forms that could appear within any service response. For example, every response might have link to the home page. Some responses will have HTML-style input forms allowing API clients to create new service data or edit existing data. There may even be service responses that list all the possible links and forms (state transitions) for the service!

Why State Transitions?

Focusing on state transitions may seem a bit unusual. First, the transition is the thing *between* states; it leads from one state to another. For example, State A might be the home page and State B might be the list of users. WeSTL documents don't describe State A or B. Instead, they describe the action that makes it possible to move from State A to State B. But this is also not quite correct. WeSTL documents do not indicate the starting state (A) or the ending state (B)—just one possible way to move from *some* state to another. This focus on the actions that enable changes of state makes WeSTL handy for creating message translators.

A simple example of how WeSTL can be used to describe transitions is shown here:

```
{
  "wstl" : {
    "transitions" : [
      {
        "name" : "home",       ❶
        "type" : "safe",
        "action" : "read",
        "prompt" : "Home Page",
      },
      {
        "name" : "user-list",  ❷
        "type" : "safe",
        "target" : "user list"
        "prompt" : "List of Users"
      }
```

```
{
  "name" : "change-password", ❸
  "type" : "unsafe",
  "action" : "append"
  "inputs" : [ ❹
    {
      "name" : "userName",
      "prompt" : "User",
      "readOnly" : true
    },
    {
      "name" : "old-password",
      "prompt" : "Current Password",
      "required" : true,
    },
    {
      "name" : "old-password",
      "prompt" : "New Password (5-10 chars)",
      "required" : true,
      "pattern" : "^[a-zA-Z0-9]{5,10}$"
    }
  ]
}
]
}
}
```

As you can see from this WeSTL document, it contains three transition descriptions named home (❶), user-list (❷), and change-password (❸). The first two transitions are marked safe. That means they don't write any data, only execute reads (e.g., HTTP GET). The third one, however (change-password) is marked unsafe since it writes data to the service (à la HTTP POST). You can also see several input elements described for the change-password transition (❹). These details will be used when creating an API resource for the User Manager service.

There are a number of details left out in this simple example, but you can see how WeSTL works; it describes the transitions that can be used within the service. What's important to note is that this document does not define *web resources* or constrain where (or even when) these transitions will appear. That work is handled by service developers elsewhere in the code.

So, this is what a WeSTL model looks like at design time, before the service is up and running. Typically, a service designer uses WeSTL in this mode. There is also another mode for WeSTL documents: runtime. That mode is typically used when *implementing* the service.

Runtime WeSTL

At runtime, an instance of the WeSTL model is created that contains only the valid transitions for a particular resource. This runtime instance also includes any data associated with that web resource. In other words, at runtime, WeSTL models reflect the current *state* of a resource—both the available data and the possible transitions.

Creating a runtime WeSTL model in code might look like this:

```
var transitions = require('./wstl-designtime.js');
var domainData = require('./domain.js');

function userResource(root) {
  var doc, coll, data;

  data = [];
  coll = [];

  // pull data for this resource ❶
  data = domain.getData('user',root.getID());

  // add transitions for this resource ❷
  tran = transitions("home");
  tran.href = root +"/home/";
  tran.rel = ["http:"+root+"/rels/home"];
  coll.splice(coll.length, 0, tran);

  tran = transitions("user-list");
  tran.href = root +"/user/";
  tran.rel = ["http:"+root+"/rels/collection"];
  coll.splice(coll.length, 0, tran);

  tran = transitions("change-password");
  tran.href = root +"/user/changepw/{id}";
  tran.rel = ["http:"+root+"/rels/changepw"];
  coll.splice(coll.length, 0, tran);

  // compose wstl model ❸
  doc = {};
  doc.wstl = {};
  doc.wstl.title = "User Management";
  doc.wstl.transitions = coll;
  doc.wstl.data =  data;

  return doc;
}
```

As the preceding code sample shows, the userResource() function first pulls any associated data for the current resource—in this case, a single user record based on the ID value in the URL (as seen in ❶) then pulls three transitions from the design-time WeSTL model (❷) and finally composes a runtime WeSTL model by combining the data, transitions, and a helpful title string (❸).

And here is some high-level code that converts that runtime WeSTL document into a HAL representation:

```
var transitions = require('./wstl-designtime.js');
var domainData = require('./domain.js');

function userResource(root) {
  var doc, coll, data;

  data = [];
  coll = [];

  // pull data for this resource ❶
  data = domain.getData('user',root.getID());

  // add transitions for this resource ❷
  tran = transitions("home");
  tran.href = root +"/home/";
  tran.rel = ["http:"+root+"/rels/home"];
  coll.splice(coll.length, 0, tran);

  tran = transitions("user-list");
  tran.href = root +"/user/";
  tran.rel = ["http:"+root+"/rels/collection"];
  coll.splice(coll.length, 0, tran);

  tran = transitions("change-password");
  tran.href = root +"/user/changepw/{id}";
  tran.rel = ["http:"+root+"/rels/changepw"];
  coll.splice(coll.length, 0, tran);

  // compose wstl model ❸
  doc = {};
  doc.wstl = {};
  doc.wstl.title = "User Management";
  doc.wstl.transitions = coll;
  doc.wstl.data =  data;

  return doc;
}
```

As this code sample shows, the userResource() function first pulls any associated data for the current resource—in this case, a single user record based on the ID value in the URL (❶) then pulls three transitions from the design-time WeSTL model (❷), and finally composes a runtime WeSTL model by combining the data, transitions, and a helpful title string (❸).

It should be pointed out that the only constraint on the `wstl.data` element is that it must be an array. It can be an array of JSON properties (e.g., name–value pairs), an array of JSON objects, or even an array of *one* JSON object that is, itself, a highly nested graph. The WeSTL document may even include a property that points to a schema document (JSON Schema, RelaxNG, etc.) describing the `data` element. The related schema information can be used by the format module to help locate and process the contents of the `data` element.

So, WeSTL documents allow service developers to define web resources in a general way. First, service *designers* can create design-time WeSTL documents that describe all the possible transitions for the service. Second, service *developers* can use the design-time document as source material for constructing runtime WeSTL documents that include selected transitions plus associated runtime data.

Now we can finally write our general format modules.

A Sample Representor

Now that resources are represented using a generic interface using WeSTL, we can build a general format module that converts the standardized WeSTL model into an output format. Basically, the code accepts a runtime WeSTL document and then translates domain data, element by element, into the target message format for an API response.

To see how this might look, here is a high-level look at a simplified implementation of a general HAL representor.

The example representor shown here has been kept to the bare minium to help illustrate the process. A fully functional HAL representor will be covered in Chapter 4, *HAL Clients*.

```
function haljson(wstl, root, rels) { ❶
  var hal;

  hal = {};
  hal._links = {};

  for(var segment in wstl) {
    hal._links = getLinks(wstl[segment], root, segment, rels);
    if(wstl[segment].data && wstl[segment].data.length===1) {
      hal = getProperties(hal, wstl[segment]);
    }
  }
  return JSON.stringify(hal, null, 2); ❷
}
```

```
// emit _links object ❷
function getLinks(wstl, root, segment, relRoot) {
  var coll, items, links, i, x;

  links = {};

  // list-level actions
  if(wstl.actions) {
    coll = wstl.transitions;
    for(i=0,x=coll.length;i<x;i++) {
      links = getLink(links, coll[i], relRoot);
    }

    // list-level objects
    if(wstl.data) {
      coll = wstl.data;
      items = [];
      for(i=0,x=coll.length;i<x;i++) {
        item = {};
        item.href = coll[i].meta.href;
        item.title = coll[i].title;
        items.push(item);
      }
      links[checkRel(segment, relRoot)] = items;
    }
  }
  return links;
}

// emit root properties ❸
function getProperties(hal, wstl) {
  var props;

  if(wstl.data && wstl.data[0]) {
    props = wstl.data[0];
    for(var p in props) {
      if(p!=='meta') {
        hal[p] = props[p];
      }
    }
  }
  return hal;
}

/* additional support functions appear here */
```

While this code example is just a high-level view, you should be able to figure out the important details. The first argument of the top level function (haljson()) accepts a WeSTL model along with some runtime request-level data (❶). That function "walks" the WeSTL runtime instance and (a) processes any links (transitions) in the model (❷) and then (b) deals with any name–value pairs in the WeSTL instance (❸). Once all the processing is done, the resulting JSON object (now a valid HAL document) is returned to the caller (❹). An example of what this code might produce follows:

```
{
  "_links" : { ❶
    "self" : {
      "href": "http://localhost:8282/user/mamund"
    },
    "http://localhost:8282/rels/home": {
      "href": "http://localhost:8282/",
      "title": "Home",
      "templated": false
    },
    "http://localhost:8282/rels/collection": {
      "href": "http://localhost:8282/user/",
      "title": "All Users",
      "templated": false
    },
    "http://localhost:8282/rels/changepw": {
      "href": "http://localhost:8282/user/changepw/mamund",
      "title": "Change Password"
    }
  },
  "userName": "mamund", ❷
  "familyName": "Amundsen",
  "givenName": "Mike",
  "password": "p@ss",
  "webUrl": "http://amundsen.com/blog/",
  "dateCreated": "2015-01-06T01:38:55.147Z",
  "dateUpdated": "2015-01-25T02:28:12.402Z"
}
```

Now you can see how the WeSTL document has led from design-time mode to run-time instance and finally (via the HAL translator module) to the actual HAL document. The WeSTL transitions appear in the HAL _links section (❶) and the related data for this user appears as name–value pairs called properties in HAL documents (starting at ❷).

Of course, HAL is just one possible translator implementation. Throughout this book, you'll find general message translators for a handful of formats. Hopefully, this short overview will give enough guidance to anyone who wishes to implement their own (possibly *better*) general representors for HAL and many other registered formats.

Summary

This chapter has been a bit of a diversion. I focused on the *server-side* representor even though the primary aim of this book is to explore *client-side* hypermedia. But the representor pattern is an important implementation approach and it will appear many times in the code examples throughout the book. We've built up a working example of a representor by taking lessons from Parnas's "responsibility assignment" approach to modularity, the content negotiation features of HTTP, and Gregor Hohpe's message translator pattern.

Not too shabby for a diversion.

Bob and Carol

"Hi, Carol. Ready to go over my results on multiformat support?"

"Sure, Bob. I've been anxious to hear what you found out."

"Well, it was really interesting. After doing some brainstorming with the group, we found a handful of previous work that applies to our challenge."

"Really? Let me guess. You found some old comp-sci papers from the 1980s with the solution already worked up, right?"

"Not quite. First, we discussed the pros and cons of multiformat support for APIs. They all boiled down to some key points. If we want to do this, we need to make adding format support safe, cheap, and easy."

"Right. You need to be able to start simple now and then add new formats in the future without incurring lots of recode/redeploy costs."

"Exactly. The good news is we found some great background material to help us work up a solution."

"Now here comes the old comp-sci stuff!"

"Yep. First, David Parnas described *responsibility assignment* as a modularity approach from a paper in 1972, so we pulled all the format-related stuff into a separate module. Next, we found an existing enterprise integration pattern— the message translator— that handles our challenge rather well.

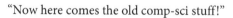

Finally, we can use HTTP's content negotiation feature as a way to select the proper output format at runtime."

"Wow, so it really *was* already built for you!"

"Not quite. We had the theory, but the next step was building the module—the representor. For that we needed to establish a common interface, and that meant using the *Web Service Transition Language* or WeSTL format. It's a model for describing transitions and even passing resource data from the internal service domain to the format-specific modules."

"Huh. We can talk about this transition model later. But now you have a full representor up and running, right? That's cool."

"Yep, the whole team contributed and we're all happy with how it's going so far. I'm really glad we took a couple days to look into this challenge and were able to come up with a general-use, loosely coupled solution."

"Well, that's great, Bob. Just one more question: What format did you finally select for the service?"

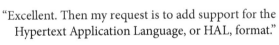

"Ha! Now that we have this pattern implemented, we can support multiple formats and we're looking for suggestions as we expand past the default HTML and plain JSON."

"Excellent. Then my request is to add support for the Hypertext Application Language, or HAL, format."

"No problem. I think the team is already working on that one."

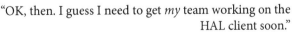

"OK, then. I guess I need to get *my* team working on the HAL client soon."

References

1. Standard Generalized Markup Language (SGML) is documented in ISO 8879:1986 (*http://g.mamund.com/zdtxd*). It is, however, based on IBM's *GML* format from the 1960s.

2. The "Simple Object Access Protocol (SOAP) 1.1" (*http://g.mamund.com/wcqhs*) specification was published as a W3C Note in May 2000. In the W3C publication model, Notes have no standing as a recommendation of the W3C. It wasn't until the W3C published the SOAP 1.2 Recommendation in 2003 that SOAP, technically, was a "standard."

3. Crockford's 50-minute talk "The JSON Saga" (*http://g.mamund.com/ztsdv*) was described as "The True Story of JSON." An unoffical transcript of this talk is available online (*http://g.mamund.com/gsqym*).

4. CSV was first specified by the IETF in RFC4180 (*http://g.mamund.com/spjhs*) "Common Format and MIME Type for Comma-Separated Values (CVS) Files" in 2005. This was later updated by RFC7111 (*http://g.mamund.com/rbexp*) (to add support for URI fragments) and additional CSV-related efforts have focused on supporting additional semantics.

5. You can learn about the binary formats mentioned in this chapter by visiting Fast Infoset, Avro, Thrift, and ProtoBuf.

6. The "Atom Syndication Format" (*http://g.mamund.com/wnqmf*) RFC4287) and the "Atom Publishing Protocol" (*http://g.mamund.com/jjbcj*) (RFC5023) form a unique pair of specifications that outline both the document format and read/write semantics in different RFCs. There are also a handful of RFCs defining Atom format extensions.

7. The YAGNI maxim is described in Ron Jeffries's blog post (*http://g.mamund.com/zeyxj*).

8. Mike Kelly's Hypertext Application Language (*http://g.mamund.com/xympu*) (HAL) has proven to be one of the more popular of the hypermedia type formats (as of this writing).

9. RFC6570 specifies URI Templates (*http://g.mamund.com/pmjez*).

10. The Collection+JSON (*http://amundsen.com/media-types/collection/*) format was registered with the IANA in 2011 and is "a JSON-based read/write hypermedia type designed to support management and querying of simple collections."

11. Both Siren (*https://github.com/kevinswiber/siren*) and Zetta (*https://github.com/zettajs/zetta/wiki*) are projects spearheaded by Kevin Swiber.

12. As of this writing, the Universal Basis for Exchanging Representations (*http://uberhypermedia.com*) (UBER) is in stable draft stage and has not been registered with any standards body.

13. Beck's 1997 article "The Past and Future of Cognitive Therapy" (*http://g.mamund.com/osucx*) describes his early experiences that led to what is now known as cognitive reframing.

14. Parnas's "On the Criteria to be Used in Decomposing Systems into Modules" (*http://g.mamund.com/bbyni*) is a very short (and excellent) article written for the ACM in 1972.

15. Details on HTTP content negotiation are covered in Section 3.4 of RFC7231 (*http://g.mamund.com/olyrb*). One of a series of HTTP-related RFCs (7230 through 7240).

16. The full title of the "Gang of Four" book is *Design Patterns: Elements of Reusable Object-Oriented Software* by Eric Gamma, Richard Helm, Ralph Johnson, and John Vlissides (Addison-Wesley Professional).

17. A good source for learning more about Christopher Alexander and his work can be found at the Pattern Language (*https://www.patternlanguage.com/ca/ca.html*) website.

18. Gregor Hohpe covers message translator in his book *Enterprise Integration Patterns* (Addison-Wesley Professional).

Image credits

- Diogo Lucas, Figures 3-1 and 3-2

CHAPTER 4

HAL Clients

"It is a mistake to look too far ahead. Only one link of the chain of destiny can be handled at a time."

—Winston Churchill

Bob and Carol

"OK, Bob. After talking with my team, we decided we want to build a new web client that uses the HAL media type."

"That's the one Amazon Web Services uses for a couple of APIs, right?"

"Right. It is one of the most frequently used of these new hypermedia formats. And I think it can help us on our quest to create a general client that adapts to backend changes in the API."

"Really? How is a HAL-based client better than a plain JSON client like the one you built a couple weeks ago?"

"Well, HAL is all about putting links in the responses and I think that's one of the things that keeps changing in your TPS web API, right?"

"Yes, we definitely need to change the URLs sometimes. It was a bit of a hassle recently when we moved the TPS API to the new servers."

 "Sure was. My team had to recode, retest, and redeploy the JSON client even though there was no new functionality updates."

"So you think using HAL as the message format for the API will help, Carol? Since the server-side team implemented the representor pattern, generating a new output format doesn't seem to be such a big job now."

 "Great. You get your server team working on the HAL representor and I'll get my team building a new HAL client app. Let's meet again next week."

"OK, Carol. See you next week."

As we saw in Chapter 2, *JSON Clients*, baking all OBJECT, ADDRESS, and ACTION information into the client app means that even minor changes to the service API will be ignored by that client. The common practice is for services to do their best to make non-breaking changes to the API and then inform clients of the new features and hope that client developers will recode and redeploy their apps sometime soon. This can be acceptable when both the client and server teams are in the same company, but becomes harder to support as more and more client developers start building against a single web API—especially when those client developers are not part of the organization that is responsible for the web API releases.

Around 2010, API developers started to tackle this problem head on by defining some new message formats for API responses. These formats were based on JSON but were more structured. The media type designs included definitions for links and, in some cases, even for query and update actions. Essentially, these formats started to restore some of the lost features of HTML (links and forms) to the plain JSON message format that was so common for web APIs.

One of the most popular of these structured formats is the Hypertext Application Language (HAL). We'll explore HAL in this chapter by building a general HAL client for our TPS web API and then, as before, modifying the web API to see how the HAL client holds up when the backend changes.

But first, let's take a brief look at the HAL format itself.

The HAL Format

Mike Kelly designed the Hypertext Application Language (HAL) in early 2011 and registered it with the Internet Authority for Names and Addresses (IANA) in July 2011. Initially created to solve a specific problem Kelly was having with a product release, HAL has gone on to become one of the more popular of the new hypermedia-style media formats created in the last several years.

HAL's design goal is rather simple—to make it easier for client applications to handle changes in backend service URLs. As he explained in a 2014 interview:

> The roadmap for the product [I was working on] included significant backend changes which were going to affect URL structures in the API. I wanted to design the API so that we could roll out those changes with as little friction as possible, and hypermedia seemed like the ideal style for that.

For Kelly, the HAL model focuses on two concepts: Resources and Links. *Links* have an identifier and a target URL along with some additional metadata. *Resources* carry state data, while Links carry other (embedded) Resources. Figure 4-1 shows a diagram of the HAL model.

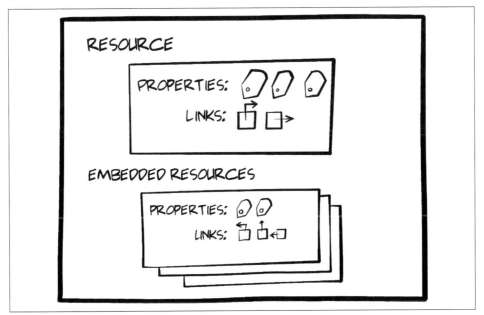

Figure 4-1. The HAL Design Model

Example 4-1 shows a simple HAL message (we'll cover the details in the following section).

Example 4-1. A simple HAL message

```
{
  "_links": {
    "self": {"href": "/orders"},
    "next": {"href": "/orders?page=2"},
    "find": {"href": "/orders{?id}", "templated": true},
    "admin": [
      {"href": "/admins/2", "title": "Fred"},
      {"href": "/admins/5", "title": "Kate"}
    ]
  },
  "currentlyProcessing": 14,
  "shippedToday": 20,
  "_embedded": {
    order": [
      {
        "_links": {
          "self": {"href": "/orders/123"},
          "basket": {"href": "/baskets/98712"},
          "customer": {"href": "/customers/7809"}
        },
        "total": 30.00,
        "currency": "USD",
        "status": "shipped"
      },
      {
        "_links": {
          "self": {"href": "/orders/124"},
          "basket": {"href": "/baskets/97213"},
          "customer": {"href": "/customers/12369"}
        },
        "total": 20.00,
        "currency": "USD",
        "status": "processing"
      }
    ]
  }
}
```

The model is very simple and, at the same time, powerful. With HAL, Kelly introduces the idea that a link is more than just a URL. It also has an identifier (rel) and other important metadata (e.g., type, name, title, templated and other properties). Kelly also points out in his 2013 blog post that he had some other important goals when designing HAL. These can be summed up as:

- HAL reduces coupling between client and server through the _link elements.

- HAL's `_link` convention makes the APIs "browsable by developers."
- The practice of connecting HAL's `_link` elements to human-readable documentation "makes the API discoverable by developers."
- Services can use HAL `_link` elements to introduce changes "in a granular way."

When considering the three important things API clients need to deal with—OBJECTS, ADDRESSES, and ACTIONS—we can see that HAL is optimized to support varying ADDRESSES (Links) at runtime. HAL's use of the `_link` as a key design element makes it possible for services to change URL values without breaking client applications.

HAL and the OAA Challenge

While HAL makes changing the ADDRESSES easy, its design doesn't attempt to optimize for changes in the exposed OBJECTS or the associated ACTIONS on those objects. That's not what Kelly was aiming for. We'll look at other hypermedia-style formats that tackle the other aspects of the web client challenge in later chapters.

Links

By far, the most important element in the HAL format is the way it standardizes Links in JSON. Here's what a link looks like in a HAL document:

```
"_links": {
  "self": { "href": "/orders" },
  "next": { "href": "/orders?page=2" },
  "find": { "href": "/orders{?id}", "templated": true } ❶
},
```

Note that each `link` object has an identifier (`self`, `next`, `find`). This is required for HAL documents. It is the identifier that the client application will store in code, not the actual URL value. The URLs appear in the `href` property and these URLs may actually be URL templates (see ❶). HAL leverages the URI Template specification (RFC6570) and the `templated:"true"` property for these.

In HAL, all link objects appear as part of a `"_links"` collection. These collections can appear in several places within a single HAL document.

Objects and Properties

HAL also supports passing plain JSON objects and name–value pairs. These typically appear as a collection of properties at the root of a HAL document. For example, the Amazon API Gateway service emits HAL responses. Following are a couple of examples of the 26 resource models the AWS Gateway API produces:

```
{
  "domainName" : "String",
  "certificateName" : "String",
  "certificateUploadDate" : "Timestamp",
  "distributionDomainName" : "String"
}

{
  "id" : "String",
  "description" : "String",
  "createdDate" : "Timestamp",
  "apiSummary" : {
    "String" : {
      "String" : {
        "authorizationType" : "String",
        "apiKeyRequired" : "Boolean"
      }
    }
  }
}
```

As we discussed in Chapter 2, *JSON Clients*, tracking domain objects is an important aspect of API clients. By design, the HAL format does not offer any additional design elements to make this any different than working with plain JSON responses. So HAL clients will need to know all the possible objects and models the API will be emitting before that client app can interact with the API.

Embedded Links and Objects

Finally, the HAL design allows for additional resources (and their associated links and properties) to appear as *embedded* models within responses. This makes it possible to return a single HAL document that includes multiple server-side resources. This acts as a way to reduce the number of HTTP requests and improves the perceived responsiveness of the service.

Following is a more extensive HAL document that includes all the features we've covered so far:

```
{
  "_links": {
    "self": { "href": "/orders" },
    "curies": [{ "name":"ea", "href":"http://example.com/docs/rels/{rel}", ❶
      "templated": true }],
    "next": { "href": "/orders?page=2" },
    "ea:find": {
      "href": "/orders{?id}",
      "templated": true
    },
    "ea:admin": [{
      "href": "/admins/2",
      "title": "Fred"
```

```
    }, {
      "href": "/admins/5",
      "title": "Kate"
    }]
  },
  "currentlyProcessing": 14,
  "shippedToday": 20,
  "_embedded": {
    "ea:order": [{
      "_links": {
        "self": { "href": "/orders/123" },
        "ea:basket": { "href": "/baskets/98712" },
        "ea:customer": { "href": "/customers/7809" }
      },
      "total": 30.00,
      "currency": "USD",
      "status": "shipped"
    }, {
      "_links": {
        "self": { "href": "/orders/124" },
        "ea:basket": { "href": "/baskets/97213" },
        "ea:customer": { "href": "/customers/12369" }
      },
      "total": 20.00,
      "currency": "USD",
      "status": "processing"
    }]
  }
}
```

The preceding example also shows HAL's curies support (❶). HAL uses the W3C Compact URI Syntax (CURIES) as a way to shorten long unique link identifiers. This is an optional HAL element but one that you may encounter "in the wild."

CURIES

The CURIES syntax was documented in 2010 by a W3C Working Group Note. The acronym CURIE (pronounced *cure-ee*) stands for Compact URI (the E is added for pronunciation). It was created by the XHTML group and is used in XML and RDF documents similar to the way XML namespaces are used. You can learn more about CURIEs by reading the W3C documents.

Quick Summary

So the HAL hypermedia format focuses on making it possible for services to change URLs at runtime without breaking client applications. It does this by formalizing the way URLs are expressed in responses using the HAL **Link** element (e.g., "_links: {"self":{"href":"/home/"}}). HAL also supports passing state data in plain JSON properties or objects and provides the ability to nest **Resources** using the "_embed ded":{...} element.

That gives us enough information to add HAL support for our TPS web API. First we'll modify the TPS API to emit HAL-compliant responses. Then we'll build a general HAL client that reads those responses.

The HAL Representor

As we learned in Chapter 3, *The Representor Pattern*, our TPS server allows us to separately create representor modules based on the WeSTL format to support multiple output formats. For our TPS web API to support HAL clients, we first need to write that representor module and add it to the existing service in production. This can be done in just a few hundred lines of server-side JavaScript by accounting for the three main aspects of the HAL format:

- Links
- Properties
- Embedded resources

The source code for the HAL edition of the TPS web API can be found in the associated GitHub repo (*https://github.com/RWCBook/hal-client*). A running version of the app described in this chapter can be found online (*http://rwcbook06.herokuapp.com/task/*).

The top-level routine in the representor creates the empty HAL document and populates it with Links, Properties, and (if available) embedded objects. The code looks like Example 4-2.

Example 4-2. The top-level routine in the HAL representor

```
function haljson(wstlObject, root, relRoot) {
  var hal;

  hal = {};
  hal._links = {};

  for(var segment in wstlObject) {
    hal._links = getLinks(wstlObject[segment], root, segment, rels); ❶
    if(wstlObject[segment].content) { ❷
      hal.content = wstlObject[segment].content;
    }
    if(wstlObject[segment].related) { ❸
      hal.related = wstlObject[segment].related;
```

```
  }
  if(wstlObject[segment].data && wstlObject[segment].data.length===1) { ❹
    hal = getProperties(hal, wstlObject[segment]);
  }
  else {
    hal._embedded = getEmbedded(wstlObject[segment], root, segment, rels); ❺
  }
  }
  }
  return JSON.stringify(hal, null, 2); ❻
}
```

After initializing an empty HAL document, this routine does the following:

❶ Add all the related Links to the _link collection.

❷ If there is any associated content for this response, add that as a root-level property.

❸ If there are any related records for this response, add them as another property.

❹ If there is only one data record associated with the response, add it as a set of properties.

❺ Otherwise, add the collection of data objects to the optional _embedded element in the HAL document.

❻ Finally, the results are returned as a plain-text JSON object for sending back to the client over HTTP.

That's it. Not too hard. Now let's look at the main subroutines for generating HAL responses: Links, Properties, and Embedded.

Links

The getLinks routine searches through the runtime internal WeSTL document and composes the appropriate link elements for the response. It looks like this:

```
// emit _links object
function getLinks(wstlObject, root, segment, relRoot) {
  var coll, items, links, i, x;

  links = {};

  // list-level actions
  if(wstlObject.actions) { ❶
    coll = wstlObject.actions;
    for(i=0,x=coll.length;i<x;i++) {
      links = getLink(links, coll[i], relRoot);
    }
```

```
// list-level objects
if(wstlObject.data) { ❷
  coll = wstlObject.data;
  items = [];
  for(i=0,x=coll.length;i<x;i++) {
    item = {};
    link = getItemLink(wstlObject.actions);
    if(link.href) {
      item.href = link.href.replace(/{key}/g, coll[i].id)||"#";
    }
    item.title = coll[i].title||coll[i].nick;
    items.push(item);
  }
  links[checkRel(segment, relRoot)] = items; ❸
  }
 }
}
```

There are just a few interesting elements to the getLinks routine:

❶ If there are actions in the WeSTL document, compose them as valid HAL links (that's the getLink routine) and add them to the document.

❷ If there is data associated with the response, walk through all the objects and resolve any direct item link data and add it to the document.

❸ Finally, check each of the links (with the checkRel routine) to see if it's a registered IANA link relation value or an application-specific link identifier.

That last step makes sure to follow the rules for link relations (from RFC5988) and include a fully qualified domain name (FQDN) to the link's rel value for any identifiers that are not already registered.

Properties

The next step is to emit any HAL properties in the response. Our TPS API could emit some plain HTML (via the internal content element). It may also have some related data objects (via the internal related object collection) to help support drop-down lists or other rendering. We also need to emit root-level HAL properties if the response has just *one* associated data object. This is not a requirement of HAL—it just makes emitting compliant HAL documents easy for our representor.

 The content and related elements are part of the TPS web API and are not defined by HAL. I'm using them here to make sure the new HAL edition of the TPS web API provides the same features and functionality as the JSON edition.

The code that handles the content and related elements appears in the haljson routine (refer back to Example 4-2). The code that emits the data object as properties (getProperties) looks like this:

```
// emit root properties
function getProperties(hal, wstlObject) {
  var props;

  if(wstlObject.data && wstlObject.data[0]) { ❶
    props = wstlObject.data[0]; ❷
    for(var p in props) {
      hal[p] = props[p]; ❸
    }
  }
  return hal;
}
```

The getProperties routine does the following:

❶ If there is only *one* data object in the resource collection…

❷ Get an index collection of that object's property names.

❸ Add each property name–value pair to the HAL document.

Embedded

The last step in supporting valid HAL responses is dealing with the optional _embedded section. This element of the HAL design is meant to optimize long lists of HAL link elements by including the associated objects in the response. This is a kind of internal caching helper. For our HAL representor, we will generate an _embedded section (using the getEmbedded function) whenever the resource behind the HAL response has multiple objects in the internal WeSTL data collection.

The code looks like this:

```
// emit embedded content
function getEmbedded(wstlObject, root, segment, relRoot) {
  var coll, items, links, i, x;

  links - {};

  // list-level objects
  if(wstlObject.data) {
    coll = wstlObject.data;
    items = [];
    for(i=0,x=coll.length;i<x;i++) { ❶
      item = {};
      link = getItemLink(wstlObject.actions); ❷
      if(link.href) {
```

```
          item.href = link.href.replace(/{key}/g, coll[i].id)||"#"; ❸
        }
        for(var p in coll[i]) {
          item[p] = coll[i][p]; ❹
        }
        items.push(item); ❺
      }
      links[checkRel(segment, relRoot)] = items;
    }

    return links; ❻
  }
```

There are a number of things going on here. After grabbing the collection of resource data objects, the getEmbedded routine does the following:

❶ Walk through the object collection to create an embedded item object.

❷ Pull that item's direct link (using the getItemLink function).

❸ Resolve the direct link (if there is a URI Template).

❹ Populate the embedded item with the internal object's properties.

❺ Add the completed item to the embedded collection.

❻ Finally, after checking the item link for RFC5988 compliance, return the _embedded collection for inclusion in the HAL document.

There are a couple of internal routines not shown here. They handle finding the data object's direct link template (getItemLink), creating valid HAL links (getLink), and RFC5988 compliance (checkRel). You can check the source code for details behind these.

Sample TPS Output from the HAL Representor

With the HAL representor completed, the TPS web API now emits proper HAL representations. Example 4-3 shows the output from the TPS server for the Home resource.

Example 4-3. HAL Response for TPS web API Home Resource

```
{
  "_links": {
    "self": {
      "href": "http://rwcbook06.herokuapp.com/home/",
      "title": "Home",
      "templated": false,
```

```
      "target": "app menu hal"
    },
    "http://rwcbook06.herokuapp.com/files/hal-home-task": {
      "href": "http://rwcbook06.herokuapp.com/task/",
      "title": "Tasks",
      "templated": false,
      "target": "app menu hal"
    },
    "http://rwcbook06.herokuapp.com/files/hal-home-user": {
      "href": "http://rwcbook06.herokuapp.com/user/",
      "title": "Users",
      "templated": false,
      "target": "app menu hal"
    },
    "http://rwcbook06.herokuapp.com/files/hal-home-home": []
  },
  "content": "<div class=\"ui segment\"><h3>Welcome to TPS at BigCo!</h3> _
  <p><b>Select one of the links above.</b></p></div>",
  "related": {},
  "_embedded": {
    "http://rwcbook06.herokuapp.com/files/hal-home-home": []
  }
}
```

And Example 4-4 shows the HAL output for a single TPS Task object.

Example 4-4. A single TPS Task object as a HAL document

```
{
  "_links": {
    "http://rwcbook06.herokuapp.com/files/hal-task-home": {
      "href": "http://rwcbook06.herokuapp.com/home/",
      "title": "Home",
      "templated": false,
      "target": "app menu hal"
    },
    "self": {
      "href": "http://rwcbook06.herokuapp.com/task/",
      "title": "Tasks",
      "templated": false,
      "target": "app menu hal"
    },
    "http://rwcbook06.herokuapp.com/files/hal-task-user": {
      "href": "http://rwcbook06.herokuapp.com/user/",
      "title": "Users",
      "templated": false,
      "target": "app menu hal"
    },
    "http://rwcbook06.herokuapp.com/files/hal-task-item": {
      "href": "http://rwcbook06.herokuapp.com/task/{key}",
      "title": "Detail",
      "templated": true,
```

```
      "target": "item hal"
    },
    "http://rwcbook06.herokuapp.com/files/hal-task-edit": {
      "href": "http://rwcbook06.herokuapp.com/task/{key}",
      "title": "Edit Task",
      "templated": true,
      "target": "item edit hal"
    },
    "http://rwcbook06.herokuapp.com/files/hal-task-remove": {
      "href": "http://rwcbook06.herokuapp.com/task/{key}",
      "title": "Remove Task",
      "templated": true,
      "target": "item edit hal"
    },
    "http://rwcbook06.herokuapp.com/files/hal-task-markcompleted": {
      "href": "http://rwcbook06.herokuapp.com/task/completed/{id}",
      "title": "Mark Completed",
      "templated": true,
      "target": "item completed edit post form hal"
    },
    "http://rwcbook06.herokuapp.com/files/hal-task-assignuser": {
      "href": "http://rwcbook06.herokuapp.com/task/assign/{id}",
      "title": "Assign User",
      "templated": true,
      "target": "item assign edit post form hal"
    },
    "http://rwcbook06.herokuapp.com/files/hal-task-task": [
      {
        "href": "//rwcbook06.herokuapp.com/task/1m80s2qgsv5",
        "title": "Run client-side tests"
      }
    ]
  },
  "id": "1m80s2qgsv5",
  "title": "Run client-side tests",
  "tags": "test",
  "completeFlag": "false",
  "assignedUser": "alice",
  "dateCreated": "2016-01-28T07:14:07.775Z",
  "dateUpdated": "2016-01-31T16:49:47.792Z"
}
```

 The output would be greatly improved if my representor used CURIEs for the URL keys. CURIEs don't make the service or the client work better, but they make the API responses much more browsable and discoverable for developers. And, you may recall from Mike Kelly's design guidelines, these were two very important goals in the design of HAL messages. I leave it to readers to improve my simple HAL representor by adding support for CURIEs and submitting the update to GitHub.

Note that the output includes link objects marked with the target property. This is not a defined HAL property. Our TPS server emits this property to help the HAL client know how to handle the link—whether it should be rendered at the top of every page ("app"), just for object lists ("list"), or only when there is a single object to display ("item"). We'll cover more of that in the next section of this chapter.

The HAL SPA Client

OK, now let's walk through the HAL client SPA implementation. As we did in Chapter 2, *JSON Clients*, we'll review the HTML container, the top-level parse loop, and how our client handles HAL's Links, Properties, and Embedded elements.

 The source code for the HAL client can be found in the associated GitHub repo (*https://github.com/RWCBook/hal-client*). A running version of the app described in this chapter can be found online (*http://rwcbook06.herokuapp.com/files/hal-client.html*).

The HTML Container

Like all single-page apps (SPAs), this one starts with a single HTML document acting as the *container* for all the client–server interactions. Our HAL client container looks like this:

```
<!DOCTYPE html>
<html>
  <head>
    <title>HAL</title>
    <link href="./semantic.min.css" rel="stylesheet" />
    <style>#dump {display:none;}</style>
  </head>
  <body>
    <div id="toplinks"></div> ❶
    <h1 id="title" class="ui page header"></h1>
    <div id="content"></div>
    <div id="links"></div>
    <div class="ui two column grid" style="margin-top: 2em">
      <div class="column">
        <div id="embedded" class="ui segments"></div>
        <div id="properties"></div>
      </div>
      <div class="column">
        <div id="form"></div>
      </div>
    </div>
    <div>
      <pre id="dump"></pre>
    </div>
```

```
    </body>
    <script src="uritemplate.js">//na</script>  ❷
    <script src="dom-help.js">//na</script>
    <script src="hal-client.js">//na </script>
    <script>
      window.onload = function() {
        var pg = hal();
        pg.init("/home/", "TPS - Task Processing System");  ❸
      }
    </script>
  </html>
```

Most of the content should look familiar. Our HTML layout for the app (starting at
❶) is a bit more involved than in previous apps in order to accommodate the HAL
elements (links, properties, embedded) but the rest is similar to our JSON client app.
Note that there are three scripts for this client (❷). The familiar dom-help.js file, the
expected hal-client.js library and a new JS module: uritemplate.js. The HAL
design relies upon RFC5988 (URI Template) compliant links so we'll use a standard
library to handle these.

Finally, at ❸, the initial URL is supplied and the hal-client.js library is kicked off.
We'll spend the rest of our walk-through in the hal-client.js file.

The Top-Level Parse Loop

After making the initial HTTP request, the response is passed to the parseHAL routine. Like all our SPA apps, the HAL client relies on a simple request, parse, render
loop. Here's the top-level parse loop for this app.

```
// primary loop
function parseHAL() {
  halClear();
  title();
  setContext();  ❶
  if(g.context!=="") {  ❷
    selectLinks("app", "toplinks");
    selectLinks("list", "links");
    content();
    embedded();
    properties();
  }
  else {
    alert("Unknown Context, can't continue");  ❸
  }
}
```

After clearing the user interface of any previously rendered content and setting the
title, the web client kicks off a set of HAL-specific routines. Here are the highlights:

❶ First, the setContext routine determines which OBJECT is being returned (Home, Task, or User).

❷ If we have a valid context, the HAL-specific elements are parsed and rendered (including filtering the link pile for display in the proper locations).

❸ Finally, if the service returned a context the client is not prepared to deal with, an alert is displayed.

Note that we're hardcoding the OBJECT knowledge into this app (via setContext). We are also expecting special information from the service about each link object to know how and where to display it. We'll see more on that in the next section.

Links

HAL's strength is the ability to return well-identified link objects for API clients. For our client, the selectLinks routine parses the HAL _links collection and determines how to build and render the link information in the proper place on the screen.

Here's the code:

```
// select and render HAL links
function selectLinks(filter, section, itm) { ❶
  var elm, coll;
  var menu, item, a, sel, opt, id;

  elm = d.find(section);
  d.clear(elm);
  if(g.hal._links) { ❷
    coll = g.hal._links;
    menu = d.node("div");
    menu.className = "ui blue menu";

    for(var link in coll) {
      if(coll[link].target && coll[link].target.indexOf(filter)!==-1) { ❸
        id = (itm && itm.id?itm.id:"");

        a = d.anchor({ ❹
          rel:link,
          href:coll[link].href.replace('{key}',id),
          title:(coll[link].title||coll[link].href.replace('{key}',id)),
          text:(coll[link].title||coll[link].href.replace('{key}',id))
        });

        // add internal attributes ❺
        a.setAttribute("templated", coll[link].templated||"false");
        a = halAttributes(a,coll[link]);

        item = d.node("li");
```

```
        item.onclick = halLink;  ❻
        item.className = "item";

        d.push(a, item);
        d.push(item, menu);
      }
    }
    d.push(menu, elm);  ❼
  }
}
```

There is a lot going on in this routine. That's because most of the information in a HAL response is stored in the _links collection. Let's do the walk-through…

First (at ❶) the signature of the selectLinks function takes up to three values: The string (filter) to use against the our custom link.target field, the name of the HTML DOM element (section) where we'll render the links, and (optionally) the current data object (itm) to use when resolving item-level links. We'll see this last argument in use when we scan the code for handling HAL's _embedded collection.

After making sure this response actually has links (❷) and filtering the collection to match our needs (❸), the code builds up an HTML <a>…</a> element (❹), adds some local attributes the code uses to handle user clicks at runtime, marks the link if it is using a URL template (❺), and then (at ❻) attaches a local click event (halLink) that can sort out just how to handle the requested action. Finally, (❼) the resulting links are added to the HTML DOM and rendered on the screen.

Figure 4-2 shows how the elements in the HAL _links collection is rendered on the screen for the list of Task objects.

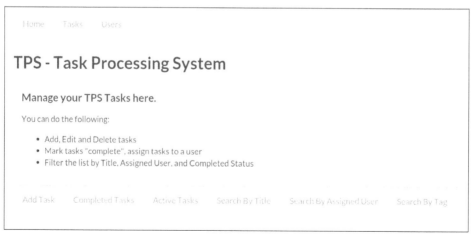

Figure 4-2. Rendering HAL _links for task objects

Embedded

HAL's _link collection doesn't just contain a list of action links (like the ones rendered before). The HAL response may also contain one or more links to associated resources. For example, the TPS web API returns a list of Task objects as link elements in a HAL response. The same response also includes the associated Task objects in the _embedded section:

```
{
  "_links": {
    "self": {
      "href": "http://rwcbook06.herokuapp.com/task/",
      "title": "Tasks",
      "templated": false,
      "target": "app menu hal"
    },
    "http://rwcbook06.herokuapp.com/files/hal-task-task": [
      {
        "href": "//rwcbook06.herokuapp.com/task/1m80s2qgsv5",
        "title": "Run client-side tests"
      },
      {
        "href": "//rwcbook06.herokuapp.com/task/1sog9t9g1ob",
        "title": "Run server-side tests"
      },
      {
        "href": "//rwcbook06.herokuapp.com/task/1xya56y8ak1",
        "title": "Validate client-side code changes"
      }
    ]
  },
  "_embedded": {
    "http://rwcbook06.herokuapp.com/files/hal-task-task": [
      {
        "href": "//rwcbook06.herokuapp.com/task/1m80s2qgsv5",
        "id": "1m80s2qgsv5",
        "title": "Run client-side tests",
        "tags": "test",
        "completeFlag": "false",
        "assignedUser": "alice",
        "dateCreated": "2016-01-28T07:14:07.775Z",
        "dateUpdated": "2016-01-31T16:49:47.792Z"
      },
      {
        "href": "//rwcbook06.herokuapp.com/task/1sog9t9g1ob",
        "id": "1sog9t9g1ob",
        "title": "Run server-side tests",
        "tags": "test",
        "completeFlag": "false",
        "assignedUser": "",
        "dateCreated": "2016-01-28T07:16:53.044Z",
```

```
      "dateUpdated": "2016-01-28T07:16:53.044Z"
    },
    {
      "href": "//rwcbook06.herokuapp.com/task/1xya56y8ak1",
      "id": "1xya56y8ak1",
      "title": "Validate client-side code changes",
      "completeFlag": "true",
      "assignedUser": "",
      "dateCreated": "2016-01-14T17:46:32.384Z",
      "dateUpdated": "2016-01-16T04:50:57.618Z"
    }
  ]
 }
}
```

Our HAL client takes advantage of the _embedded objects and renders them on screen. That's handled by the embedded routine, which looks like this:

```
// handle any embedded content
function embedded() {
  var elm, embeds, links;
  var segment, table, tr;

  elm = d.find("embedded");
  d.clear(elm);

  if(g.hal._embedded) {
    embeds = g.hal._embedded;
    for(var coll in embeds) { ❶

      p = d.para({text:coll, className:"ui header segment"});
      d.push(p,elm);

      // get all the objects in each collection
      items = embeds[coll];
      for(var itm of items) { ❷
        segment = d.node("div");
        segment.className = "ui segment";
        links = d.node("div");
        links.id = itm.id;
        d.push(links,segment);

        // emit all the properties for this item
        table = d.node("table"); ❸
        table.className = "ui very basic collapsing celled table";
        for(var prop of g.fields[g.context]) {
          if(itm[prop]) {
            tr = d.data_row({className:"property "+prop,text:prop+" ",
            value:itm[prop]+" "});
            d.push(tr,table);
          }
        }
```

```
        // push the item element to the page
        d.push(table,segment);
        d.push(segment, elm);

        // emit any item-level links
        selectLinks("item",itm.id, itm); ❹
      }
    }
  }
}
```

Here is a quick rundown of what's happening in this routine:

❶ Our embedded routine is able to handle *multiple* object collections in the response since the HAL spec allows this.

❷ After collecting a set of objects, the code loops through each item in the collection for rendering.

❸ Each of the embedded objects has their properties rendered within an HTML table.

❹ And, lastly, any item-level links (from the _link collection) associated with the object are rendered, too.

Caching or Object Lists?

It should be noted that our HAL client treats the _embedded section as a list of one or more object collections. This (technically) pushes the boundaries of caching intent of the HAL _embedded design. We can get by with that here, but it might not work with just any service that returns HAL responses.

Figure 4-3 shows a screenshot of our HAL client rendering a list of User objects.

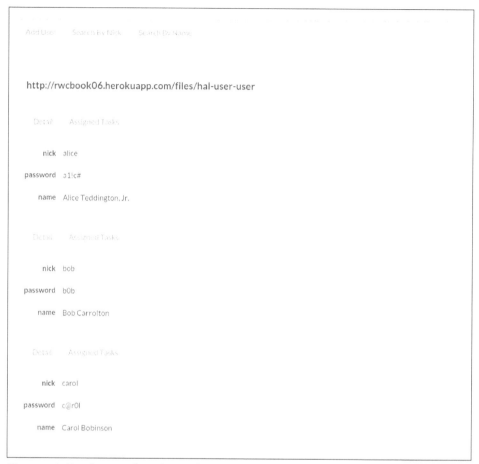

Add User   Search by Nick   Search By Name

http://rwcbook06.herokuapp.com/files/hal-user-user

Detail   Assigned Tasks

nick   alice

password a1!c#

name   Alice Teddington, Jr.

Detail   Assigned Tasks

nick   bob

password b0b

name   Bob Carrolton

Detail   Assigned Tasks

nick   carol

password c@r0l

name   Carol Bobinson

Figure 4-3. Rendering a list of user objects with the HAL client

We have one more HAL element to deal with: Properties.

Properties

The HAL design includes support for sending objects or name–value pairs at the root level of the response. We saw an example of this earlier in Example 4-1. Our routine to handle these root elements is the `properties` function:

```
// emit any root-level properties
function properties() {
  var elm, coll;
  var segment, table, tr;

  elm = d.find("properties");
  d.clear(elm);
  segment = d.node("div");
```

```
segment.className = "ui segment";
if(g.hal && g.hal.id) { ❶
  links = d.node("div");
  links.id = g.hal.id;
  d.push(links,segment);
}

table = d.node("table");
table.className = "ui very basic collapsing celled table";

for(var prop of g.fields[g.context]) { ❷
  if(g.hal[prop]) {
    tr = d.data_row({className:"property "+prop,text:prop+" ",
      value:g.hal[prop]+" "});
    d.push(tr,table);
  }
}

d.push(table,segment);
d.push(segment,elm);

// emit any item-level links
if(g.hal && g.hal.id) {
  selectLinks("item",g.hal.id, g.hal); ❸
}
}
```

This routine is a bit less busy than the one handling the _links section.

First (at ❶), we confirm that we have one or more root level properties. Note the check for hal.id. This is a specific bit of knowledge of TPS OBJECTS (they always have an id property) baked into the client. This would not work with just *any* HAL service response. Once we have a set of properties, we loop through the internal collection of fields for this context (❷) using the g.fields[g.context] state value and only display properties the client knows about ahead of time. Finally, at ❸, we insert any item-level links associated with this object. This is another TPS-specific element.

Figure 4-4 shows the HAL client rendering a single Task record.

That covers all the HAL response elements. But we still have a very important aspect of the web client that we have not shown: handling the ACTIONS for Tasks and Users. You may recall that HAL doesn't include any ACTION metadata in responses. It is up to the client application to handle these details.

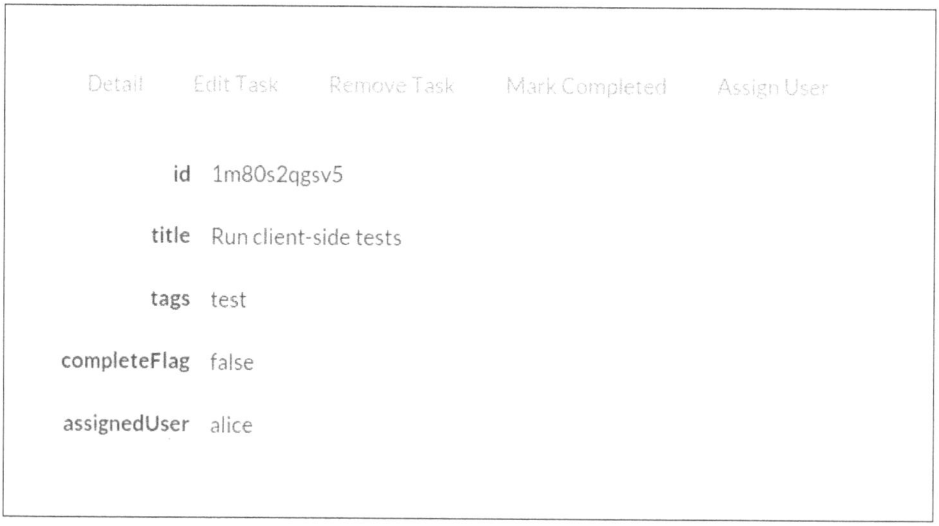

Figure 4-4. *Rendering a single item in HAL*

Handling Actions for HAL

Since HAL doesn't include ACTION details such as HTTP methods and arguments, our client needs to handle these instead. For the JSON client, we used a set of `action` objects to hold all the information (see "Addresses" on page 62). In the HAL client, we'll do something similar. Since HAL links all have a unique identifier, we can use that identifier as a pointer to a list of ACTION definitions in code. And we can write a short routine to access these definitions. I created a small `halForms` JavaScript library for this.

Here is an example of the `halForms` ACTION definition:

```
{
  rel:"/files/hal-task-edit",  ❶
  method:"put",  ❷
  properties:   [ ❸
    {name:"id",required:true, value:"{id}", prompt:"ID", readOnly:true},
    {name:"title",required:true, value:"{title}", prompt:"Title"},
    {name:"tags", value:"{tags}", prompt:"Tags"},
    {name:"completeFlag",value:"{completeFlag}", prompt:"Completed"},
    {name:"assignedUser",value:"{assignedUser}", prompt:"Assigned User"}
  ]
};
```

Note the use of the `rel` property to hold the ACTION identifier at ❶. This is used to match the same value found in a `link` element in the _links section of a HAL response. The HTTP method to use (❷) and all the input arguments (❸) are included, too. There is an ACTION definition for every query and write operation documented for the TPS web API. These are then accessed at runtime when someone clicks on an action link in the user interface.

To use these at runtime in the HAL client, every link in the UI is tied to a single function—the halLink function. That function looks like this:

```
// handle GET for links
function halLink(e) {
  var elm, form, href, accept;

  elm = e.target;
  accept = elm.getAttribute("type");

  form = forms.lookUp(elm.rel); ❶
  if(form && form!==null) {
    halShowForm(form, elm.href, elm.title); ❷
  }
  else {
    req(elm.href, "get", null, null, accept||g.ctype); ❸
  }
  return false;
}
```

As you can see, when a person clicks on a link in the HAL client, this code checks to see if there is an ACTION definition available (❶) and, if it is, shows the HTML FORM in the UI (❷). Otherwise, the HAL client just executes a simple HTTP GET on the clicked link (❸).

The halShowForm routine knows how to convert the ACTION definition into a valid HTML FORM and can associate any current task or user record with the inputs (to make it easy to render existing objects for editing). Figure 4-5 shows a screen showing the TaskEdit operation at runtime.

Figure 4-5. Handling inputs in the HAL client

Quick Summary

In building our HAL client, we learned how to create a general HAL response parser that would render the data in a user interface. Along the way, we built a few key HAL-aware operations into our general library:

selectLinks

> This routine was used to find and filter the collection of link elements in the HAL _links collection and render them when and where they are needed.

embedded

> We used the HAL _embedded section to carry object lists (tasks and users) and wrote code that rendered these at runtime as well as any associated item-level links (using the selectLinks function again).

properties

> Finally, the properties function handles any root-level name–value pairs (or objects) and also uses the selectLinks routine to render any item-level links associated with the root object.

There is more to the hal-client.js library that we didn't cover here including the same low-level HTTP routines we used in all the other SPA examples and some HAL-specific functions to support URI Templates, manage screen display, and handle other small chores.

Now that we have a fully functioning HAL client, let's introduce some change on the service API to see how our client adapts.

Dealing with Change

Just as we did in Chapter 2, *JSON Clients*, we'll now test the HAL client to see how it stands up to changes that occur on the backend API *after* the initial release. We saw that the JSON client didn't do very well. When the service added a new data field and filter option, the JSON client just ignored them. It didn't break, but we needed to recode and redeploy the app before the new API functionality would appear in the client.

From our earlier review of HAL and the OAA Challenge, we know that the HAL design is focused on handling changes to ADDRESSES. As long as we keep the initial URL for the API the same—the *entry* URL—the HAL spec allows us to change all the other URLs and the client will work just fine.

For example, if the TPS service changed the URL used for handling the ChangePassword operation from /user/pass/{id} to user/changepw/{id}, the HAL application would continue working. That's because the HAL client doesn't have the actual operation URLs baked into the code.

However, since HAL responses do not include OBJECT metadata or ACTION definitions, changes to these elements—even *adding* them—can cause problems for HAL client apps.

Adding an Action

For our example, let's assume the TPS team decides to add a new ACTION element to the web API—the `TaskMarkActive` operation. This one allows people to mark any single `Task` object as "active" by setting the `completeFlag="false"`. We can do something similar with the `TaskMarkCompleted` already.

Updating the docs

So, we can add the following ACTION definition to the API documentation (Table 4-1).

Table 4-1. TPS TaskMarkActive action

Operation	URL	Method	Returns	Inputs
TaskMarkActive	/task/active/{id}	POST	TaskList	none

The source code for the HAL client with the new `MarkActive` feature built in can be found in the associated GitHub repo (*https://github.com/RWCBook/hal-client-active*). A running version of the app described in this chapter can be found online (*http://rwcbook07.herokuapp.com/files/hal-client.html*).

Updating the TPS web API

With the docs done, we can update our server-side task connector with the new functionality (see ❶):

```
case 'POST':
  if(parts[1] && parts[1].indexOf('?')===-1) {
    switch(parts[1].toLowerCase()) {
      case "completed":
        markCompleted(req, res, respond, parts[2]);
        break;
      case "active":
        markActive(req, res, respond, parts[2]); ❶
        break;
      case "assign":
        assignUser(req, res, respond, parts[2]);
        break;
      default:
        respond(req, res,
          utils.errorResponse(req, res, 'Method Not Allowed', 405)
```

```
      );
   }
```

Now, when we make a request for a single task record against the API—for example, GET /task/1m80s2qgsv5)—we'll see the new TaskMarkActive appear (**❶** in the following code):

```
{
  "_links": {
    "collection": {
      "href": "http://localhost:8181/task/",
      "title": "Tasks",
      "templated": false,
      "target": "app menu hal"
    },
    "http://localhost:8181/files/hal-task-item": {
      "href": "http://localhost:8181/task/{key}",
      "title": "Detail",
      "templated": true,
      "target": "item hal"
    },
    "http://localhost:8181/files/hal-task-edit": {
      "href": "http://localhost:8181/task/{key}",
      "title": "Edit Task",
      "templated": true,
      "target": "item edit hal"
    },
    "http://localhost:8181/files/hal-task-remove": {
      "href": "http://localhost:8181/task/{key}",
      "title": "Remove Task",
      "templated": true,
      "target": "item edit hal"
    },
    "http://localhost:8181/files/hal-task-markcompleted": {
      "href": "http://localhost:8181/task/completed/{id}",
      "title": "Mark Completed",
      "templated": true,
      "target": "item completed edit post form hal"
    },
    "http://localhost:8181/files/hal-task-assignuser": {
      "href": "http://localhost:8181/task/assign/{id}",
      "title": "Assign User",
      "templated": true,
      "target": "item assign edit post form hal"
    },
    "http://localhost:8181/files/hal-task-markactive": {  ❶
      "href": "http://localhost:8181/task/active/{id}",
      "title": "Mark Active",
      "templated": true,
      "target": "item active edit post form hal"
    },
    "http://localhost:8181/files/hal-task-task": [
```

```
    {
        "href": "//localhost:8181/task/1m80s2qgsv5",
        "title": "Run client-side tests"
    }
    ]
  },
  "id": "1m80s2qgsv5",
  "title": "Run client-side tests",
  "tags": "test",
  "completeFlag": "false",
  "assignedUser": "alice",
  "dateCreated": "2016-01-28T07:14:07.775Z",
  "dateUpdated": "2016-01-31T22:30:25.578Z"
}
```

The failing HAL client

The new link ("Mark Active") will appear in the HAL client *automatically* since HAL understands how to deal with links. However, since the `TaskMarkActive` operation requires using an HTTP `POST`, the HAL client fails (see Figure 4-6).

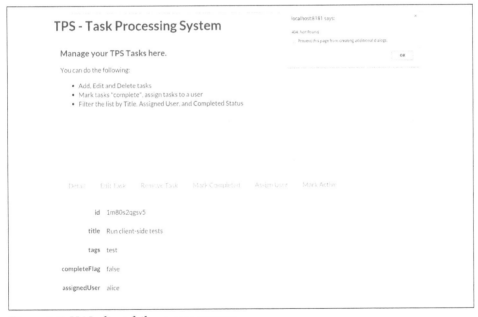

Figure 4-6. HAL client fails on new ACTION

HAL responses don't include ACTION definitions. For this new functionality, it is not enough to recognize the link, the client also needs to know what to do with it. And that only appears in the human documentation.

Recoding the ACTION definition on the HAL client

To fix this, we need to translate the new API documentation into a new ACTION definition and recode and redeploy our app again:

```
{
  rel:"/files/hal-task-markactive",  ❶
  method:"post",
  properties: [
    {name:"id",value:"{id}", prompt:"ID",readOnly:true},
    {name:"completeFlag",value:"false", prompt:"Completed",readOnly:true}
  ]
};
```

Note in the preceding ACTION definition (❶), the `rel` value is set to match that of the link identifier in the HAL response output by the TPS web API.

Now, as Figure 4-7 shows, the HAL client knows how to handle the new link, shows the proper HTML `form`, and successfully marks the `Task` object as "active."

Figure 4-7. New ACTION *definition for HAL client*

We can actually improve the HAL client's ability to deal with unexpected ACTIONS by relying on a custom HAL extension. We'll take a quick look at that in the last section of this chapter.

The HAL-FORMS Extension

One way to improve the HAL client is to extend the HAL format to include more OBJECT or ACTION information than the current design contains. This kind of extension is not *explicitly* described in the original HAL spec. However, as long as your extensions do not *break* existing clients or redefine existing features of HAL, they should be OK.

For this book, I created an extension to hold all the ACTION definitions that I've been adding to code. With this extention in place *and* a client that understands how to use it, it is possible to add new ACTION definitions at runtime without having to recode and redeploy the HAL client.

The source code for the HAL client that supports HAL-FORMS can be found in the associated GitHub repo (*https://github.com/RWCBook/hal-client-forms*). A running version of the app described in this chapter can be found online (*http://rwcbook08.herokuapp.com/files/hal-client.html*).

The Specification

The HAL-FORMS specification is a more formalized version of the in-app ACTION definitions used earlier in this chapter. However, that simple JSON object has been updated to be more in line with Mike Kelly's HAL specification and offers a few more future possibilities including the ability to load the definitions on-demand at run-time.

I won't go into the details on the HAL-FORMS extension here—you can read all about it in the associated GitHub (*https://github.com/RWCBook/hal-forms*) repo and read the latest documentation online (*http://rwcbook.github.io/hal-forms/*). For now, I'll just show what a HAL-FORMS document looks like and then get into how it's used in our updated HAL client.

A HAL-FORMS document

Here is the standalone HAL-FORMS document for adding a task to the TPS system:

```
{
  "_links" : {
    "self": {
      "href": "/files/hal-task-create-form" ❶
    }
  },
  "_templates" : {
    "default" : {
      "title" : "Add Task",
      "method":"post", ❷
      "properties": [ ❸
        {"name":"title", "required":true, "value":"", "prompt":"Title"},
        {"name":"tags", "value":"", "prompt":"Tags"},
        {"name":"completeFlag", "required":false,
         "value":"false", "prompt":"Completed"]
      ]
    }
  }
}
```

In the preceding document three things are worth pointing out:

❶ The rel value used to locate this document is included here since it is standard practice to include a "self" reference in HAL docs.

❷ The HTTP method is included. This is usually POST, PUT, or DELETE but might be a GET for complex query forms.

❸ The properties array contains all the details for rendering the HTML form and then sending the data to the service.

Notice that there is no href in this document. That is because the client app gets the ADDRESS for this operation from the HAL document at runtime. That makes these HAL-FORMS a bit more reusable, too.

Requesting HAL-FORMS documents

The HAL-FORMS document are returned with a unique IANA media type string (application/prs.hal-forms+json) in HTTP's content-type header. That's also how HAL-FORMS documents are *requested*—using the application/prs.hal-forms +json media type string in HTTP's accept header. The HAL client uses the link identifier as the URL to see if there is an associated ACTION definition for this link.

 The prs in the media type string is part of the IANA registration standard for media types covered in RFC6838. It indicates a "personal" registration. As this book goes to press, I've applied for the registration but it has not yet been completed.

Here's how it works:

If the client app sees this link in the HAL response:

```
"http://localhost:8181/files/hal-task-create-form": {
  "href": "http://localhost:8181/task/",
  "title": "Add Task",
  "templated": false
},
```

When someone activates (clicks) the Add Task link in the app, the client makes an HTTP request that looks like this:

```
GET /files/hal-task-create-form HTTP/1.1
accept: application/prs.hal-forms+json
...
```

If it exists, the server responds with a HAL-FORM like this:

```
HTTP/1.1 200 OK
content-type: application/prs.hal-forms+json
....
{
  ... HAL-FORMS document here
}
```

Once the document is loaded by the client, it can be used to build and render an HTML FORM for user input. Some sample implementation details are in the next section.

The Implementation

Adding support for the HAL-FORMS extension at runtime is pretty simple. I needed to make some adjustments to the low-level HTTP calls to make them aware of HAL-FORMS responses. I also needed to modify the way the client responds to the initial link clicks (halLink), and to update the way the halShowForm routine worked to make sure it included information from the new HAL-FORMS document.

Here is an excerpt from the client library that shows the halLink routine and related code:

```
// handle GET for links
function halLink(e) {
  var elm, form, href, accept, fset;

  elm = e.target;
  accept = elm.getAttribute("type");

  // build stateless block ❶
  fset = {};
  fset.rel = elm.rel;
  fset.href = elm.href;
  fset.title = elm.title;
  fset.accept = elm.accept;
  fset.func = halFormResponse;

  // execute check for a form
  formLookUp(fset); ❷

  return false;
}

function formLookUp(fset) { ❸
  req(fset.rel, "get", null, null, "application/prs.hal-forms+json", fset);
}

function halFormResponse(form, fset) {
  if(form && form!==null && !form.error && fset.status<400) {
```

```
    // valid form resonse? show it
    halShowForm(form, fset.href, fset.title);  ❹
  }
  else {
    // must be a simple HAL response, then
    req(fset.href, "get", null, null, fset.accept||g.ctype, null);  ❺
  }
}
```

The highlights are:

❶   Build up a shared block of properties to send to the low-level HTTP caller.

❷   Use that information to make a request for a HAL-FORMS document.

❸   This is the line that makes the HAL-FORMS request (not the media type string).

❹   If a valid HAL-FORMS document was returned, pass it to the halShowForm routine.

❺   Otherwise, just perform a simple HTTP GET on the original URL that initiated the click.

There is more to making the mod work and you can check out the associated repo for details.

So, with this new extension, I've moved the ACTION definitions to a standalone set of files that can be updated by the API service in a way that our HAL client application can understand and use safely without the need to recode and redeploy the client code. That means when the service API adds new functionality—for example, MarkTaskActive or any other new interaction—the service can just offer up a new HAL-FORMS document and the existing client will be able to handle the details (e.g., URL, HTTP method, arguments, etc.).

 Benjamin Greenberg, Senior Software Engineer at Comcast, gave a talk on how they created their own custom HAL-FORMS implementation (called _forms). I wasn't able to find a written specification for it as I was writing this chapter, but I added a pointer to a video of his presentation to the References section of this chapter.

Summary

OK, we covered quite a bit in this chapter. Let's do a quick summary:

Changing URLs is safe

Thanks to HAL's design, we no longer need to store many URLs in the code. I was able to get by with storing only one (the starting URL), but you could even have users supply that at runtime. Now the TPS API can modify URLs any time it wants without breaking the client application (as long as that *first* URL is still honored).

OBJECTS and ACTIONS are still missing

While the HAL responses have lots of available information about ADDRESSES, it supplies almost nothing about OBJECTS and ACTIONS. We needed to handle that ourselves. We included a `setContext` routine in the client code to look for OBJECTS we already expected (Home, Task, and User). We also used the `halForms` routine and custom ACTION definitions baked into the code to handle the query and write operations. Adding this information into our app makes it tightly bound to both the service OBJECT model and the predefined ACTION elements from the human documentation.

The HAL-FORMS extension solves the ACTIONS challenge

I was able to create a custom extension to the HAL spec that allowed me to store all my ACTIONS in a separate document and load them at runtime. This means my HAL client doesn't need to know about all the ACTIONS ahead of time and that the TPS API can add new ACTIONS in the future without breaking my app. The bad news is that this is just a convention I invented. It's not going to be available from other HAL servers and even my extension will likely be ignored by any other HAL client that accesses the TPS service.

An update on HAL clients and the OAA Challenge

HAL clients do OK in our OAA Challenge. They are built to handle changes to ADDRESSES (URLs), but they need to be recoded and redeployed any time an OBJECT or ACTION is added, removed, or changed. We can improve our OAA Challenge standing by implementing our custom HAL-FORMS extension, but that is not likely to work for any other HAL services or clients.

So, we are certainly better off than we were when relying on just JSON clients—those that only receive custom JSON object graph responses. But we *can* do better. As we'll see later in the book, there are a couple of more media type designs to review, and both of them do better at the OAA Challenge.

Bob and Carol

 "So, Carol. How did we do this week?"

 "Well, not bad. I think this HAL client is definitely a step in the right direction. But we still need to do more work on this adaptability challenge. How did things go on the API side this week?"

 "Really well. It was not hard at all for one of our team members to implement the HAL representor. She just studied up on the spec, spent some time in chat rooms and the discussion list to share some samples, and within a day had a simple working version up and running."

 "That's great, Bob. We did pretty much the same thing— spec, chats, discussion list—but it took us a bit longer to build our first working client. Turns out HAL was missing a few things important to our team."

 "Like what, Carol?"

 "Well, the HAL links stuff is excellent—really happy to see that the URLs can change without breaking our app or us having to do production updates. But we are still stuck dealing with the API's custom object models and all the details of executing queries and write operations."

 "Oh, I see. HAL doesn't include the OBJECT and ACTION metadata, does it? But you implemented that HAL-FORMS extension to fix that, right?"

 "Yep, that's a nice private extension for the ACTIONS element. And we can share that library with teams around the company and maybe even customers. But we can't expect all the HAL clients out there to use *our* custom extension. And we've already started running into other HAL servers where our client doesn't work since it expects that HAL-FORMS stuff."

"Right, Carol. I get it. You really want a format and client app that works with a wide range of services, right? A kind of HTML browser for APIs."

"Well, Bob. I don't need a full-blown 'browser' for APIs but I do need to improve our client app's ability to adapt to more than just URL changes. I think we need to start looking into some other hypermedia formats, too."

"OK, you let me know what you want to do next and I'll have my team ready to build another representor for you."

"OK, Bob. I'll get back to the team and let you know what we decide to try next."

"Sounds fine. Talk to you later, Carol."

References

1. When this book was released, the most reliable documentation on the Hypertext Application Language (*http://stateless.co/hal_specification.html*) (HAL) was hosted on Mike Kelly's web server.

2. There is an IETF specification document started for JSON HAL (*http://g.mamund.com/mdfce*), but it had expired by the time this book was written. It may be revived by the time you read it, though.

3. The IANA Registration for HAL can be found at IANA (*http://g.mamund.com/kjinu*).

4. Mike Kelly agreed to an interview (*http://g.mamund.com/exses*) with me in 2014 for InfoQ Magazine.

5. Mike Kelly's 2013 blog post—"The Case for Hyperlinks in APIs"—can be found at The Stateless Blog (*http://g.mamund.com/egdvb*).

6. The URI Template IETF specification (RFC6570 (*http://g.mamund.com/pmjez*)) defines patterns for variable expansion for URLs.

7. The W3C released the CURIES 1.0 (*https://www.w3.org/TR/curie/*) Working Group Note in 2010.

8. The Web Linking spec RFC5988 (*http://g.mamund.com/dysxr*) "specifies relation types for web links, and defines a registry for them."

9. The standards for registering a media type with the IETF are written up in RFC6836 (*http://g.mamund.com/zivam*), RFC4289 (*http://g.mamund.com/unqmf*), and RFC6657 (*http://tools.ietf.org/html/rfc6657*).

10. Benjamin Greenberg, Senior Software Engineer at Comcast, did a presentation on a forms extension for HAL. You can watch a video of his talk on YouTube (*http://g.mamund.com/xzdlf*).

Image Credits

- Diogo Lucas: Figure 4-1

CHAPTER 5

The Challenge of Reusable Client Apps

"Everything does go in a circle."

—Cyndi Lauper

Bob and Carol

 "OK, Bob. I wanted to go over a few things from the client-side team working on this reusable client idea."

"Sounds good. I know the JSON client project went well and the HAL client seemed successful, too. I'm looking forward to more from your team."

 "Right, that's what we need to discuss. As we look ahead to creating clients for additional media types, we're starting to see a pattern emerge."

"You mean there is probably some kind of model that applies no matter what format you're using, right?"

 "Exactly. I've started to question how we typically build client apps. Usually we have a preset goal in mind and we just write an app to solve that one problem."

"You mean like an app to compute late fees or an app to edit our catalog and so forth. That's fine, right?"

 "Well, it's fine as long as you want to keep creating new apps each time you come up with a new task. But our team needs to build apps that have some level of reusability."

"Sure, I see that. We use apps like spreadsheets and word processing software all the time. They're a kind of general client, right?"

 "Right, Bob. A spreadsheet app is really a 'canvas' for creating all sorts of solutions. Even for problems that were not thought of by the people who created the spreadsheet software."

"And you want to build those kinds of apps? That seems like a huge task, Carol."

 "Maybe. But people on the team have been coming up with papers that describe some models for creating interactive interfaces. There might be some simple principles or patterns that we can use."

"Right, like the server-side team did when implementing the representor. I see your point. We can afford to do some digging into some background and see what emerges."

 "OK, Bob. I'm going to go back to the team and see what they have for us. We can meet up again at the end of the week."

"Sounds good to me, Carol. See you later this week."

The challenge of building client applications is that we often *start* with a solution in mind. That might seem like a good thing, but sometimes it is not. Sometimes, it is more important to start with the *problem* in mind; more specifically, the *problem domain*.

This notion of starting with the problem domain has some important implications. Instead of using the problem itself as the design model, we'll need something else. This is usually referred to as the interaction model. At this level, the interaction model becomes one of the first-class aspects of the application design. There are a handful of different ways to model interaction and we'll explore two of them in this chapter along with coming up with a model of our own that we can use when implementing our hypermedia clients.

Finally, using information from the interaction models, we'll be able to identify one of the key differences between hypermedia clients (what I'll be calling *map-style* clients) and non-hypermedia clients (*path-style* clients). Hypermedia clients have a key aspect of the interaction model (the ability to understand action details and interpret the structure of responses) *missing* from the code. Instead of being hardcoded in the client, these details are supplied by the messages sent from the service. When you can build a client that doesn't have to memorize the solution ahead of time (e.g., have all the possible actions and workflow baked into the code), you can start building clients that can solve previously unknown problems and who are "smart" enough to adapt to new possible actions as the service presents them.

How can you build "smarter" client apps by teaching them *less* about how to solve a particular problem? Well, that depends on what problem you are trying to solve in the first place. And that's where we'll start this chapter on creating general-use client applications.

What Problem Are You Solving?

Thinking about the general problem space gives us a chance to consider a wide range of solutions to the same problem. It also gives us a chance to think up lots of related problems. In fact, if we're not careful, we can rush to come up with a solution to the *wrong* problem. When working on a design, it is important to make sure you understand the "real" problem to solve. In his book *The Design of Everyday Things*, Donald Norman, one of the leading thinkers in the human–computer interaction (HCI) space, put it this way:

> Good designers never start out by trying to solve the problem given to them: they start by trying to understand what the real issues are.

A similar approach is part of the *Toyota Way* and is called "The Five Whys." In his 1988 book, *Toyota Production System* (Productivity Press) Taiichi Ohno states:

> By asking why five times and answering each time, the real cause of a problem can be discovered.

Double Diamond Model of Design

The act of taking a single problem and expanding the problem space even larger is a common technique for designers. This is sometimes referred to as the *Double Diamond Model of Design* (see Figure 5-1). Created by the UK Design Council in 2005, the Double Diamond illustrates the four-part process of DISCOVER, DEFINE, DEVELOP, and DELIVER. The DISCOVER and DEVELOP phases aim to *expand* the area of consideration in order to explore alternatives, and the DEFINE and DELIVER phases aim to *narrow* the list of options to find the best available solution.

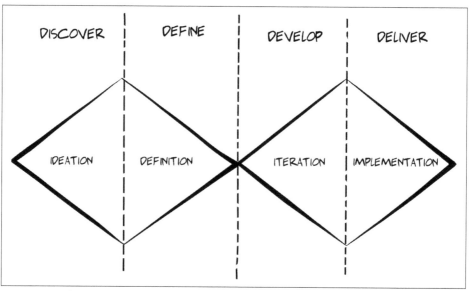

Figure 5-1. The UK Design Council's Double Diamond Model of Design

So, being ready to explore the problem more in depth is important. But how can we go about doing that?

Closed Solution Versus Open Solution

One way you can get beyond writing a bespoke application for each and every problem is to rethink how you *design* the client itself. Most web client applications are crafted and tailored to solve a single problem or a small set of closely related problems. These apps are what I call *closed-solution* apps. The problems they are designed to solve (and the solutions) are known ahead of time—before the app is built. In these cases, programmers are there to translate the predetermined solution into code and deploy the results for use.

But there is a class of applications that are designed to allow users to solve *their own* problems. These apps are what I call *open-solution* apps. The solution is not defined ahead of time and supplied by the code. Instead, the app is created in order to allow users to define and solve problems that the app designer/programmer may have never imagined. Easy examples of this class of apps are spreadsheets, word processors, drawing tools, and the like. It is this second class of apps—the open-solution apps —that can be the most valuable over time and the most challenging to implement.

What separates open-solution app designs form more typical single-use client apps? One way to think about it is that closed-solution apps are usually designed to provide a single, static *path* through a domain space—a path that leads from the start of the problem to the completed solution. Think of a wizard-style interface that leads the user through a series of steps until the job is complete. That's a path-style application.

For example, here's some pseudo-code for a path-style application:

```
START
  COLLECT userProfile THEN
  COLLECT productToBuy THEN
  COLLECT shoppingCart THEN
  COLLECT shippingInfo THEN
  COLLECT paymentInfo THEN
  FINALIZE checkOut
END
```

The advantage of "closed-solution" apps is that they are often very easy for users to navigate and are relatively easy to implement and deploy. They solve a narrow-focused problem like a fixed set of steps or *workflow* through a problem domain (e.g., online retail sales). The downside is that any changes to the workflow mean the current app is "broken" and needs to be recoded and redeployed. For example, if the workflow was changed so that it no longer requires users to identify themselves (COLLECT userProfile) *before* shopping (COLLECT productToBuy) then this app would need to be rewritten. The same would happen if the service was able to use a default shipping service, thus skipping the COLLECT shippingInfo step. And the list goes on…

However, in an open-solution style app, there is no direct path from start to finish. Instead, there are a series of *possible actions* that may (or may not) be needed. The user (or sometimes another service) helps determine which actions to take depending on what is being accomplished and the "state of things" at any point in time.

Here's how we might recode the shopping client as more of an open-solution style app:

```
WHILE NOT EXIT
  IF-NEEDED COLLECT userProfile OR
  IF-NEEDED COLLECT productToBuy OR
  IF-NEEDED COLLECT shoppingCart OR
  IF-NEEDED COLLECT shippingInfo OR
  IF-NEEDED COLLECT paymentInfo OR
  IF-ALLOWED FINALIZE checkOut OR
```

```
IF-REQUESTED EXIT
WHILE-END
```

As you can see from the second example, the app is designed as a continuous loop, and within that loop a number of things could possibly happen based on a check of the "state of things" (IF-NEEDED, IF-ALLOWED) at any time along the way. And this loop continues until the job is completed (FINALIZE checkout and IF-REQUESTED EXIT). This kind of implementation doesn't look like a path through the problem domain. Instead, it looks more like a list or *map* of interesting possibilities (locations) within the problem domain (the map). Just looking at this imaginary code, you can see that the app is now something that allows for solving all sorts of problems within the online retail sales domain, such as:

- Creating/updating a user profile
- Selecting products to purchase
- Loading and managing a shopping cart
- Managing shipping details
- Managing payment information
- Authorizing and completing a purchase

And, most important, the *order* in which these are done is not very important. There is certainly a check (IF-ALLOWED) to see that all things are supplied before allowing the user to complete the checkOut action. In a nontrivial app, this "if allowed" pattern would occur often and cover things like the status of the logged-in user (IF-ALLOWED delete user), the state of content on the server (IF-INSTOCK selectForPurchase), or the user's account (IF-AUTHORIZED purchaseOnConsignment).

It turns out this repeated loop style of apps is quite common. Most computer games use loops to manage user interaction. All windowing software uses loops and events to handle user interaction, and advanced robotics uses loops to sense the surroundings and continually act accordingly to adjust to external inputs.

So, one way to avoid falling into the trap of making every client app a bespoke or custom affair is to start thinking of clients as applications that enable users to *explore* a domain space. And an important way to do that is to think carefully about whether you want your application to offer a fixed *path* from start to finish or a detailed *map* of the general domain space itself. Path-style implementations get us to a predetermined destination quickly. Map-style implementations offer many possible ways to get similar results.

Whether you are implementing path-finders or map-makers, you need some model that underpins these general explorer applications. And that means we need to learn a little bit about modeling interaction before we make our ultimate decision.

Modeling Interaction

The process of modeling interaction can help provide a high-level guidance to designers and developers. The phrase *interaction design* was first coined in the 1980s, but thinking about how machines and humans would interact in the electronic age goes back further than that—at least as far as the 1960s for teachers at the School of Design in Ulm, Germany. And before that, the field of industrial design (from eighteenth-century England) established many of the principles used in interaction design today.

Multiple Views of Interaction Modeling

There's a great ACM article from 2009, "What Is Interaction? Are There Different Types?" (*http://g.mamund.com/eawdy*), that covers the topic in more depth than I can do in this book. It also introduces the notion of varying *views* of interaction modeling such as Design-Theory, HCI, and Systems-Theory views. If you want to explore this topic further, that article is a great place to start.

When thinking about the features of a general-use hypermedia client, it is important to get a feel for the field of interaction design and the models that have dominated the space over the last half-century. To that end, I've selected two individuals (and their models) to review:

- Tomás Maldonado's "Ulm Model"
- Bill Verplank's DO-FEEL-KNOW

Maldonado's Mechanisms

One early example of thinking about how humans and machines interact comes from the German Ulm School for Design (Hochschule für Gestaltung, or HfG). In 1964, a paper (*Science and Design* by Maldonado & Bonsiepe) was published in the school's journal. It included the notion of human–machine interface. The model assumes a relationship between **Humans** and **Mechanisms** mediated by **Controls** and **Displays**.

Argentine painter, designer, and philosopher Tomás Maldonado was a major force at the cutting-edge Ulm School of Design in the 1950s and 1960s, and the Ulm Model (see Figure 5-2) described in his 1964 paper is one of the lasting legacies of his work there. The work of Maldonado and his German colleague Gui Bonsiepe are, to this day, thought of as the standard of design theory.

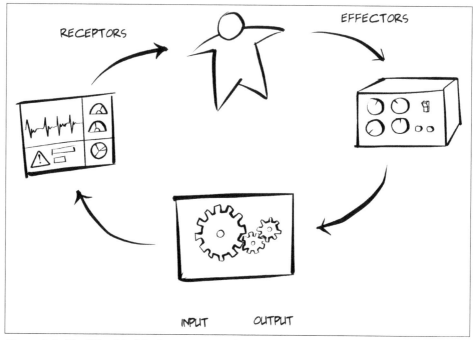

Figure 5-2. The Ulm Model of Human–Machine Interaction

As you can see from the diagram:

- **Humans** can manipulate…
- **Controls**, which produce inputs for…
- **Mechanisms**, which produce outputs that may appear on…
- **Displays**, which are viewed by **Humans** (and the loop continues).

This is essentially the way the web browser operates. **Humans** manipulate the interface (e.g., they supply a URL and press Enter). Then the browser uses its own internal **Mechanisms** (code) to execute the request, parse the response, and **Display** it on the screen. The screen typically contains some level of information (data and context) and usually includes additional **Controls** (links and forms). The **Human** reviews the **Displays** and determines which **Controls** (if any) need to be manipulated to continue the process.

The good news is that all this work is done in modern software today by the web browser without any need for additional coding. The only required element is the HTML response provided by servers. Of course, the downside is that this important interaction model is hidden from us and difficult to observe directly. It didn't take long before this changed with the introduction of client-side scripting for browsers.

Paying Attention to the Man Behind the Curtain

Much like the character Dorothy in the movie *The Wizard of Oz*, web developers were not content with keeping the **Mechanisms** of the web browser hidden. Not long after the release of web browsers, added support for client scripting allowed developers to use local code to improve the user interaction experience. Soon (around the year 2000) programmers gained access to the HTTP request/response interactions with the XMLHttpRequest object. By the 2010s, there was a movement to gain access to much more of the web browser's internal mechanisms with the *Extensible Web Manifesto* movement (*https://extensiblewebmanifesto.org/*).

A simple pseudo-code example of what the Ulm Model might look look like is:

```
WHILE
  WAIT-FOR CONTROLS("user-action")
  THEN EXECUTE MECHANISM(input:"user-action", output:"service-response")
  THEN DISPLAY("service-response")
END-WHILE
```

Note that the preceding sample doesn't have any domain-specific information. There is nothing about user access management or accounting, and so on. At this level, the general interaction is the focus, not some specific problem that needs to be addressed. Writing general-purpose applications often means focusing *first* on the interaction model.

This simple interaction model from 1964 is not the only one to consider. In fact, when Maldonado and Bonsiepe published the Ulm Model, there was no notion of interaction design as we know it.

Verplank's Humans

It was Bill Verplank (along with William Moggridge) who coined the term *interaction design* in the 1980s. Much like the work of Maldonado and Bonsiepe at the Ulm School, Verplank and Moggridge codeveloped important theories on how humans and machine interactions are described and designed (see Figure 5-3). From Verplank's point of view, interaction designers should ask three key questions:

- How do you **Do**?
- How do you **Feel**?
- How do you **Know**?

Figure 5-3. Verplank's Do-Feel-Know Interaction Model

In Interaction Design Sketchbook, he offers a simple example of this interaction model by referring to the act of manipulating the light switch in a room:

> Even the simplest appliance requires doing, feeling, and knowing. What I **Do** is flip a light switch and see (**Feel?**) the light come on; what I need to **Know** is the mapping from switch to light.

What's compelling about Verplank's model is that the human aspects of **Feel** (the ability to perceive change in the world) and **Know** (the information needed to act accordingly) is accounted for directly. This leads to an important aspect of creating client-side applications that is rarely discussed in the API world—human understanding. Although quite a bit of interesting and powerful programming can be written into client applications, these applications are still often standing in as *user-agents* for humans. It is the humans that know the ultimate goal (e.g., "I wonder if that bicycle is still on sale?") and it is the humans who have the power to interpret responses and decide which step(s) are still needed to accomplish the goal.

Hypermedia Clients are Dumb

One comment I hear when talking to people about hypermedia goes like this: "It doesn't make sense to include hypermedia links and forms in responses because hypermedia clients won't know what to do with them anyway." This is, of course, true. Just sending links and forms in responses does not magically make client applications smart enough to understand goals or make choices that lead to them. But including hypermedia controls makes it possible for *humans* to make choices. That's the first role of hypermedia—to allow humans the opportunity to make their own choices about what happens next. Hypermedia is not there to take the place of human understanding and choice; it is there to enable it.

So, with Verplank's model, we can isolate parts of the interaction loop where *humans* play a role (**Feel** and **Know**) and where machines play a role (**Do**). Similar to the Ulm Model, humans are an important feature of the interaction loop. But, with Verplank, the contributions humans make are more specific than in the Ulm Model. That gives developers a chance to approach the process of implementing client applications with a clear separation of concerns. This is a well-known concept that is discussed in computing, too.

The Origin of Separation of Concerns

The phrase *separation of concerns* is thought to have been coined by E. W. Dijkstra in his 1974 essay "On the Role of Scientific Thought."" Initially, he was discussing the importance of taking differing points of view when evaluating the same program (correctness, efficiency, etc.). Later the phrase was used to describe programs that kept various aspects of the work clearly separated (e.g., algorithms, user input, memory management, etc.).

Again, what would an application's interaction approach look like if it followed Verplank's DO-FEEL-KNOW model? Probably something like this:

```
WHILE
  WITH-USER:
    FEEL(previously-rendered-display)
    KNOW(select-action)
  WITH-MACHINE:
    DO(RUN selected-action on TARGET website and RENDER)
END-WHILE
```

Here we can see that the HUMAN is responsible for scanning the display for information (**Feel**) and then deciding what action to take (**Know**). Once that happens, the MACHINE will **Do** the selected action and render the results before starting the loop again.

When human and machine roles are separated, it's possible to see that client applications do not need to be designed to *solve* a particular problem (shopping for bicycles). Instead, they can be designed to provide a set of *capabilities* (finding stores that sell bicycles, filtering a list of bicycles within a store, ordering a bicycle, etc.). This makes it possible to allow machines to **Do** what they know how to do based on humans' ability to **Feel** and **Know**.

So, how can we apply this knowledge to our hypermedia client implementations? What we need is our own model for creating general-use hypermedia clients—our own interaction loop.

A Hypermedia Interaction Loop

The client applications in this book deal mostly with Verplank's **Do** level. They are focused on executing the actions specified by humans and reflecting the results of those actions back to the human user. This gets us close to the map-style implementations that can have a long shelf life and support a wide range of solutions in more than one problem domain space.

Using the previous interaction models as a guide, I'll describe a simple model that can help when building hypermedia client applications—what I call the **RPW** model. This model is used as an implementation pattern for all the hypermedia clients we'll see in this book.

The Request, Parse, Wait Loop

From a programmatic standpoint, a very straightforward interaction model is that of the web browser:

1. Wait for some input (e.g., a URL or field inputs, etc.).
2. Execute the request (using the inputs supplied).
3. Parse and render the response (text, images, etc.).
4. Go back to step 1.

This pattern is at the heart of all user-centric web applications, too, and is shown in Figure 5-4. Get some inputs, make a request, and render the results. Starting from the request step, I call this the *Request, Parse,* and *Wait* loop (RPW).

Sometimes it is easy to see the pattern, but sometimes it is hidden or muddled behind lots of code or multiple interaction modules. For example, in event-based client implementations, there are dozens of isolated RPW interactions happening throughout the life of the client application. Some of the RPWs are initiated by the client, but many of them are simple reactions to incoming messages from the service. In those cases the, "R" of RPW (the request) exists in the form of a *subscription*—a general request made by the client one time that says "Please send me any notifications related to the User object" or some other similar statement. There are a number of programming frameworks that adopt this style of RPW including React, Meteor, AngularJS, and others.

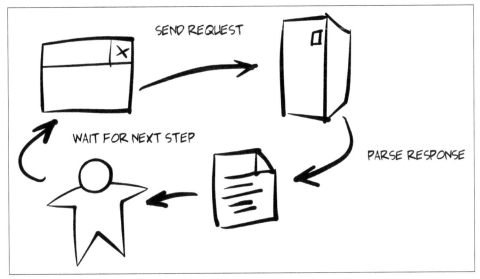

Figure 5-4. The Request, Parse, and Wait model

Another form of the RPW loop exists for asynchronous implementations. A client might initiate a request and not expect to parse the response immediately. In asynchronous clients, multiple requests may be sent before any of the responses need to be parsed. The RPW loops are stretched out over time and sometimes overlap with each other. JavaScript is based on support for async operations. This is essentially how NodeJS works, too. When using NodeJS to write API consumer code, you can fire off one or more requests, register callback functions for each, and assemble the results once all calls have been resolved.

Whether your user-centric client implements the client–server model (e.g., classic HTML-only apps), an event-based model (AngularJS, etc.), or an asynchronous model (NodeJS-style callbacks), at the heart of all the interactions between the client and the target service is some form of the **RPW** loop. This RPW-style loop exists outside of computer programming, too. Consider calling ahead for a dinner reservation and then traveling to the restaurant to retrieve your table. Or telling your friend to call you the minute they get home and then going about your business until the call arrives. Or using a thermostat to adjust the temperature of an overheated office and then waiting for the air conditioner to turn on to start cooling the room. These are all examples of RPW-type loops.

So what does this look like in code?

Implementing RPW in Code

In Chapter 2, *JSON Clients*, we saw that the initial entry point for the single-page app (SPA) was the act of passing an initial URL to the client library:

```
window.onload = function() {
  var pg = jsonClient();
  pg.init("http://localhost:8181/", "TPS");
}
```

After validating the initial call, this URL is used to make the first request:

```
// init library and start
function init(url) {
  if(!url || url==='') {
    alert('*** ERROR:\n\nMUST pass starting URL to the library');
  }
  else {
    httpRequest(url,"get");
  }
}
```

And, when the response comes back, it is parsed and rendered in the browser:

```
// primary loop
function parseMsg() {
  processTitle();
  processItems();
  processActions();
}
```

Once the parsing is completed, the application **Wait**s for the user to activate a link or fill in a form. When that happens, another **Request** is made and the response is **Parse**d. This repeats until the application is closed by the user.

The **Request** and **Parse** steps correspond closely to the **Do** step of Verplank's model. The **Wait** step in our model is the part where the human steps in. The application simply *waits* for the human to do all the other work—in this case, Verplank's **Feel** step.

But it turns out something is missing from the RPW model. What about Verplank's **Know** step? Once a human reacts to the rendered response, gets the **Feel**ing that what is needed is adding a new user to the database, fills in the proper inputs, and presses the Enter key, how does the client application **Know** how to turn those inputs into a valid action to **Do**?

The answer to this question goes to the primary differences between path-style and map-style client applications. And this difference is what sets hypermedia client applications apart from others.

Handling Verplank's KNOW Step

We saw in the JSON client application built in Chapter 2, *JSON Clients* that it relies on a simple loop. But what we glossed over is that there is another level of functionality baked into the JSON client app—the functionality that **Know**s how to construct and execute network requests. This changes the nature of the JSON client as it relates to Verplank's **Know** level. The app has code that predefines all the possible behaviors so that it *knows* how to handle all the operations ahead of time. In this way, I (as the programmer of that app) have narrowed the app's ability to solve problems. It can only **Do** the things it **Know**s in advance.

Most of the **Know** content of the example JSON client from Chapter 2 is kept in two locations:

global.actions *object collection*
>   This contains the rules that let the app **Know** which behaviors are possible and how to perform the specified actions at runtime (e.g., addTask, assignUser, etc.).

processItems() *function*
>   This function **Know**s how to interpret the responses in order to find all the objects and their properties and how to render this information on the screen.

For example, near the top of the JSON client source code file, you can see the collection actions:

```
// all URLs and action details
g.actions.task = {
    tasks:   {target:"app", func:httpGet, href:"/task/", prompt:"Tasks"},
    active:  {target:"list", func:httpGet,
                href:"/task/?completeFlag=false", prompt:"Active Tasks"
             },
    closed:  {target:"list", func:httpGet,
                href:"/task/?completeFlag=true", prompt:"Completed Tasks"
             },
    byTitle: {target:"list", func:jsonForm,
                href:"/task", prompt:"By Title", method:"GET",
                args:{
                    title: {value:"", prompt:"Title", required:true}
                }
             },
    add:     {target:"list", func:jsonForm,
                href:"/task/", prompt:"Add Task", method:"POST",
                args:{
                    title: {value:"", prompt:"Title", required:true},
                    tags: {value:"", prompt:"Tags"},
                    completeFlag: {value:"", prompt:"completeFlag"}
                }
             },
    item:    {target:"item", func:httpGet, href:"/task/{id}", prompt:"Item"},
    edit:    {target:"single", func:jsonForm,
```

```
            href:"/task/{id}", prompt:"Edit", method:"PUT",
            args:{
              id: {value:"{id}", prompt:"Id", readOnly:true},
              title: {value:"{title}", prompt:"Title", required:true},
              tags: {value:"{tags}", prompt:"Tags"},
              completeFlag: {value:"{completeFlag}", prompt:"completeFlag"}
            }
        },
   delete: {target:"single", func:httpDelete,
            href:"/task/{id}", prompt:"Delete", method:"DELETE",
            args:{}
        },
};
```

Each action element in the preceding code set contains all the information needed to
fully describe one of the possible domain actions. These are the static set of *paths* the
client **Knows** about. They are *fixed* within the client source code and the list cannot
be updated without also updating and redeploying the client app itself.

The same is true for the code that represents the client's ability to parse the response
and render it on the screen:

```
// the only fields to process
global.fields = ["id","title", "tags", "dateCreated", "dateUpate", "assignedUser"];

for(var item of itemCollection) {
  li = domHelp.node("li");
  dl = domHelp.node("dl");
  dt = domHelp.node("dt");

  // emit item-level actions ❶
  dt = processitemActions(dt, item, (itemCollection.length===1));

  // emit the data elements
  dd = d.node("dd");
  for(var f of global.fields) { ❷
    p = domHelp.data({className:"item "+f, text:f, value:item[f]+" "});
    domHelp.push(p,dd);
  }

  domHelp.push(dt,dl,dd,li,ul);
}
```

In the function that handles each item in the response (just shown), we can see the
code that filters through the list of item properties and only shows the ones that are
in the client's global.fields array (❷). This client already **Knows** which data elements to display and parses the response in order to find and render them.

There is also code in the preceding example that parses the response to emit additional actions (❶) to expose to the human user. That routine (processItemActions)
looks like this:

```
// handle item-level actions
function processItemActions(dt, item, single) {
  var a, link;

  // item link
  link = global.actions.item;
  a = domHelp.anchor({
    href:link.href.replace(/{id}/,item.id), ❶
    rel:"item",
    className:"item action",
    text:link.prompt
  });
  a.onclick = httpGet;
  domHelp.push(a,dt);

  // only show these for single item renders
  if(single===true) { ❷
    // edit link
    link = global.actions.edit;
    a = domHelp.anchor({
      href:link.href.replace(/{id}/,item.id),
      rel:"edit",
      className:"item action",
      text:link.prompt
    });
    a.onclick = jsonForm;
    a.setAttribute("method",link.method);
    a.setAttribute("args",JSON.stringify(link.args));
    domHelp.push(a,dt);

    // delete link
    link = global.actions.remove;
    a = domHelp.anchor({
      href:link.href.replace(/{id}/,item.id),
      rel:"remove",
      className:"item action",
      text:link.prompt
    });
    a.onclick = httpDelete;
    domHelp.push(a,dt);
  }
  return dt;
}
```

Note that the JSON client not only knows how to construct valid URLs (❶). It also knows *when* selected actions will be valid (❷). Again, this kind of knowledge (URL rules for each action and when an action is possible) are now hardcoded into the app. Changes in these rules will invalidate the app itself.

We can now see that the JSON client app contains code that covers not just the ability to **Do** actions and parse the results. It also has a set of rules baked into the code to handle all the possible actions—the capability to **Know** how each action is constructed and understand the semantic content of responses.

In hypermedia-style clients, this information is *left out of the client* completely. All the information that describes how to formulate requests and parse responses is part of the *message* itself. And hypermedia clients have additional skills to recognize this descriptive information, giving them the ability to execute actions that do not appear in the source code. These clients are able to read the *map* supplied by the message instead of just following a predetermined *path*.

For example, the HAL client we covered in Chapter 4 has the ability to understand the _link elements in each response in order to compose (**Do**) simple requests. It is important to note that we also decided to implement the HAL-FORMS extension in order to help the client app **Know** how deal with additional information on formulating requests.

And that's what we're focusing on as we build our hypermedia-style clients. We are exploring ways to allow client apps to improve their ability interact with API services based on their ability to **Know** the interaction information (LINKS and FORMS) contained in responses and use this information to **Do** things on behalf of the user.

Essentially, we're creating adaptable map-makers instead of just static path-finders.

Summary

In this chapter, we looked at the challenges of implementing general-use API clients. We learned about the difference between path-style and map-style app designs. We also explored the background interactive design through the works of Tomás Maldonado (the Ulm Model) and Bill Verplank (**Do-Feel-Know**). From that exploration, we came up with our own interaction model (**RPW**) to use as a guide for implementing our client applications.

Finally, we reviewed the JSON client app from Chapter 2 and saw how that implementation illustrates the path-style approach. And we noted that hypermedia client apps, such as the HAL client app discussed in Chapter 4, get their action information from the messages they receive instead of from the source code itself. This **RPW** model will also act as a guide as we explore other client implementations in future chapters like the ones that support the Siren format (Chapter 6) and the Collection +JSON format (Chapter 8).

Bob and Carol

"Hi, Carol. What did you find out about a model for general-use client apps?"

"Well, Bob, quite a bit—mostly due to some great research and review from the team."

"OK, then. Let's hear it."

"Well, you remember we were talking about the difference between client apps that solve one problem and those that are able to solve lots of problems, right? The single-problem solutions are like path-finder apps—they use a predetermined set of steps to navigate a path through a problem space to a solution destination."

"Hm. So the apps that let you solve multiple problems are less likely to have any predetermined solution (or path) built into the code, right?"

"Right, we're calling those apps *map-makers*. They have a kind of map of the problem space, but no fixed navigation plan. Humans *using* the apps determine the path at runtime."

"OK, Carol. But this map-maker style app is probably harder to write and even to use. We'd still need some guidance for designing and building these map-makers, right."

"Yep. I won't cover all the details here since you can read the background materials I sent you. But it comes down to thinking about the whole human–computer interaction model."

"Yeah, I read that. What Bill Verplank calls **Feel-Know-Do**. If I remember it right, your team wants to remove the client code that hardcodes the actions and start to use hypermedia controls in the API responses to hold that information."

"Exactly, Bob. By doing that, we improve the chances that our clients can be more flexible, can adapt to new workflows and operations without the need for additional code-and-deploy cycles."

"That makes sense. I know that the JSON client your team built needed an update almost the day we released it."

"Right. And the HAL client was better at adapting to changes in ADDRESSES."

"Right, but that's only part of the solution. What about adapting to changes in ACTIONS and OBJECTS? Can a hypermedia format handle that, too?"

"Well, let's find out. My team wants to explore the Siren hypermedia format now. You up for it, Bob?"

"Sure, Carol. We can add Siren support in a matter of days with the representor pattern. Let's see how this new format behaves."

References

1. *The Design of Everyday Things, Revised and Expanded Edition* (*http://g.mamund.com/irhmy*) is the 2013 update of Donald Norman's classic 1988 book on usability and interaction design.

2. A short paper from 1978 with the title "The Toyota Production System" is available online (*http://g.mamund.com/axqkj*). This is dated ten years before the 1988 release of the book with the same name.

3. Peter Merholz has a nice blog post (*http://g.mamund.com/nrmyc*) about the UK Design Council's *Double Diamond Design Model*.

4. The article "What Is Interaction? Are There Different Types?" (*http://g.mamund.com/nrmyc*) was published in the January 2009 issue of *Interactions* magazine.

5. The Ulm Model and the *Ulm School of Design* (*http://g.mamund.com/osbxt*) has a colorful history and it is well worth exploring.

6. You can learn more about the *Extensible Web* movement by visiting their website and reading their Manifesto (*https://extensiblewebmanifesto.org/*).

7. Bill Verplank has a unique presentation style that includes sketching as he speaks. There are a number of videos online where you can see this in action. He also released a short pamphlet online called Interaction Design Sketchbook (*http://g.mamund.com/ecpud*).

8. Moggridge's book *Designing Interactions* (*http://g.mamund.com/jrldk*) is a collection of interviews with many important figures in the history of interaction design.

9. Dijkstra's 1974 essay, "On the role of scientific thought," is available online (*http://g.mamund.com/cibtn*).

Image Credits

- Diogo Lucas: Figures 5-1, 5-2, 5-3, and 5-4

CHAPTER 6

Siren Clients

"First you will come to the Sirens who enchant all who come near them."

—The Odyssey, *Circe*

Bob and Carol

 "Hi, Bob. Just stopping by to talk to you about our work on creating more adaptable API clients."

"Hello, Carol. Glad you stopped by. So, what's our next move?"

 "Well, the team has decided they want to explore using the Siren hypermedia type this time. It seems to have more hypermedia features than HAL."

"Yes, I heard about Siren. It's being used for some Internet of Things work, right?"

 "Right. Zetta is the IoT platform. Siren looks like it has lots of support for describing actions within the responses themselves."

"Yes, these look a lot like HTML FORMS, don't they? A URL, a method, and a set of arguments. Nice. But didn't you solve this problem for HAL with the HAL-FORMS extension?"

"The problem with the HAL-FORMS solution is that it is a private convention, not a shared standard. We can't rely on HAL-FORMS when we want to consume HAL responses from other companies."

"OK, Carol. I'll get my team working on a Siren representor module while you and your group work up a Siren client. Let's meet back here at the end of the week and see how it goes."

 "Thanks, Bob. See you in a few days."

It's time to move along in our quest for a hypermedia type that handles the three aspects of API client applications: OBJECTS, ADDRESSES, and ACTIONS. We learned in Chapter 2, *JSON Clients* that developers relying on plain JSON responses need to hardcode details for all three aspects. That means changing just one of these aspects on the server can cause problems for client apps (the best case being the client *ignores* the changes). This is when developers, in an effort to at least *identify* changes in the API, resort to "versioning" tactics. Of course, adding a version to the API doesn't help the client adapt to the changes; it just protects the client from ever seeing them.

 We'll take an in-depth look at dealing with change over time and the technique of versioning in Chapter 7, *Versioning and the Web*.

In Chapter 4, *HAL Clients* we explored a media type that does a good job handling the ADDRESSES aspect of the OAA Challenge. Since HAL is designed to include `link` objects in responses, client apps receive not only the URL but also lots of metadata *about* the URL including link identifiers, names, titles, and other important information. This means changes to the URL values themselves (e.g., moving the service to a new server, changing the folder hierarchy or a particular resource name, etc.) can be done safely and *quietly* without bothering clients with versioning information. In fact, as long as the new URLs don't introduce unknown variables (like a new variable in a URI Template), HAL clients can successfully adapt to the backend URL changes without the need for any additional code/test/deploy cycles.

But HAL doesn't do well with the other two aspects of the OAA Challenge: OBJECTS and ACTIONS. So, in this chapter we'll explore another hypermedia format design— the Structured Interface for Representing Entities, aka Siren. And, as in previous chapters, we'll go beyond a review of the format. We'll cover the code behind a server-side Siren representor. Then we'll create a general-use Siren client. Finally, we'll introduce changes to the backend API to see how Siren clients hold up when APIs change over time.

The Siren Format

Siren was registered with the IANA in November of 2012. Designed by Kevin Swiber, Siren focuses on providing rich metadata on the ACTIONS element of web APIs. In an online discussion (*https://github.com/kevinswiber/siren/issues/15*) comparing different hypermedia formats, Swiber said:

> The biggest differentiator of Siren is Actions. … Siren also has a concept of "class." The class attribute may contain multiple descriptors of the current representation. I've avoided calling these "type descriptors." They act more like "mixin descriptors."

The preceding quote points out another valuable feature of Siren—the `class` concept. This maps rather well to the OBJECT aspect of our OAA Challenge. So, in theory, Siren has features for all three of our OAA elements.

 It is important to point out that Siren's `class` identifier is *not* the equivalent of the typical source code `class` keyword. For Siren, the `class` identifier is roughly the same as the HTML `class` attribute. This is actually a broader use of the term than the code-centric use, which makes it possible to use Siren's `class` identifiers as both an OBJECT type *and* as a more general way to "tag" entities as belonging to a category.

The Siren design (illustrated in Figure 6-1) also has `Links` (the ADDRESS aspect of our OAA Challenge) and they look very similar to HAL's `_links`. There is the concept of `Properties` for name–value pairs, and `Entities` that can be nested collections of JSON objects (called `SubEntities`), which may also have `Class`, `Links`, and `Properties` elements. And the nesting can continue—it's `Entities` all the way down.

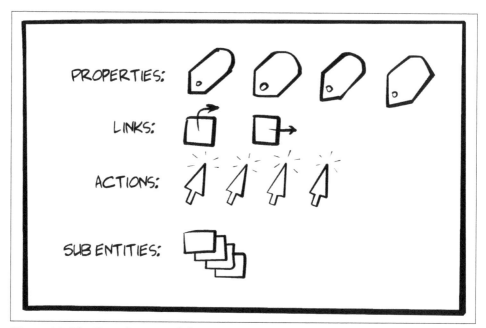

Figure 6-1. The Siren design model

Here's a simple Siren message that we'll dive into in the next section of this chapter:

```
{
  "class": ["order"],
  "properties": {
      "orderNumber": 42,
      "itemCount": 3,
      "status": "pending"
  },
  "entities": [
    {
      "class": ["items", "collection"],
      "rel": ["http://x.io/rels/order-items"],
      "href": "http://api.x.io/orders/42/items"
    },
    {
      "class": ["info", "customer"],
      "rel": ["http://x.io/rels/customer"],
      "properties": {
        "customerId": "pj123",
        "name": "Peter Joseph"
      },
      "links": [
        { "rel": ["self"], "href": "http://api.x.io/customers/pj123"}
      ]
    }
  ],
```

```
"actions": [
  {
    "name": "add-item",
    "title": "Add Item",
    "method": "POST",
    "href": "http://api.x.io/orders/42/items",
    "type": "application/x-www-form-urlencoded",
    "fields": [
      {"name": "orderNumber", "type": "hidden", "value": "42"},
      {"name": "productCode", "type": "text"},
      {"name": "quantity", "type": "number"}
    ]
  }
],
"links": [
  {"rel": ["self" ], "href": "http://api.x.io/orders/42"},
  {"rel": ["previous" ], "href": "http://api.x.io/orders/41"},
  {"rel": ["next" ], "href": "http://api.x.io/orders/43"}
]
}
```

I won't dig too deep into the Siren media type design here. You can get a much better picture of Siren and the tooling that has grown up around it by reading the Siren docs mentioned in "References" on page 218.

The Siren message design is slightly more involved than the HAL model and that makes it both more powerful and a bit more of a challenge to understand and put into practice. But the added effort can really pay off.

Let's review the key design elements a bit more.

Entities

Each Siren response is an addressable entity resource. In Siren terms, the response is a "root" Entity. Entities usually have one or more Links and several Properties. They may have one or more Action elements and possibly some nested entities (called SubEntities). Finally, an Entity may have one or more associated Class elements.

Here is what the basic structure of a Siren Entity looks like:

```
{
  "class" : [...],
  "properties" : {...}.
  "entities" : [...],
  "actions" : [...],
  "links" : [...]
}
```

The Entity is the thing that gets returned when an API call is made to a valid URL.

Class

Siren's Class element is used to identify the kind of entity. The Siren docs are careful to say the class array is not a type descriptor (e.g., source code class) and emphasizes that it is used to "describe the nature of the entity." Since it is an array, it is common for the class element to contain a list of descriptors. For example, this is how a Siren class element can be used to indicate that the current entity is representing both a customer and a person:

```
"class": ["person", "customer"]
```

The consuming client application can use this information to decide when and where to render the entity. It is also important to point out the Siren docs say the valid values of the class element are "implementation-dependent and should be documented." In other words, the client should know ahead of time what class values will appear in responses. This will come up when we work on our Siren client implementation later in the chapter.

 The Siren documentation makes it a point to explain that the class property identifies "the nature of the element" and the rel property defines the "relationship between two resources." Siren is the only hypermedia type covered in this book that makes a clear distinction between annotating ADDRESSES (with rel) and annotating OBJECTS (with class).

Properties

The Siren Properties object is a simple JSON set of name–value pairs. For example, here is a set of properties for a Siren Entity:

```
"properties": {
  "id": "8f06d3ef-4c67-4a2c-ae8e-1e7d23ab793f",
  "hubId": "001788fffe10857f",
  "ipAddress": "10.1.10.12",
  "auth": "3dac9ce5182f73e727d2b0b11c280b13",
  "colorValue": [255, 255, 255],
  "other" : {
    "type": "huehub",
    "name": "Hue Hub",
    "state": "on"
  }
}
```

Note that the value of a property may be an array or even another set of name–value pairs. Essentially, the `properties` element is a JSON graph.

Links

The `Links` array in a Siren document contains one or more `link` elements. A single `link` element has the following JSON properties:

```
"links" : [
  {
    "class" : ["customer", "person"],
    "href" : "http://api.example.org/customers/q1w23e",
    "rel" : ["item"],
    "title" : "Moab",
    "type" : "application/vnd.siren+json"
  },
  ... more links here
]
```

You'll notice that looks very similar to the HAL `_links` collection (see "Links" on page 119).

Actions

The Siren `Actions` array contains a collection of valid operations for the associated entity. They look and behave much the same as HTML `FORM` elements. They indicate the operation's internal `name`, HTTP `method`, associated `href`, `type` of content body to send, and possibly a set of `field` objects that describe the arguments for the operation.

Here's an example Siren Action element:

```
"actions": [
  {
    "name": "add-item",
    "title": "Add Item",
    "method": "POST",
    "href": "http://api.x.io/orders/42/items",
    "type": "application/x-www-form-urlencoded",
    "fields": [
      {"name": "orderNumber", "type": "hidden", "value": "42"},
      {"name": "productCode", "type": "text"},
      {"name": "quantity", "type": "number"}
    ]
  }
],
```

It's worth pointing out that Siren has a very rich set of `field` objects. Basically, Siren's `field` list matches the full set of HTML5 `input` types (currently up to 19 different input types). It also has `name`, `title`, `value`, and `class` properties.

Check out all the possible field types in the Siren online docs listed at the end of this chapter.

That completes the basic set of elements for Siren responses except one that we'll turn to in the following section: the SubEntities collection.

SubEntities

Siren SubEntities are simply Siren Entity objects nested within a Siren representation. That means all the properties just listed (Class, Properties, Actions, and Links) are valid elements of SubEntities. All of these elements are optional for a SubEntity. However, there are two additional required properties: rel and href. Every SubEntity must have these two properties.

The name for the element that holds the SubEntities in a Siren response is "entities". That might be a bit confusing, but it makes sense. The response is an Entity and it can have an entities property that contains one or more "sub" entities.

Of course, Siren Entities can be nested infinitely within Siren Entities. That means something like the following is a valid Siren response:

```
{
  "class":["item"],
  "properties":{"name" : "value"},
  "actions":[
    {
      "name":"search-box",
      "method":"GET",
      "href":"/search-results/",
      "fields":[{"name" : "search", "value" : "", "title" : "Search"}]
    }
  ],
  "links" : [
    {"rel":["self"],"href":"."}
  ],
  "entities" : [
    {
      "rel" : ["item"],
      "href" : "/search-page1/",
      "class":["item"],
      "properties" : {"name" : "value"},
      "actions" : [
        {
          "name" : "search-box",
```

```
        "method" : "GET",
        "href" : "/search-results/",
        "fields" : [{"name" : "search", "value" : "", "title" : "Search"}]
      }
    ],
    "links" : [{"rel":["self"],"href":"."}],
    "entities" : [
      {
        "rel" : ["item"],
        "href" : "/search-page2/",
        "class":["item"],
        "properties" : {"name" : "value"},
        "actions" : [
          {
            "name" : "search-box",
            "method" : "GET",
            "href" : "/search-results/",
            "fields" : [
              {"name" : "search", "value" : "", "title" : "Search"}
            ]
          }
        ],
        "links" : [{"rel":["self"],"href":"."}]
      }
    ]
  }
]
}
```

Representational and Linked SubEntities

It is important to point out that there are essentially two "flavors" of SubEntities that can be embedded in an Entity: linked and representational. *Linked* SubEntities *must* have the href and rel attributes. *Representational* SubEntities are only *required* to have a rel attribute to identify the relationship. They *should* also contain a self relation and MAY contain a links array.

Typically, representational SubEntities are used to display lists. The linked variety is useful if the server instance has little information regarding the SubEntities.

This is a bit of a tricky distinction and has been the subject of much debate over the years in the Siren community.

Quick Summary

So, a Siren message has four basic elements:

- class
- properties
- actions
- links

There is a fifth element: entities that can also contain all the first four elements. Siren has a recursive design that allows for expressing very intricate object trees with a concise set of elements.

Armed with our basic understanding of the Siren hypermedia type, it's time to implement our Siren representor for the TPS web API.

The Siren Representor

Again, we'll get a chance to create a new representor for our TPS web API—the one that converts the internal WeSTL document that represents the collection of valid actions and data for a request into a Siren document to be shared with the outside world. And, just like our Siren review, the Siren representor will handle the five elements of a Siren document:

- class
- properties
- actions
- links
- entities

 The source code for the Siren representor can be found in the associated GitHub repo (*https://github.com/RWCBook/siren-client*). A running version of the Siren-generating TPS API described in this chapter can be found online (*http://rwcbook09.herokuapp.com/home/*).

The Top-Level Loop

The top-level loop for the Siren representor creates a valid Siren JSON object and then walks through the WeSTL document to produce a valid Siren document for output via the HTTP server. Here's the routine followed by some comments:

```
// emit valid siren body
function siren(wstlObject, root) {
  var siren;

  siren = {}; ❶

  for(var segment in wstlObject) {
    if(!siren.class) {
      siren.class = [];
    }
    siren.class.push(segment); ❷

    if(wstlObject[segment].data) {
      if(wstlObject[segment].data.length===1) {
        siren = getProperties(siren, wstlObject[segment].data, o); ❸
      }
      else {
        siren.entities = getSubEntities(wstlObject[segment], o); ❹
      }
    }
    if(wstlObject[segment].actions) {
      siren.actions = getActions(wstlObject[segment].actions, o); ❺
      siren.links = getLinks(wstlObject[segment].actions, o); ❻
    }
  }
  return JSON.stringify(siren, null, 2); ❼
}
```

❶ We first create an empty Siren object.

❷ Then insert the current WesTL object name as the Siren `class`.

❸ If there is only one data element, emit that object as a Siren `Properties` object.

❹ Otherwise, emit the collection of data objects as `SubEntities`.

❺ Then if the WeSTL document has any action elements, emit the ones that require arguments as Siren `Actions`.

❻ And then emit any other actions as Siren `Links`.

❼ Finally, convert the JSON graph into a string for returning to the API caller.

Simple, but Effective

I took a few shortcuts in creating this representor. First, it never outputs both `properties` and `entities` in the same response. That's technically valid, but simplifies support a bit. Also, this representor does not support *nested* `entities` collections. I left these out to keep the code simple for the book and to give you, the reader, a little project to work on.

Class

There's not much to say about support for the Siren `class` element except that our representor simply emits the internal object name (`"task"` or `"user"`) as the value for a single-item array (see the previous code example). I don't support multivalued `class` arrays in this representor.

Properties

The `getProperties` routine handles cases where the internal data collection has only one element. As I mentioned before, this is a simplification of the possible Siren representor and is perfectly valid.

The code looks like this:

```
// handle single entity
function getProperties(siren, data, segment) {
  var props, properties;

  props = data[0];
  properties = {}; ❶
  for(var p in props) {
    properties[p] = props[p]; ❷
  }

  siren.class = [segment] ❸
  siren.properties = properties;

  return siren; ❹
}
```

The highlights are:

❶   Create an empty `property` object.

❷   Fill it with the internal data object's name–value pairs.

❸   Set the `class` value for this collection.

❹ After updating the `siren` object, return it to the caller.

Again, more could be done here, but this generates valid Siren content for our API.

Entities

The `getSubEntities` routine in our Siren representor handles cases where the internal WeSTL document holds more than one data object for the current representation response. This is a pattern that uses Siren's `entities` element to return a list of objects while we use Siren's `properties` element to return a *single* object.

Here's what the code looks like:

```
// handle collection of subentities
function getSubEntities(wstlObject, segment) {
  var items, item, i, x, data, actions;

  data = wstlObject.data;
  actions = wstlObject.actions;
  items= [];

  if(data) {
    for(i=0,x=data.length;i<x;i++) {  ❶
      item = {};  ❷
      item.class = [segment];
      item.href = "#";
      item.rel = [];
      item.type = g.atype;

      for(var p in data[i]) {  ❸
        item[p] = data[i][p];
      }

      if(actions) {
        link = getItemLink(actions);  ❹
        if(link) {
          item.href = link.href.replace(/{key}/g,item.id);  ❺
          item.rel = link.rel;
          item.type = link.contentType||g.atype;
        }
      }

      items.push(item);  ❻
    }
  }

  return items;  ❼
}
```

The important points in this routine are:

❶ Loop through the collection of internal data objects.

❷ Create an empty `item` element for each Siren subentity.

❸ Fill that `item` with the data object's properties.

❹ Get the associated `ItemAction` transition.

❺ Update the `item` with the transition details.

❻ Add that `item` to the list of subentities.

❼ Return the completed list to the caller for including in the Siren response.

We now have covered Siren's `class`, `properties`, and `entities` elements. All we have left are the two hypermedia-centric elements: `actions` and `links`.

Actions

Siren's `Actions` element is the one that carries all the information needed to perform an API action—such as add a record, update the existing record, remove a record, etc. In the HAL media type (see Chapter 4), all this information was left in the human-readable documentation and developers were responsible for encoding those details into the client app *and* figuring out how to associate the details with user clicks at runtime.

But Siren makes it the responsibility of the API *service* to share the appropriate ACTION details *at runtime* via the Siren `action` collection in the response. This lightens the burden for client developers because they only need to *recognize* the `action` elements as they appear in responses. The Siren model allows clients to focus on the parsing and rendering steps for `actions`.

The representor code for handling ACTIONS in Siren responses is detailed, but not complicated. Essentially, the representor needs to figure out if there are any forms that are needed for the current response and, if there are, send them as valid Siren `action` elements.

Here's the `getActions` function that does that:

```
// handle actions
function getActions(actions,segment) {
  var coll, form, action, input, i, x;

  coll = [];
  for(i=0, x=actions.length; i<x; i++) { ❶
```

```
    if(actions[i].inputs && actions[i].inputs.length!==0) { ❷
      action = actions[i];
      form = {}; ❸
      form.name = action.name;
      form.title = action.prompt||action.name;
      form.href = action.href||"#";
      if(action.type!=="safe") { ❹
        form.type = action.contentType||g.ctype;
        form.method = utils.actionMethod(action.action)
      }
      else {
        form.method = "GET";
      }
      form.fields = [];
      for(j=0,y=action.inputs.length; j<y; j++) { ❺
        input = action.inputs[j];
        field = {};
        if(input.name) { ❻
          field.name = input.name;
          field.type = input.type||"text"
          field.value = input.value||"";
          field.title = input.prompt||input.name;
          field.class = [segment];
          form.fields.push(field);
        }
      }
      coll.push(form); ❼
    }
  }
  return coll; ❽
}
```

There is a good deal of activity in this routine. It's the most involved one of the Siren representor because Siren's support for the ACTION aspect of hypermedia is very rich. Here's the breakdown:

❶ Loop through the list of all the WeSTL document's action elements for this resource response

❷ If the WeSTL action has one or more input objects associated, we'll convert that to a Siren action.

❸ Start an empty form object.

❹ After some basic setup, determine the property HTTP method to use from the WeSTL metadata.

❺ Loop through the WeSTL input objects for this action.

❻ Use the WeSTL input data to populate a Siren field element.

❼ After loading up all the fields, add the completed form to the Siren action collection.

❽ Finally, return the resulting action collection to the caller to add to the siren object.

 It's worth noting that the code at ❹ is the first time we've actually populated an API response with an HTTP method value. The Siren hypermedia type happens to be the *only* media type we're using in this book that allows service to indicate HTTP methods directly.

OK, just one more Siren element left: the Links collection.

Links

Like the _links element in the HAL hypermedia type, the Siren links collection carries all the *immutable* links (the unchangeable ones with no query arguments) associated with the current response. And, like HAL, Siren supports a number of metadata properties for each link such as rel, title, and others.

The code for the getLinks routine in our Siren representor is pretty simple and looks like this:

```
// handle links
function getLinks(actions, segment) {
  var coll, link, action, i, x;

  coll = [];
  for(i=0, x=actions.length; i<x; i++) { ❶
    if(actions[i].type==="safe" &&
      (actions[i].inputs===undefined || actions[i].inputs.length===0) ❷
    ) {
      action = actions[i];
      link = {}; ❸
      link.rel = action.rel;
      link.href = action.href||"#";
      link.class = [segment];
      link.title = action.prompt||"";
      link.type = action.contentType||g.atype;
      coll.push(link); ❹
    }
  }
  return coll; ❺
}
```

There is only one interesting line of code in the getLinks routine and that's at ❷—
making sure the WeSTL action object represents a "safe" operation (e.g., HTTP GET)
and that there are no input objects associated with the action. The rest is pretty
basic:

❶ Loop through the available WeSTL action objects.

❷ Make sure the WesTL action is both "safe" and has no associated arguments.

❸ Start an empty link element and populate it with WeSTL action data.

❹ Add the resulting link to the Siren collection.

❺ Finally, return the completed collection to the caller to insert into the Siren
    response.

And that's the high-level review of our Siren representor. There are a few support
routines in the representor, but we don't need to review them here. You can check out
the source code for details.

Sample TPS Output from the Siren Representor

With the Siren representor up and running, the TPS web API now emits proper Siren
representations. Here's the output from the TPS server for the Home resource:

```
{
  "class": [
    "home"
  ],
  "properties": {
    "content": "<div class=\"ui segment\"><h3>Welcome to TPS at BigCo!</h3>
    <p><b>Select one of the links above.</b></p></div>"
  },
  "entities": [],
  "actions": [],
  "links": [
    {
      "rel": ["self","home","collection"],
      "href": "http://rwcbook09.herokuapp.com/home/",
      "class": ["home"],
      "title": "Home",
      "type": "application/vnd.siren+json"
    },
    {
      "rel": ["task","collection"],
      "href": "http://rwcbook09.herokuapp.com/task/",
      "class": ["home"],
      "title": "Tasks",
      "type": "application/vnd.siren+json"
```

```
      },
      {
        "rel": ["user","collection"],
        "href": "http://rwcbook09.herokuapp.com/user/",
        "class": ["home"],
        "title": "Users",
        "type": "application/vnd.siren+json"
      }
    ]
  }
```

And here is the Siren output for a single Task object:

```
{
  "class": ["task"],
  "properties": {
    "content": "<div class=\"ui segment\">...</div>",
    "id": "1l9fz7bhaho",
    "title": "extension",
    "tags": "forms testing",
    "completeFlag": "false",
    "assignedUser": "fred",
    "dateCreated": "2016-02-01T01:08:15.205Z",
    "dateUpdated": "2016-02-06T20:02:24.929Z"
  },
  "actions": [
    {
      "name": "taskFormEdit","title": "Edit Task",
      "href": "http://rwcbook09.herokuapp.com/task/1l9fz7bhaho",
      "type": "application/x-www-form-urlencoded",
      "method": "PUT",
      "fields": [
        {"name": "id","type": "text","value": "",
         "title": "ID","class": ["task"]},
        {"name": "title","type": "text","value": "",
         "title": "Title","class": ["task"]},
        {"name": "tags","type": "text","value": "",
         "title": "Tags","class": ["task"]},
        {"name": "completeFlag","type": "select","value": "false",
         "title": "Complete","class": ["task"]}
      ]
    },
    {
      "name": "taskFormRemove","title": "Remove Task",
      "href": "http://rwcbook09.herokuapp.com/task/1l9fz7bhaho",
      "type": "application/x-www-form-urlencoded",
      "method": "DELETE",
      "fields": [
        {"name": "id","type": "text","value": "",
         "title": "ID","class": ["task"]}
      ]
    },
    {
```

```json
      "name": "taskCompletedForm","title": "Mark Completed",
      "href": "http://rwcbook09.herokuapp.com/task/completed/1l9fz7bhaho",
      "type": "application/x-www-form-urlencoded",
      "method": "POST",
      "fields": [
        {"name": "id","type": "text","value": "",
         "title": "ID","class": ["task"]}
      ]
    },
    {
      "name": "taskAssignForm","title": "Assign User",
      "href": "http://rwcbook09.herokuapp.com/task/assign/1l9fz7bhaho",
      "type": "application/x-www-form-urlencoded",
      "method": "POST",
      "fields": [
        {"name": "id","type": "text","value": "",
         "title": "ID","class": ["task"]},
        {"name": "assignedUser","type": "select","value": "",
         "title": "User Nickname","class": ["task"]}
      ]
    },
    {
      "name": "taskActiveForm","title": "Mark Active",
      "href": "http://rwcbook09.herokuapp.com/task/active/1l9fz7bhaho",
      "type": "application/x-www-form-urlencoded",
      "method": "POST",
      "fields": [
        {"name": "id","type": "text","value": "",
         "title": "ID","class": ["task"]}
      ]
    }
  ],
  "links": [
    {"rel": ["home","collection"],
     "href": "http://rwcbook09.herokuapp.com/home/",
     "class": ["task"],"title": "Home"},
    {"rel": ["self","task","collection"],
     "href": "http://rwcbook09.herokuapp.com/task/",
     "class": ["task"],"title": "Tasks"},
    {"rel": ["user","collection"],
     "href": "http://rwcbook09.herokuapp.com/user/",
     "class": ["task"],"title": "Users"},
    {"rel": ["item"],
     "href": "http://rwcbook09.herokuapp.com/task/1l9fz7bhaho",
     "class": ["task"],"title": "Detail"}
  ]
}
```

You can compare this output with that of the HAL representor (see Example 4-4 in
Chapter 4) and recognize that a big difference is the existence of the actions section
in the Siren response. As I mentioned at the start of this chapter, one of the key
strengths of the Siren format is its ability to describe the available ACTIONS for the

current API response. We'll take advantage of this feature when we build the Siren SPA client next.

The Siren SPA Client

OK, just as we did in Chapter 2, *JSON Clients*, and Chapter 4, *HAL Clients*, let's walk through the code for the Siren SPA client. We'll hit the highlights of the tour including the HTML container, the top-level parse loop, and the key Siren elements (Class, Properties, SubEntities, Actions, and Links). We'll also see how Siren can handle error displays—something we left out of the HAL client.

 The source code for the HAL client can be found in the associated GitHub repo (*https://github.com/RWCBook/siren-client*). A running version of the app can be found online (*http://rwcbook09.hero kuapp.com/files/siren-client.html*).

The HTML Container

Again, like all the sample apps in this book, we're using the single-page app (SPA) pattern to keep things simple and transparent. Here is the static HTML for our Siren SPA:

```
<!DOCTYPE html>
<html>
  <head>
    <title>Siren</title>
    <link href="siren-client.css" rel="stylesheet" />
  </head>
  <body>
    <h1 id="title"></h1> ❶
    <div id="links"></div>
    <div id="error"></div>
    <div id="content"></div>
    <div id="properties"></div>
    <div id="entities"></div>
    <div id="actions"></div>
    <div>
      <pre id="dump"></pre>
    </div>
  </body>
  <script src="dom-help.js">//na</script>
  <script src="siren-client.js">//na </script> ❷
  <script>
    window.onload = function() {
      var pg = siren();
      pg.init("/home/", "TPS - Task Processing System");
    }
```

```
      </script>
    </html>
```

This is our third SPA, so things should look very familiar. The Siren layout starts at ❶ and you can see DIVs to hold each of the major Siren elements (links, properties, entities, and actions) along with a couple other DIVs to help the SPA manage things like the title, errors, content, and the debug dump.

There is only one major script file to deal with (siren-client.js at ❷) and we kick off the client with a relative URL call to the /home/ resource of the TPS web API.

The Top-Level Parse Loop

The initial code for the siren-client.js library fires off the first HTTP request and then, when the response comes in, calls the top-level routine (parseSiren) to render the page for humans. Here's the code:

```
// init library and start
function init(url, title) {

  global.title = title||"Siren Client";

  if(!url || url==='') {
    alert('*** ERROR:\n\nMUST pass starting URL to the library');
  }
  else {
    global.url = url;
    req(global.url,"get");
  }
}

// primary loop
function parseSiren() { ❶
  sirenClear();
  title();
  getContent();
  links(); ❷
  entities(); ❸
  properties(); ❹
  actions(); ❺
  dump();
}
```

Not much to talk about here. You can see the parseSiren routine handles the incoming response (❶) and, after some local cleanup and state-handling, the Siren message is rendered (❷, ❸, ❹, and ❺). Note that this top-level parser doesn't show handling of the Siren class element—that's taken care of within each of the other routines since the class element can appear in multiple places within the Siren response.

Links

Handling the link elements that appear in Siren responses is pretty simple. Just loop through them and render them as HTML anchor tags (<a>...</a>) with all the associated attributes:

```
// links
function links() {
  var elm, coll;

  elm = domHelp.find("links");
  domHelp.clear(elm);

  if(global.msg.links) {  ❶
    ul = domHelp.node("ul");
    ul.onclick = httpGet;  ❹
    coll = global.msg.links;
    for(var link of coll) {  ❷
      li = domHelp.node("li");
      a = domHelp.anchor({
        rel:link.rel.join(" "),
        href:link.href,
        text:link.title||link.href,
        className:link.class.join(" "),
        type:link.type||""
      });
      domHelp.push(a, li, ul);
    }
    domHelp.push(ul, elm);  ❸
  }
}
```

The main points are:

❶   Make sure we have links in the Siren response.

❷   If we do, loop through the collection to create <a> tags

❸   And add the resulting collection to the HTML DOM.

Note (in ❹) that the <ul> gets registered to capture user clicks with the httpGet routine. This is a shortcut way to allow all child clicks to "bubble up" to the enclosing <ul> tag.

Figure 6-2 shows what the rendered links look like in the running client app.

Figure 6-2. Rendering links in the Siren SPA

Entities

As I mentioned earlier in this chapter, the TPS web API uses Siren's `entities` element to hold a collection of similar TPS objects (`Task` and `User`). So, parsing the Siren document here means generating a list of objects to display. That code looks a bit interesting, too:

```
// entities
function entities() {
  var elm, coll, cls;
  var ul, li, dl, dt, dd, a, p;

  elm = domHelp.find("entities");
  domHelp.clear(elm);

  if(global.msg.entities) { ❶
    ul = domHelp.node("ul");

    coll = global.msg.entities;
    for(var item of coll) { ❷
      cls = item.class[0]; ❸
      if(g.fields[cls]) {
        li = domHelp.node("li");
        dl = domHelp.node("dl");
        dt = domHelp.node("dt");

        a = domHelp.anchor({ ❹
          href:item.href,
          rel:item.rel.join(" "),
          className:item.class.join(" "),
          text:item.title||item.href});
        a.onclick = httpGet;
        domHelp.push(a, dt, dl);

        dd = domHelp.node("dd");
        for(var prop in item) {
          if(global.fields[cls].indexOf(prop)!==-1) { ❺
            p = domHelp.data({
              className:"item "+item.class.join(" "),
```

```
                    text:prop+" ",
                    value:item[prop]+" "
                });
                domHelp.push(p,dd);
            }
        }
        domHelp.push(dd, dl, li, ul);
    }
}
domHelp.push(ul, elm); ❻
    }
}
```

And the tour is:

❶ Make sure you have some entities to deal with.

❷ If so, start looping through them.

❸ Right away, capture the `class` value for each rendered object (we'll use this in ❺).

❹ Generate an "Item" link for each rendered object.

❺ Loop through the object properties and only render the ones this client "knows about" (see the following explanation).

❻ Finally, after rendering each object and all its properties, add the results to the HTML DOM and exit.

The line of code at ❺ compares the properties returned from the server to the internal list of properties the client "knows" about (based on the human-readable documentation). This "knowledge" is captured in some initialization code at the start of the `siren-client.js` file and looks like this:

```
global.fields = {};
global.fields.home = [];
global.fields.task = ["id","title","tags","completeFlag","assignedUser"];
global.fields.user = ["nick","password","name"];
global.fields.error = ["code","message","title","url"];
```

You can see that this client has been told to watch out for four possible objects (home, task, user, and error) and that three of those objects have fields worth showing on the screen to humans. These object values will appear in Siren responses as class values—that's how our client knows what each object is about and how to render them (see Figure 6-3). Our TPS API uses simple, flat name–value pairs as class objects. If we had a more involved set of objects with arrays and additional nested elements, we'd need to teach our clients how to recognize all those elements, too.

extension	
id	1I9fz7bhaho
title	extension
tags	forms testing
completeFlag	false
assignedUser	bob
Run client-side tests	
id	1m80s2qgsv5
title	Run client-side tests
tags	test
completeFlag	true
assignedUser	alice

Figure 6-3. Rendering objects in the Siren client

Properties

The client deals with Siren `properties` pretty much the same way it handles
`entities`, but there is a twist. For the TPS API, Siren responses usually have a
`content` property (this TPS-specific object property is described in the TPS documentation). And the `content` property gets special treatment. Here's how the code
does it:

```
// get response content
function getContent() {
  var elm, coll;

  if(global.msg.properties) {
    coll = global.msg.properties;
    for(var prop in coll) { ❶
      if(prop==="content") {
        elm = domHelp.find("content");
        elm.innerHTML = coll[prop];
```

```
        break;
      }
    }
  }
}
```

Basically, the `getContent` routine loops through all the properties in the response and if there is one named `content`, the value of that property is rendered in the user's content area of the HTML page (see Figure 6-4).

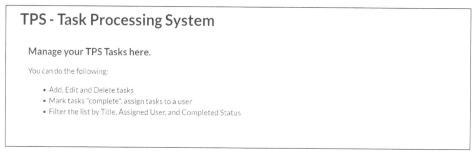

TPS - Task Processing System

Manage your TPS Tasks here.

You can do the following:

- Add, Edit and Delete tasks
- Mark tasks "complete", assign tasks to a user
- Filter the list by Title, Assigned User, and Completed Status

Figure 6-4. Rendering the content property

With this special property taken care of, our Siren client can go on working with the Siren `properties` element (see the following code). You'll notice another bit of special handling going on this this routine, too:

```
// properties
function properties() {
  var elm, coll, cls;
  var table, a, tr_data;

  elm = domHelp.find("properties");
  domHelp.clear(elm);

  if(global.msg.class) { ❶
    cls = g.msg.class[0];
  }

  if(global.msg.properties) {
    table = domHelp.node("table");
    table.className = "ui table";

    if(cls==="error") { ❷
      a = domHelp.anchor({
        href:g.url,
        rel:"error",
        className:"error",
        text:"Reload"});
      a.onclick = httpGet;
      domHelp.push(a, elm);
    }
```

```
      coll = g.msg.properties;
      for(var prop in coll) { ❸
        if(global.fields[cls].indexOf(prop)!==-1) {
          tr_data = domHelp.data_row({
            className:"item "+global.msg.class.join(" ")||"",
            text:prop+" ",
            value:coll[prop]+" "
          });
          domHelp.push(tr_data,table);
        }
      }
      if (table.hasChildNodes()) {
        domHelp.push(table, elm); ❹
      }

      if (elm.hasChildNodes()) {
        elm.style.display = "block";
      } else {
        elm.style.display = "none";
      }
    }
  }
```

❶ Capture any class element associated with the properties collection.

❷ If it turns out the class value is set to "error", emit a Reload link for the user.

❸ Now loop through all the name–value pairs and render them on screen as long as
   the object is one we "know" about.

❹ Finally, after all the properties are processed, add the results to the HTML DOM
   for display.

You may recall from some discussion early in the chapter (see Simple, but Effective)
that the TPS web API emits single item responses (e.g., a request for a single Task
or User) via the Siren properties element and emits lists of items using the Siren
entities element. One of the reasons for this is that it is a pattern that makes handling error responses relatively easy. Here is what one of those error responses looks
like in Siren:

```
{
  "class": [
    "error"
  ],
  "properties": {
    "code": 404,
    "message": "File Not Found",
    "url": "http://rwcbook09.herokuapp.com/task/pc-load-letter"
```

```
    }
  }
```

Figure 6-5 shows how that would look in the Siren client.

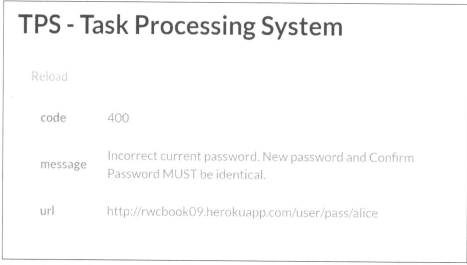

TPS - Task Processing System

Reload

code	400
message	Incorrect current password. New password and Confirm Password MUST be identical.
url	http://rwcbook09.herokuapp.com/user/pass/alice

Figure 6-5. Rendering an error in the Siren client

That leaves one more major Siren element to work out: the `actions` element.

Actions

The code that parses Siren's `action` element is the one with the most moving parts. This one not only handles the form rendering but also populates the values in the form if they are available:

```
// actions
function actions() {
  var elm, coll;
  var segment, frm, header, field, submit;

  elm = d.find("actions");
  d.clear(elm);

  if(g.msg.actions) {
    coll = g.msg.actions;

    for(var act of coll) { ❶
      segment = d.node("div");
      segment.className = "ui green segment";
      frm = d.node("form");
      frm.className = "ui form";
      frm.id = act.name;
```

```
      frm.setAttribute("smethod",act.method); ❷
      frm.method = act.method;
      frm.action = act.href;
      frm.onsubmit = httpForm;
      header = d.node("div");
      header.className = "ui dividing header";
      header.innerHTML = act.title;
      d.push(header, frm);
      for (var fld of act.fields) { ❸
        field = d.node("p");
        field.className = "inline field";
        input = d.input({
          "prompt" : fld.title||fld.name,
          "name" : fld.name,
          "className" : fld.class.join(" "),
          "value" : g.msg.properties[fld.name]||fld.value,
          "type" : fld.type||"text",
          "required" : fld.required||false,
          "readOnly" : fld.readOnly||false,
          "pattern" : fld.pattern||""
        });
        d.push(input, field);
        d.push(field, frm);
      }

      submit = d.node("input"); ❹
      submit.className = "ui positive mini submit button";
      submit.type = "submit";
      d.push(submit, frm);

      d.push(frm, segment); ❺
      d.push(segment, elm); ❻
    }
  }
}
```

OK, one more walk-through:

❶ Assuming you have discovered that there are action elements to deal with, start looping through them here.

❷ Stash the HTTP method in a custom attribute of the HTML FORM element (HTML ignores any value except GET and POST if you try to save it to the default FORM.method property).

❸ Loop through the input arguments (fields) defined for this Siren action and be sure to include any object values, if they are available.

❹ Be sure to include a "submit" button to each HTML FORM you render.

❺ Add the complete FORM set to the collection.

❻ Push the results into the HTML DOM for rendering.

Figure 6-6 shows what a set of rendered forms looks like in the client.

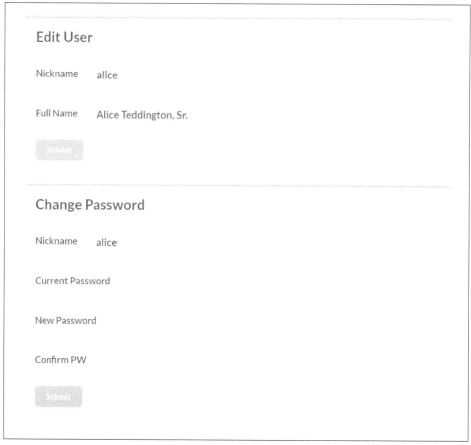

Figure 6-6. Rendering user forms in the Siren client

There are a few other client-side routines to fill out all the Siren client's functionality, but I won't take up pages reviewing them. You can scan the source code if you're interested in the details.

Quick Summary

So, building a Siren SPA was not too complicated. We had to parse and render the key Siren document elements into the HTML DOM.

They are:

Links

Any static links that appear in the Siren `link` section are rendered as simple HTML `<a>...</a>` tags.

Entities

The TPS web API uses the Siren `entities` section to hold a list of one or more domain objects. These are marked with the Siren `class` property and our client knows just which objects to expect ahead of time (`home`, `task`, `user`, and `error`).

Properties

Siren's `properties` holds a set of name–value pairs associated with the response. The TPS API uses this to return any single objects in the response (e.g., a single `Task` or `User`) as well as returning the page `content` element. Our client was taught to look for the `content` element specifically—this is domain-specific information.

Actions

This is the Siren section that includes all the details handling parameterized reads and writes for the API. The Siren format has very rich support for describing forms and our client took advantage of that.

Now that we have a fully functional Siren client, it's time to see how it deals with change over time.

Dealing with Change

From our experience building the Siren client, we know that we can safely add new ACTIONS (forms) and ADDRESSES (links) to the API responses and, as long as we make the changes backward-compatible, the client should have no problem handling them. So that's what we'll do. This time, we'll update the interface to allow people to enter an email address for the user screen and filter the list of users based on email address.

 The source code for this updated TPS API and Siren client can be found in the associated GitHub repo (*https://github.com/RWCBook/siren-client-email*). A running version of the app described in this section can be found online (*http://rwcbook10.herokuapp.com/files/siren-client.html*).

You probably expect this to go quite easily, but there's a hitch. Can you guess what it will be?

Adding the Email Field and Filter

So, we just need to update the WeSTL document on the server to add the email field to the userFormAdd and userFormEdit, as well as create a new WeSTL entry to describe the userFormListByEmail operation. Once that's done, we can see how the Siren client deals with this change to the backend API.

Here are two updates to the WeSTL document that add the new email field to the User operations:

```
trans.push({
  name : "userFormAdd",
  type : "unsafe",
  action : "append",
  kind : "user",
  target : "list add hal siren",
  prompt : "Add User",
  inputs : [
    {name : "nick", prompt : "Nickname", required: true,
      pattern: "[a-zA-Z0-9]+"},
    {name : "email", prompt : "Email", value: "", type: "email"}, ❶
    {name : "name", prompt : "Full Name", value: "", required: true},
    {name : "password", prompt : "Password", value: "", required: true,
      pattern: "[a-zA-Z0-9!@#$%^&*-]+"}
  ]
});

trans.push({
  name : "userFormEdit",
  type : "unsafe",
  action : "replace",
  kind : "user",
  prompt : "Edit User",
  target : "item edit form hal siren",
  inputs : [
    {name : "nick", prompt : "Nickname", value : "", readOnly: true},
    {name : "email", prompt : "Email", value: "", type: "email"}, ❷
    {name : "name", prompt : "Full Name", value : ""}
  ]
});
```

Scanning the WeSTL document, you can see the new email field (❶ and ❷). Notice that there is a new property on the input element: the type property. Siren automatically supports the expanded set of HTML5 input types (about 20 in all) and we can take advantage of this by setting the email field description to force the Siren client to validate the inputs for us.

The other thing we need to add to the WeSTL document is the new userForm ListByEmail transition. Here it is:

```
trans.push({
  name : "userFormListByEmail",
  type : "safe",
  action : "read",
  kind : "task",
  target : "list query hal siren",
  prompt : "Search By Email",
  inputs : [
    {name : "email", prompt : "Email", value : ""}
  ]
});
```

You might notice that, this time, I did *not* include the `type:"email"` property. This will allow us to search using only a partial email address—and that's what we want to be able to do.

We're almost done updating the API. We need just one more step—to modify the backend `User` component code to recognize (and validate) the new `email` field. For our simple service, that means we need to add the field name (see ❶ in the following code) to the list of valid fields to read/write:

```
props = [
  "id",
  "nick",
  "email", ❶
  "password",
  "name",
  "dateCreated",
  "dateUpdated"
];
```

And we need to update the component's validation code (see ❶) to make sure we store and return the new `email` field:

```
item = {}
item.nick = (body.nick||"");
item.name = (body.name||"");
item.email = (body.email||""); ❶
item.password = (body.password||"");
```

With these changes in place, we can spin up the client and see how it handles the new field.

Testing the Email Field

First, if you make a direct call to the TPS Server, you can see that the new `email` field *does* appear in Siren's `actions` section (see ❶):

```
{
  "class": [
    "user"
  ],
```

```
...
    "actions": [
      {
        "name": "userFormAdd",
        "title": "Add User",
        "href": "http://localhost:8181/user/",
        "type": "application/x-www-form-urlencoded",
        "method": "POST",
        "fields": [
          {
            "name": "nick",
            "type": "text",
            "value": "",
            "title": "Nickname",
            "class": ["user"],
            "readOnly": false,
            "required": true,
            "pattern": "[a-zA-Z0-9]+"
          },
          {
            "name": "email",    ❶
            "type": "email",
            "value": "",
            "title": "Email",
            "class": ["user"],
            "readOnly": false,
            "required": false
          },
          {
            "name": "name",
            "type": "text",
            "value": "",
            "title": "Full Name",
            "class": ["user"],
            "readOnly": false,
            "required": true
          },
          {
            "name": "password",
            "type": "text",
            "value": "",
            "title": "Password",
            "class": ["user"],
            "readOnly": false,
            "required": true,
            "pattern": "[a-zA-Z0-9!@#$%^&*-]+"
          }
        ]
      }
    ]
}
```

Also, when you load up the UI, both the `userFormListByEmail` (see Figure 6-7) and `userFormAdd` (Figure 6-8) show the `email` field on screen. When filling out the Add User screen, you can even see the "validate user" functionality for the add operation.

Figure 6-7. Viewing the new email field on the Search by Email screen

Figure 6-8. Viewing the new email field on the Add User screen

However, once you save the email data, you discover that the Siren client is not *displaying* the email field in the UI (see Figure 6-9).

It turns out the Siren client successfully supports the `email` field for Add and Search operations because the TPS API service sends the complete description of Add and Search forms (e.g., the URL, method, and field details) with each response. However, the Siren format does not include metadata details for `entities` and `properties` elements. And that's where the trouble starts.

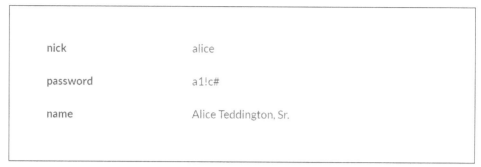

nick	alice
password	a1!c#
name	Alice Teddington, Sr.

Figure 6-9. Email field is missing on the Siren User dislplay

This "bug" in our Siren clients is due to a mismatch between client and server on the *definition* of the User object. Even though the server sends the same class value ("user") it has previously been sending, the server's definition of User has changed (it has a new email field). However, the Siren client's definition (the one in the client code) is no longer in sync with the TPS API (the client code does not have the email field). So the client just ignores the new field when it displays properties for a User.

This confusion is all because the Siren format is not designed to send OBJECT metadata in responses, it is designed to only send metadata for ACTION and ADDRESS elements. So, for our Siren client apps, we still need to "bake" the object definition into the client source code.

Remember these lines in the client code review?

```
global.fields = {};
global.fields.home = [];
global.fields.task = ["id","title","tags","completeFlag","assignedUser"];
global.fields.user = ["nick","password","name"];
global.fields.error = ["code","message","title","url"];
```

This is the object description information the client will need for displays. That was an implementation decision I made when coding this Siren client. I hardcoded the field names into the app in order to make sure I only handled fields the client already knows about. I did this mostly for safety. I also did it because I wanted to be able to select which fields to *not* render even when they appear in the response (e.g., dateCreated and dateUpdated). Again, Siren doesn't make it easy for servers to send these kind of rendering hints directly in the API response, so I added this "smarts" to the client code.

So, right now, my TPS API that emits Siren responses doesn't have a way to send object and property metadata to client apps. To solve my problem, I'll get beyond this design feature of Siren by creating a custom extension that allows the TPS API to send metadata about the User and Task objects, too.

The Profile Object Description (POD) Extension

Since Siren does not (by design) pass OBJECT metadata in responses, if we want to be able to make backward-compatible changes to the service *objects*, we need to figure out a way to pass this information to the client at runtime. The good news is that Siren already has the hooks for this in the baseline design. We can use the class value to point to a description of the API's objects.

Sharing the object metadata in a standardized way means we can teach the Siren client to use the metadata shared at runtime instead of relying on the metadata stored in the client code. We need to convert the client's internal knowledge about objects into *external* knowledge.

 The source code for the Siren client that supports the POD extension can be found in the associated GitHub repo (*https://github.com/RWCBook/siren-client-pod*). A running version of the app described in this section can be found online (*http://rwcbook11.herokuapp.com/files/siren-client.html*).

The POD Specification

What we need at this point is a reliable way to share object information between client and server—a way that the client can use at runtime to adjust the display of enti ties and properties in Siren responses. For this book, I'll outline a very simple solution. In a production app, you would likely need a more robust design. Even better, you might want to use one designed and reviewed by the Siren community.

 Siren's creator, Kevin Swiber, uses a convention in many of his implementations that is quite similar to the POD spec I'm using here. Essentially, clients can look for (and dereference) a link that indicates there is available metadata for the response.

I'll also take the time to expand the object metadata to include not just the object's property name but also a suggested human-readable prompt and a flag on whether the field should be displayed or hidden.

The Siren Profile Object Display (POD) document

My POD document design has three elements:

- The field identifier (e.g., nick)
- The prompt string (e.g., "Nickname")

- The render flag (e.g., "text", "embedded", "link", or "none")

All of that is wrapped in a JSON element whose name can be matched to the Siren class value (which is the object name). The complete POD document for the TPS User object looks like this:

```
{
  "user" : {
    "id" : {"prompt" : "ID", "render" : "none"},
    "nick" : {"prompt" : "Nickname", "render" : "text"},
    "email" : {"prompt" : "Email", "render" : "text"},
    "name" : {"prompt" : "Full Name", "render" : "text"},
    "password" : {"prompt" : "Password", "render" : "text"},
    "dateCreated" : {"prompt" : "Created", "render" : "none"},
    "dateUpdated" : {"prompt" : "Updated", "render" : "none"}
  }
}
```

 You can find the Profile Object Display (POD) specification in the associated GitHub (*https://github.com/RWCBook/pod-spec*) repo and at this web page (*http://rwcbook.github.io/pod-spec/*).

Now we need a way to retrieve it from the server.

Retrieving POD documents

To be able to retrieve the document, we'll add a new link element with the rel value of "profile" and we'll teach the Siren client to look for this link and use it to retrieve the POD for the currently loaded class. For example, if the Siren response contains the following profile link:

```
{
  "rel": ["profile"],
  "href": "/files/user.pod",
  "class": ["user"]
  "type": "application/prs.profile-object-desc+json"
}
```

then the Siren client will know it can attempt to retrieve an SOP document as follows:

```
GET /files/user.pod HTTP/1.1
accept: application/prs.profile-object-desc+json
...
```

If it exists, the server responds with a POD document like this:

```
HTTP/1.1 200 OK
content-type: application/prs.profile-object-desc+json
....
```

```
{
    ... POD document here
}
```

 The prs in the media type string is part of the IANA registration standard for media types covered in RFC6838. It indicates a *personal* registration. As this book goes to press, I've applied for the registration but it has not yet been completed.

Once the document is loaded, it can be parsed and then the contents used to control the display of the objects in the Siren response.

Let's see how a working version looks.

The Implementation

Adding support for the POD Siren extension takes a little bit of work on the server and a few modifications on the Siren client app. Similar to the way we implemented the HAL-FORMS extension (see "The HAL-FORMS Extension" on page 144), we are implementing a custom extension that doesn't require changes to the Siren specification itself.

I just need to modify the low-level HTTP calls for the client app so that it "knows" about the new application/prs.profile-object-desc+json media type calls *and* integrates the object profile into the rest of the parse/render process.

Here's the snippet that handles the profile responses (❶).

```
function rsp(ajax) {
  if(ajax.readyState===4) {
    if(ajax.getResponseHeader("content-type").toLowerCase()===global.podType) {
      global.profile = JSON.parse(ajax.responseText); ❶
      parseSiren();
    }
    else {
      global.msg = JSON.parse(ajax.responseText);
      parseMsg();
    }
  }
}
```

The new top-level code for the client follows. Now, after the initial load of the Siren response, we'll check to see if there is a profile link (❶) and, after completing the profile call (or not, depending on the response) we go ahead and finish up the Siren parse and render work (at ❷):

```
// primary loop
function parseMsg() {
  var profile;
```

```
sirenClear();
title();
dump();

profile = getProfileLink(); ❶
if(profile) {
  req(profile.href, "get", null, null, global.podType);
}
else {
  parseSiren();
}
}

// finish parsing the Siren response
function parseSiren() { ❷
  getContent();
  links();
  entities();
  properties();
  actions();
}
```

Again, there are other minor changes to the client to make it match the class value to the profile object in memory and some updates to the service to make sure it returns Profile Object Display (POD) documents when requested. You can check out the source code for the Siren-POD client for a deeper look into this custom extension.

Displaying Objects in Siren Using POD

Now that I've updated my Siren client to optionally support the Profile Object Display (POD) extension, services can send along metadata for things like Task and User objects. That means, as the service modifies the object definitions (e.g., adding fields, changing the field prompt strings, etc.), my Siren client app will be able to find this information via a request for a POD document and no longer needs to have the object metadata stored with the client source code.

For example, the current TPS API exposes four objects that the Siren client needs to deal with:

- Home
- Task
- User
- Error

That means that the TPS API service can now serve up the following four POD documents:

- `home.pod`
- `task.pod`
- `user.pod`
- `error.pod`

Now, when the TPS API service adds the `email` field to the `user.pod` document (see "The Siren Profile Object Display (POD) document" on page 211), the updated Siren client will be able to display it as expected (see Figure 6-10).

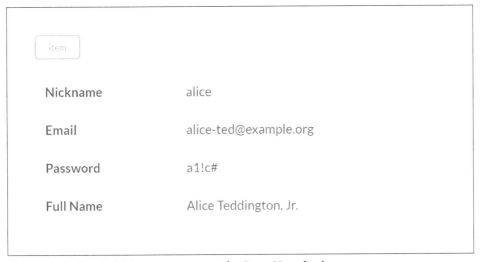

Figure 6-10. Email field now appears on the Siren User display

Notice that the new POD specification allows the TPS API server to provide updated field prompts (`"Full Name"` instead of `"name"`), too. Also, the POD specification could be expanded to support client-side input validators similar to those supported by HTML5 such as:

- Data types (`"email"`, `"url"`, `"number"`, etc.)
- Existence (`"required"`)
- Regular expression matching (e.g., HTML5's `pattern` property)

I'll leave these handy additions to the POD spec and Siren client as a project for the reader to explore.

Quick Summary

In this section on extending Siren, we learned that even though Siren does a great job sending metadata about ADDRESSES and ACTIONS in responses, it doesn't send much information about the OBJECTS (just identifiers in the class element). So we extended Siren by defining a Profile Object Display (POD) document and establishing a *private convention* in the Siren client that asks servers to send a representation of the OBJECT definitions (via the "profile" URL) and uses *that* external data as a guide in dealing with the identified objects that appear in Siren responses.

This is a handy extension but, like all custom extensions and private conventions, it is not a solution I can expect all Siren services and clients to know about or support. It has a limited reach since it is just something I made up to solve my local problem.

Summary

OK, let's summarize what we learned about Siren and creating Siren clients:

Changing ADDRESSES is Safe
> Siren does a great job supporting the ADDRESSES aspect of our OAA Challenge. Changing the URL values of any of the operations at runtime will not cause problems for Siren clients. The only URL that needs to stay constant is the initial starting URL, which is the one used to launch the app.

Changing ACTIONS is Safe
> We also learned that Siren has excellent support for describing ACTIONS for an API. Adding and changing Siren Action elements (like arguments or even entirely new operations) will not break the Siren client as long as they are done in a backward-compatible way.

Changing OBJECTS is Not Supported
> Siren does a good job of including object identifiers in responses (the class element) but does not (by design) support object metadata. For this reason, when a service changes an object (e.g., adds fields), the Siren client may not discover that at runtime unless it has been specifically coded to emit *all* unknown objects and properties (not always a safe approach). If the client is coded to only parse objects and properties it already knows about, any new fields in a response will be ignored until the client app is recoded and redeployed. We were able to create a custom extension for Siren to get around this (the POD extension), but that is a private convention, not a Siren standard shared by all Siren clients and services.

Siren and the OAA Challenge

In our review of hypermedia types that make it possible for API clients to adapt at runtime, Siren does rather well. It clearly supports the ADDRESS aspect with its `links` collection. And the `actions` collection handles our ACTIONS exactly. But Siren's `class` element, which supports the OBJECT aspect, falls a bit short of our goal. Our Siren client was not be able to handle a new OBJECT added to the backend API because, as the Siren documentation points out, "Possible values are implementation-dependent and should be documented." Our Siren extension to support the POD document helped us get over the hurdle, but that is a custom extension that general Siren clients cannot be expected to support.

Siren definitely gets us much further along on the path to a standalone API client that can support all three aspects (OBJECTS, ADDRESSES, and ACTIONS). But we're not quite there yet. We have one more hypermedia standard to explore (Collection+JSON) to see how well it does in our OAA Challenge.

Bob and Carol

"Well, Carol. We got pretty close this time, didn't we?"

"Yes, Bob. But not quite close enough. Siren is great for handling ADDRESSES and ACTIONS but still doesn't have the OBJECT support I think we need."

"You know, I got the sense even as we were making changes to the backend API just which ones the Siren client could handle and which it could not."

"Right. When you announced the new email field and filter options, the client team was able to guess the results, too. Siren clients don't get enough information about the shared objects."

"So, your Profile Object Display document includes all the important information on the object that both client and server need to share in a safe way, right?"

"That's right, Bob. But, you know, as our team worked up the POD format we discovered something else interesting. We don't need to share *all* the object information between client and server—just some of it."

"I don't think I follow you, Carol."

"Well, we were able to solve our problem by sharing just field identifiers, prompts, and some display information. We didn't need to share relationship information, data types, or other things the server deals with."

"I see. We don't need to share the *entire* object model, just parts of it. Wonder if there is a hypermedia design that takes advantage of that idea?"

"That's the question I asked my team, too, Bob. Let's see what they come up with."

References

1. The IANA registration for Siren is available online (*http://g.mamund.com/ekaqu*).

2. The GitHub conversation "What's different/better/worse than other JSON hypermedia media types?" (*http://g.mamund.com/vokzt*) from 2013 contains lots of interesting observations from some key hypermedia API players.

3. As I am writing this, the most recent official documentation for Siren (*http://g.mamund.com/rrkzz*) is hosted at Kevin Swiber's GitHub account.

4. The current set of the HTML5 `input` elements are documenting in the HTML5 documentation (*http://g.mamund.com/pwhnv*).

Image Credits

- Diogo Lucas: Figure 6-1

CHAPTER 7

Versioning and the Web

"Everything changes and nothing stands still."

 —Heraclitus

Bob and Carol

 "Carol, I've been starting to worry that we've missed something very important in our API design."

"Oh? What's that, Bob?"

 "Versioning."

"You mean handling changes in the API over time, right?"

 "Right. I think we need to account for that in our design."

"Hm. You know, now that I think about it, we've updated the API a couple times and never once talked about versioning. Wonder why that is."

 "I think we were in too much of a hurry to publish a working API and didn't think about the long-term implications."

"Maybe. You know, I've not really missed versioning at all. I mean, things seem to be working fine, right?"

"Well, that's true for now. We're doing mostly small changes and don't have too many independent clients running against the API. But what happens in a few months or even a year from now?"

"I suspect the same thing happens. We keep making small changes and things keep working just fine."

"Well, I think we are going to run into problems at some point unless we address this now."

"OK, let's take a look at it. We're using HTTP so far, right? HTTP has had a couple version updates over the last twenty or so years."

"That's true, Carol. And it all seemed to go pretty well. Hm. HTML is another example, right? Lots of versions there."

"Right. That makes me wonder what it is about the design of HTTP and HTML that made it possible to change over time without breaking existing implementations."

"Huh. Let's not make any changes to our API design yet. I want to do some more research on this."

"Sounds good to me, Bob. Spend a few days on it and let's get back together early next week."

Whether you are in charge of designing, implementing, or just maintaining a web API, at some point you start to think about how to handle change over time. The common word used in the API world is *versioning*. This idea of versioning is so deeply ingrained in the idea of API design that it is considered part of the common practice (discussed in "Web API Common Practice" on page 40) for APIs. Many API designers include versioning information (e.g., numbers in the URL, HTTP headers, or response body) without much thought about the assumption behind that practice.

And there are lots of assumptions behind the common practices of versioning APIs. Chief among them is the assumption that *any* change that is made to the API should be explicitly noted in the API itself (usually in the URL). Another common assumption is that *all* changes are breaking changes—that failing to explicitly signal changes means someone, somewhere will experience a fatal error. One more assumption worth mentioning here is that it is not possible to make meaningful changes to the functionality of web APIs *unless* you make a breaking change.

Finally, there is enough uncertainty associated with the life cycle of web APIs that many API developers decide to simply hedge their bets by adding versioning information in the API design *just in case* it might be needed at some future point. This is a kind of Pascal's Wager for API design.

Pascal's Wager

Blaise Pascal, noted seventeenth-century philosopher, mathematician, and physicist, is credited with creating Pascal's Wager. A simplified version of his argument is that when faced with a decision that cannot be made using logic alone, "a Game is being played… where heads or tails will turn up." In his case, he was illustrating, since we do not know if there is a God, we should bet that one exists since that is the bet with a better outcome.

Although his argument was more nuanced—and others have made similar observations about the nature of uncertainty—Pascal's Wager has become a *meme* that essentially states "When in doubt, hedge your bets."

OK, with this background, let's look into the assumptions behind the versioning argument and at some evidence of how web-related technology handles change over time.

Versioning for the Internet

The idea that handling change over time on the Web means employing the *explicit versioning* technique flies in the face of some very important evidence about how things have worked on the Internet (not just the Web) over the last several decades. We'll take some time here to look at just a few examples.

The examples we'll explore here are (1) the foundational transport-level protocols (TCP/IP), (2) the most common application-level protocol (HTTP), and (3) the most common markup language for the WWW (HTML). They have each undergone important modification over the years and all without causing any major breakage for existing implementations.

Each of our examples is unique, but they all have a common design element that can help us understand how to handle change over time in our own web applications.

TCP/IP's Robustness Principle

The TCP/IP protocol is an essential part of how the Internet works today. In fact, TCP/IP is actually two related protocols: the Transmission Control Protocol (TCP) and the Internet Protocol (IP). Together they are sometimes referred to as the Internet Protocol Suite. Computer scientist Alan Kay called TCP/IP "a kind of universal DNA of [the Internet]." Kay also has pointed out that the Internet has "never been stopped since it was first turned on in September 1969." That means that this set of protocols has been working 24 hours a day, seven days a week for over forty years without a "restart." That's pretty amazing.

Kay's point is that the source code for TCP/IP has been changed and improved over all these years without the need to shut down the Internet. There are a number of reasons for this and one of the key elements is that it was designed for this very situation—to be able to change over time without shutting down. Regarding this feature of the Internet Protocol Suite, Kay has been quoted as saying that the two people credited with designing TCP (Bob Kahn) and IP (Vint Cerf) "knew what they were doing."

One bit of evidence of this knowing what to do can be found in a short section of the TCP specification: section 2.10 with the title *The Robustness Principle*. The full text of this section is:

> "TCP implementations will follow a general principle of robustness: be conservative in what you do, be liberal in what you accept from others."
>
> —RFC793

The authors of this specification understood that it is important to design a system where the odds are tilted in favor of completing message delivery successfully. To do that, implementors are told to be careful to craft valid messages to send. Implementors are also encouraged to do their best to accept incoming messages—even if they are not quite perfect in their format and delivery. When both things are happening in a system, the odds of messages being accepted and processed improves. TCP/IP works, in some part, because this principle is baked into the specification.

Postel's Law

The Robustness Principle is often referred to as *Postel's Law* because Jon Postel was the editor for the RFC that described the TCP protocol.

One way to implement Postel's Law when building hypermedia-style client applications is to pass service responses through a routine that *converts* the incoming message into an internal representation (usually an object graph). This conversion process should be implemented in a way that allows successful processing even when there are flaws in the response such as missing default values that the converter can fill in or simple structural errors, such as missing closing tags, etc. Also, when forming outbound requests—especially requests that will send an HTTP body (e.g., POST, PUT, and PATCH)—it is a good idea to run the composed body through a strict validation routine that will fix formatting errors in any outbound messages.

Here is a bit of pseudo-code that illustrates how you can implement Postel's Law in a client application:

```
// handling incoming messages
httpResponse = getResponse(url);
internalObjectModel = permissiveConverter(httpResponse.body);


...


// handling outgoing messages
httpRequest.body = strictValidator(internalObjectModel);
sendRequest(httpRequest);
```

So TCP teaches us to apply the Robustness Principle to our API implementations. When we do that, we have an improved likelihood that messages sent between parties will be accepted and processed.

HTTP's Must Ignore

The HTTP protocol has been around a long time. It was running in its earliest form in 1990 at CERN labs and has gone through several significant changes in the last 25 years. Some of the earliest editions of the HTTP specification made specific reference to the need for what was then called "client tolerance" in order to make sure that client applications would continue to function even when the responses from web servers were not strictly valid. These were called "deviant servers" in a special note linked to the 1992 draft of the HTTP specs.

A key principle used in the early HTTP specifications is the MUST IGNORE directive. In its basic form, it states that any element of a response that the receiver does not understand must be ignored without halting the further processing of that response.

The final HTTP 1.0 documentation (RFC1945) has several places where this principle is documented. For example, in the section on HTTP headers, it reads:

> Unrecognized header fields should be ignored by the recipient and forwarded by proxies.

Note that in this quote, the MUST IGNORE principle is extended to include instructions for proxies to forward the unrecognized headers to the next party. Not only should the receiver not reject messages with unknown headers but, in the case of proxy servers, those unknown headers are to be included in any forwarded messages. The HTTP 1.0 specification (RFC1945) contains eight separate examples of the MUST IGNORE principle. The HTTP 1.1 specification (RFC2616) has more than 30 examples.

Must Ignore or May Ignore?

Throughout this section of the chapter, I use the phrase MUST IGNORE when referring to the principle in the HTTP specification documents. This name is also used by David Orchard in his blog article "Versioning XML Vocabularies." While the HTTP specs use the word *ignore* many times, not all uses are prefaced by *must*. In fact, some references to the ignore directive are qualified by the words *may* or *should*. The name MUST IGNORE, however, is commonly used for the general principle of ignoring what you don't understand without halting processing.

Supporting the MUST IGNORE principle for web clients means that incoming messages are not rejected when they contain elements that are not understood by the client application. The easiest way to achieve that is to code the clients to simply look for and process the elements in the message that they know.

For example, a client may be coded to know that every incoming message contains three root elements: links, data, and actions. In a JSON-based media type, the response body of this kind of message might look like this:

```
{
  "links" : [...],
  "data" : [...],
  "actions" : [...]
}
```

Some pseudo-code to process these messages might look like this:

```
WITH message DO
  PROCESS message.links
  PROCESS message.data
  PROCESS message.actions
END
```

However, that same client application might receive a response body that contains an additional root-level element named extensions:

```
{
  "links" : [...],
  "data" : [...],
  "actions" : [...],
```

```
    "extensions" : [...]
  }
```

In a client that honors the MUST IGNORE principle (as implemented in the preceding examples), this will not be a problem because the client will simply ignore the unknown element and continue to process the message as if the extensions element does not exist. This is an example of MUST IGNORE at work.

So HTTP's MUST IGNORE principle shows us that we must safely be able to process a message even when it contains portions we do not understand. This is similar to Postel's Law from the TCP specification. Both rules are based on the assumption that some percentage of incoming messages will contain elements that the receiver has not been programmed to understand. When that happens, the processing should not simply stop. Instead, processing should continue on as if the unrecognized element had never appeared at all.

HTML's Backward Compatibility

HTML is another example of a design and implementation approach that accounts for change over time. Like HTTP, the HTML media type has been around since the early 1990s. And, like HTTP, HTML has undergone quite a few changes over that time—from Tim Berners-Lee's initial "HTML Tags" document in 1990, later known as HTML 1.0, on up to the current HTML5. And those many changes have been guided by the principle of *backward compatibility*. Every attempt has been made to only make changes to the media type design that will not cause HTML browsers to halt or crash when attempting to process an HTML document.

The Earliest Known HTML Document

The earliest known HTML document is from November 1990 and is still available on the Web today (*http://g.mamund.com/xublv*). It was crafted two weeks before Tim Berners-Lee and his CERN colleague Robert Cailliau attended ECHT '90—the European Hyper-Text Convention—in Paris. The entire HTML document looks like this:

```
<title>Hypertext Links</title>
<h1>Links and Anchors</h1>
A link is the connection between one piece of
<a href=WhatIs.html>hypertext</a> and another.
```

The fact that this page still renders in browsers today—25 years later—is a great example of how both message design (HTML) and client implementation principles (web browsers) can combine to support successful web interactions over decades.

From almost the very beginning, HTML was designed with both Postel's Law and HTTP's MUST IGNORE in mind. Berners-Lee makes this clear in one of the early working documents for HTML:

> "The HTML parser will ignore tags which it does not understand, and will ignore attributes which it does not understand…"

What's interesting here is that this type of guidance shows that the message designers (those defining HTML) are also providing specific guidance to client implementors (those coding HTML parsers). This principle of advising implementors on how to use and process incoming messages is an important feature of Internet standards in general—so important that there is an IETF document (RFC2119) that establishes just *how* specifications should pass this advice to implementors. This document defines a set of special words for giving directive advice. They are MUST, MUST NOT, REQUIRED, SHALL, SHALL NOT, SHOULD, SHOULD NOT, RECOMMENDED, MAY, and OPTIONAL. Other standards bodies have adopted a similar approach to passing on guidance to implementors.

So, after reviewing lessons from TCP, HTTP, and HTML, we can come up with some general guidance for designing and maintaining APIs that need to support change over time.

Versioning, Forking, and Noncompatible Copies

One more way to think about the act of versioning is that it is really creating a new fork of your app or service. When you create a new version, you are creating a related but likely noncompatible copy of your app—one that now has its own lifeline. And each time you do this forking of your app, you get yet another noncompatible copy. If you're not careful, you'll populate the universe with lots of similar apps that you need to maintain *and* you'll need to help developers keep track of which copy they are using and make sure they don't mistakenly try to get these non-compatible copies to talk to each other.

Committing to a backward-compatible strategy for adding functionality and fixing bugs gets rid of the whole job of naming (versioning) and tracking non-compatible copies of your app or service.

Guidelines for Non-Breaking Changes

Dealing with change over time is best approached with a set of principles—a kind of change *aesthetic*. There is no one single action to take or design feature to include (or exclude). Another key thing to keep in mind is that change will *always* occur. You can certainly use energy and effort to stave off change (e.g., "I know you want that feature in the API but we are not going to be able to make that change this year."). You can even work around change with a hack (e.g., "Well, we don't support that but you can get the same effect if you first write a temp record and then filter based on the change-date of the temp file."). There are other ways to avoid facing change, but almost all long-lived and oft-used APIs will experience pressure to change, and designing-in the ability to handle select types of change can reduce the stress, cost, and danger of changing APIs over time.

So, for those who are no longer attempting to stave off inevitable changes to your APIs, here is some general guidance for web API designers, service providers, and consumer clients. I've used all these options in the past and found them helpful in many cases.

API Designers

For those in charge of designing APIs and message formats, it is important to understand enough about the general problem area to get a sense of what types of changes are likely to be needed over time. It is also important to design interfaces that lead implementors down the "happy path" of creating both API services and API clients that are able to handle common changes over time.

Taking into account the likely changes over time is tricky but important. We saw this kind of thinking when we reviewed the way HTML is documented and designed (see "HTML's Backward Compatibility" on page 225). Paul Clements, one of the authors of the book *Software Architecture in Practice* (Addison-Wesley Professional) claims that those who work in software architecture have a responsibility to deal with change as a fundamental aspect of their design:

> The best software architecture 'knows' what changes often and makes that easy.

With this in mind, here are three valuable principles for those tasked with designing web APIs.

Promise media types, not objects

Over time, object models are bound to change—and these models are likely to change often for new services. Trying to get all your service consumers to learn and track all your object model changes is not a good idea. And, even if you *wanted* all API consumers to keep up with your team's model changes, that means your feature velocity will be limited to that of the slowest API consumer in your ecosystem. This can be especially problematic when your API consumers are customers and not fellow colleagues within the same company.

Instead of exposing object models in your APIs, promise standard message formats (e.g., HTML, Atom, HAL, Cj, Siren, etc.). These formats don't require consumers to understand your service's internal object model. That means you're free to modify your internal model without breaking your promise to API consumers. This also means providers will need to handle the task of translating internal domain data into external message formats, but we covered that already in Chapter 3, *The Representor Pattern*.

Well-designed formats *should* allow API designers to safely introduce *semantic* changes (e.g., data carried within the message model), and well-implemented API consumers will be able to parse/render these content changes without the need for code updates. These same formats might support *structural* changes to messages (e.g., format extensions) in order to safely introduce changes that can be ignored by clients that do not understand them.

Document link identifiers, not URLs

Your API *should not* bake static URLs into the design. URLs are likely to change over time, especially in cases where your initial service is running in a test bed or small online community to start. Tricking API consumers into baking explicit URLs into their source code increases the likelihood that their code will become obsolete, and that forces consumers into unwanted recode-test-deploy cycles if and when your URLs change.

Instead, your API design *should* promise to support a named operation (`shopping CartCheckOut`, `computeTax`, `findCustomer`) instead of promising exact addresses for those operations (e.g., *http://api.example.org/findCustomer*). Documenting (and promising operations by name) is a much more stable and maintainable design feature.

If you want new operations to be ignored by existing clients, make it part of the *structure* of the message (e.g., `<findCustomer ... />`). However, when you want the operation to be automatically parsed and/or rendered, favor formats that allow you to include the operation identifiers as part of the message's *semantic* content (e.g., `<operation name="findCustomer" ... />`). Good candidates for semantic identifers are properties such as `id`, `name`, `class`, and `rel`.

Publish vocabularies, not models

The notion of *canonical models* has been around a long time—especially in large enterprise IT shops. The hope is that, with enough hard work, a single grand model of the company's business domain will be completely defined and properly described so that everyone (from the business analyst on through to the front-line developer) will have a complete picture of the entire company's domain data. But this never works out.

The two things conspiring against canonical models are (1) scope and (2) time. As the scope of the problem grows (e.g., the company expands, product offerings increase, etc.), the model becomes unwieldy. And as time goes on, even simple models experience modifications that complicate a single-model view of the world. The good news is there is another way to solve this problem: vocabularies.

Once you move to promising formats instead of object models (see "Promise media types, not objects" on page 227), the work of providing shared understanding of your API's domain data and actions needs to be kept somewhere else. A great place for this is in a *shared vocabulary*. Eric Evans refers to this using the name *ubiquitous language* —a common rigorous language shared between domain experts and system implementors. By focusing on a shared vocabulary designers can constantly probe domain experts for clarification, and developers can implement features and share data with a high degree of confidence.

 Eric Evans's book *Domain-Driven Design* (Addison-Wesley Professional) offers a number of valuable lessons in scoping problem domains. While the book was written primarily for those who favor OOP code and XML-based messages over local networks, there is still quite a bit of value in his DDD approach to building up a shared language for a domain and marking the boundaries of components (services) using what he calls *bounded context*.

Another important reason to rely on vocabularies is that you can define consistent binding rules between the vocabulary terms and the output formats used in your API. For example, you might document that data element names in the vocabulary will always appear in the `class` property of HTML responses and the `name` property of Collection+JSON responses, and so forth. This also helps API providers and consumers write general-use code that will work even when new vocabulary terms are added over time.

So, when designing APIs you should:

- Promise media types, not objects
- Document link identifiers, not URLs
- Publish vocabularies, not models

Server Implementors

Like API designers, service implementors have a responsibility to create a software implementation that can account for change over time in an effective way. This means making sure local service changes can be made without any unnecessary complexity or instability. It also means you need to ensure that changes made to the service over time are not likely to break existing client implementations—even implementations that the service knows nothing about!

Maintaining backward compatibility is the primary principle for service implementors when supporting change over time. Essentially, this constrains the types of changes a service can make to those which will not invalidate existing implementations. We saw this principle in play, for example, when reviewing HTTP's design principles (see "HTTP's Must Ignore" on page 223).

With this in mind, here are three principles I've used to help support change over time while reducing the likelihood of breaking existing implementations.

Don't take things away

One of the most important aspects of maintaining a backward-compatible service implementation is *don't take things away* such as operations or data elements. In API projects I work on, I make this an explicit promise. Once API consumers know that you will not take things away, the value of your API will go up. That's because API consumers will be assured that, even when you add new data elements and actions to the API, the existing API consumer code will still be valid.

One big reason to make this promise is that it allows API consumer teams to move at their own pace. They don't need to stop current sprints or feature work in order to deal with potentially breaking changes from some service API they are using in their application. That also means the services don't need to wait for the slowest API consumer team before they introduce new elements and actions in the API. This loose-coupling in the API update process can result in overall faster development processes since it reduces potential blocking scenarios.

So, what does this backward-compatibility promise look like? Here's an example I learned from Jason Rudolph at GitHub a few years ago. This is an example of what they call *evolutionary design* for APIs. He says:

> When people are building on top of our API, we're really asking them to trust us with the time they're investing in building their applications. And to earn that trust, we can't make changes [to the API] that would cause their code to break.

Here's an example of evolutionary design in action. They supported an API response that returned the current status of an account's request rate limit. It looked like this:

```
*** REQUEST ***
GET rate_limit
Accept: application/vnd.github+json
...

*** RESPONSE ***
200 OK HTTP/1.1
Content-Type: application/vnd.github+json
...

{
  "rate" {
```

```
      "limit" : 5000,
      "remaining : 4992,
      "reset" : 1379363338
   }
}
```

Over time, the GitHub team learned that this response was more coarse-grained than was needed. It turns out they wanted to separate search-related rate limits from typical core API calls. So the new design would look like this:

```
*** REQUEST ***
GET rate_limit
Accept: application/vnd.github+json
...

*** RESPONSE ***
200 OK HTTP/1.1
Content-Type: application/vnd.github+json
...

{
  "resources" : {
    "core" : {
      "limit" : 5000,
      "remaining : 4992,
      "reset" : 1379363338
    },
    "search" : {
      "limit" : 20,
      "remaining : 19,
      "reset" : 1379361617
    }
  }
}
```

Now, they had a dilemma on their hands. How could they make this important change to the interface without breaking existing implementations? Their solution was, I think, quite smart. Rather than *changing* the response body, they *extended* it. The new response for the rate_limit request now looks like this:

```
*** REQUEST ***
GET rate_limit
Accept: application/vnd.github+json
...

*** RESPONSE ***
200 OK HTTP/1.1
Content-Type: application/vnd.github+json
...

{
  "rate" : { ❶
```

```
    "limit" : 5000,
    "remaining : 4992,
    "reset" : 1379363338
  },
  "resources" : { ❷
    "core" : {
      "limit" : 5000,
      "remaining : 4992,
      "reset" : 1379363338
    },
    "search" : {
      "limit" : 20,
      "remaining : 19,
      "reset" : 1379361617
    }
  }
}
```

Notice that GitHub applied a *structural* change to the response. The original structure (❶) and the new structure (❷) *both* appear in the response message. This results in a change that can be safely ignored by clients that don't understand the new, detailed structural element ("resources"). This is just one example of implementing backward-compatibility by not taking things away. The same general approach can be made for links and forms in a response, too.

Don't change the meaning of things

Another important backward-compatibility principle for service providers is *don't change the meaning of things*. That means that, once you publish a link or form with an identifier that tells API consumers what is returned (e.g., <a href="…" rel="users" /> returns a list of users), you should not later use that same identifier to return something completely different (e.g., <a href="…" rel="users" /> later only returns a list of inactive users). Consistency of what the link identifier and/or data element *represents* is very important for maintaining backward compatibility over time.

In cases where you want to represent some new functionality to the API, it is much better to make a *semantic* change by adding the new feature. And you should do this without removing any existing functionality. To use the preceding example, if you want to add the ability to return a list of inactive users, it is better to introduce an additional link (and identifier) while maintaining the existing one:

```
*** REQUEST ***
GET /user-actions HTTP/1.1
Accept: application/vnd.hal+json
...

**** RESPONSE ***
200 OK HTTP/1.1
```

```
Content-Type: application/vnd.hal+json
...

{
  "_links" :  {
    "users" : {"href" : "/user-list"},
    "inactive" : {"href" : "/user-list?status=inactive"}
  }
}
...
```

In cases where the preceding response is used to create a human-driven UI, both the links will appear on the screen and the person running the app can decide which link to select. In the case of a service-only interface (e.g., some middleware that is tasked with collecting a list of users and processing it in some unique way), the added semantic information (e.g., the `inactive` link) will not be "known" to existing apps and will be safely ignored. In both cases, this maintains backward compatibility and does not break existing implementations.

All new things are optional

Another important change over time principle for service implementors is to make sure *all new things are optional*. This especially applies to new arguments (e.g., filters or update values)—they cannot be treated as required elements. Also, any new functionality or workflow steps (e.g., you introduce a new workflow step between login and checkout) cannot be required in order to complete the process.

One example of this is similar to the GitHub case just described (see "Don't take things away" on page 230). It is possible that, over time, you'll find that some new filters are needed when making requests for large lists of data. You might even want to introduce a default `page-size` to limit the load time of a resource and speed up responsiveness in your API. Here's how a filter form looks before the introduction of the `page-size` argument:

```
*** REQUEST ***
GET /search-form HTTP/1.1
Accept: application/vnd.collection+json
...

*** RESPONSE ***
200 OK HTTP/1.1
Content-Type: application/vnd.collection+json
...

{
  "collection" : {
    "queries" : [
      {
        "rel" : "search"
```

```
        "href" : "/search-results",
        "prompt" : Search Form",
        "data" : [
          {
            "name" : "filter",
            "value" : "",
            "prompt" : "Filter",
            "required" : true
          }
        ]
      }
    ]
  }
}
```

And here is the same response after introducing the page-size argument:

```
*** REQUEST ***
GET /search-form HTTP/1.1
Accept: application/vnd.collection+json
...

*** RESPONSE ***
200 OK HTTP/1.1
Content-Type: application/vnd.collection+json
...

{
  "collection" : {
    "queries" : [
      {
        "rel" : "search"
        "href" : "/search-results",
        "prompt" : Search Form",
        "data" : [
          {
            "name" : "filter",
            "value" : "",
            "prompt" : "Filter",
            "required" : true
          },
          {
            "name" : page-size",
            "value" : "all",
            "prompt" : "Page Size",
            "required" : false
          }
        ]
      }
    ]
  }
}
```

In the updated rendition, you can see that the new argument (`page-size`) was explicitly marked optional (`"required" : false`). You can also see that the a default value was provided (`"value" : "all"`). This may seem a bit counterintuitive. The update was introduced in order to *limit* the number of records sent in responses. So why set the default value to `"all"`? It is set to `"all"` because that was the initial promise in the first rendition of the API. We can't change the results of this request now to only include *some* of the records. This also follows the *don't change the meaning of things* principle.

So, as service implementors, you can go a long way toward maintaining backward compatibility by supporting these three principles:

- Don't take things away
- Don't change the meaning of things
- Make new things optional

Client Implementors

Those on the consuming end of APIs also have some responsibility to support change over time. We need to make sure we're prepared for the backward-compatible features employed by API designers and service implementors. But we don't need to wait for designers and providers to make changes to their own work before creating stable API consumer apps. We can adopt some of our own principles for creating robust, resilient API clients. Finally, we also need to help API designers and service providers understand the challenges of creating adaptable API consumers by encouraging them to adopt the kinds of principles described here when they create APIs.

Code defensively

The first thing API consumers can do is adopt a coding strategy that protects the app from cases where expected data elements and/or actions are missing in a response. This can be accomplished when you *code defensively*. You can think of this as honoring *Postel's Law* (see "TCP/IP's Robustness Principle" on page 222) by being "liberal in what you accept from others." There are a couple of very simple ways to do this.

For example, when I write client code to process a response, I almost always include code that first checks for the existence of an element before attempting to parse it. Here's some client code that you'll likely find in the examples associated with this book:

```
// handle title
function title() {
  var elm;
```

```
        if(hasTitle(global.cj.collection)===true) { ❶
          elm = domHelper.find("title");
          elm.innerText = global.cj.collection.title;
          elm = domHelper.tags("title");
          elm[0].innerText = global.cj.collection.title;
        }
      }
```

You can see that I first check to see if the collection object has a title property (❶).
If so, I can continue processing it.

Here's another example where I supply local default values for cases where the service
response is missing expected elements (❶, ❷, ❸, ❹, ❺) *and* check for the existence of
a property (❻):

```
      function input(args) {
        var p, lbl, inp;

        p = domHelper.node("p");
        p.className = "inline field";
        lbl = domHelper.node("label");
        inp = domHelper.node("input");
        lbl.className = "data";
        lbl.innerHTML = args.prompt||""; ❶
        inp.name = args.name||""; ❷
        inp.className = "value "+ args.className;
        inp.value = args.value.toString()||""; ❸
        inp.required = (args.required||false); ❹
        inp.readOnly = (args.readOnly||false); ❺
        if(args.pattern) { ❻
          inp.pattern = args.pattern;
        }
        domHelper.push(lbl,p);
        domHelper.push(inp,p);

        return p;
      }
```

There are other examples of coding defensively that I won't include here. The main
idea is to make sure that client applications can continue functioning even when any
given response is missing expected elements. When you do this, even most unexpected changes will not cause your API consumer to crash.

Code to the media type

Another important principle for building resilient API consumer apps is to *code to
the media type*. Essentially, this is using the same approach that was discussed in
Chapter 3, *The Representor Pattern*, except that this time, instead of focusing on creating a pattern for converting internal domain data into a standard message format (via
a *Message Translator*), the opposite is the goal for API consumers: convert a standar-

dized message format into a useful internal domain model. By doing this, you can go a long way toward protecting your client application from both semantic and structural changes in the service responses.

For all the client examples I implement in this book, the media type messages (HTML, HAL, Cj, and Siren) are converted into the same internal domain model: the HTML Document Object Model (DOM). The DOM is a consistent model, and writing client-side JavaScript for it is the way most browser-based API clients work.

Here is a short code snippet that shows how I convert Siren `entities` into HTML DOM objects for rendering in the browser:

```javascript
// entities
function entities() {
  var elm, coll;
  var ul, li, dl, dt, dd, a, p;

  elm = domHelper.find("entities");
  domHelper.clear(elm);

  if(global.siren.entities) {
    coll = global.siren.entities;
    for(var item of coll) {
      segment = domHelper.node("div");  ❶
      segment.className = "ui segment";

      a = domHelper.anchor({  ❷
        href:item.href,
        rel:item.rel.join(" "),
        className:item.class.join(" "),
        text:item.title||item.href});
      a.onclick = httpGet;
      domHelper.push(a, segment);

      table = domHelper.node("table");  ❸
      table.className = "ui very basic collapsing celled table";
      for(var prop in item) {
        if(prop!=="href" &&
          prop!=="class" &&
          prop!=="type" &&
          prop!=="rel") {
          tr = domHelper.data_row({  ❹
            className:"item "+item.class.join(" "),
            text:prop+" ",
            value:item[prop]+" "
          });
          domHelper.push(tr,table);
        }
      }
      domHelper.push(table, segment, elm);  ❺
    }
```

```
        }
    }
```

It might be a bit tough to see how the HTML DOM is utilized in this example since I use a helper class (the `domHelper` object) to access most of the DOM functions. But you can see that, for each Siren `entity` I create an HTML `div` tag (❶). I then create an HTML anchor tag (❷) for each item. I set up an HTML `<table>` to hold the Siren `entity`'s properties (❸) and add a new table row (`<tr>`) for each one (❹). Finally, after completing all the rows in the table, I add the results to the HTML page for visible display (❺).

This works because all the implementation examples in this book are intended for common HTML browsers. For cases where the target clients are mobile devices or native desktop applications, I need to work out another strategy. One way to handle this is to create *reverse representors* for each platform. In other words, create a custom `Format-to-Domain` handler for iOS, Android, and Windows Mobile, etc. Then the same for Linux, Mac, and Windows desktops, and so forth. This can get tedious, though. That's why using the browser DOM is still appealing and why some mobile apps rely on tools like Apache Cordova, Mono, Appcelerator, and other cross-platform development environments.

Client-Side Representors

As of this writing, there are a number of efforts to build representor libraries that focus on the client—the reverse of the example I outlined in Chapter 3, *The Representor Pattern*. The team at Apiary are working on the Hyperdrive project (*http://g.mamund.com/hhdno*). The Hypermedia Project (*http://g.mamund.com/zfxno*) is a Microsoft.NET-specific effort. And Joshua Kalis has started a project (to which I am a contributor) called Rosetta (*https://github.com/ubiquitary*). Finally, the Yaks (*https://github.com/plexus/yaks*) project is an independent OSS effort to create a framework that includes the representor pattern to support plug-ins for new formats. There may be more projects by the time you read this book, too.

Leverage the API vocabulary

Once you start building clients that *code to the media type*, you'll find that you still need to know domain-specific details that appear in responses. Things like:

- Does this response contain the list of users I asked for?
- How do I find all the inactive customers?
- Which of these invoice records are overdue?

- Is there a way for me to find all the products that are no longer in stock in the warehouse?

All these questions are *domain-specific* and are not tied to any single response format like HAL, Cj, or Siren. One of the reasons the HTML browser has been so powerful is that the browser source code doesn't need to know anything about accounting in order to host an accounting application. That's because the *user* driving the browser knows that stuff. The browser is just the *agent* of the human user. For many API client cases, there is a human user available to interpret and act upon the domain-specific information in API responses. However, there are cases where the API client is not acting as a direct user agent. Instead, it is just a middleware component or utility app tasked with some job by itself (e.g., find all the overdue invoices). In these cases, the client app needs to have enough domain information to complete its job. And that's where API vocabularies come in.

There are a handful of projects focused on documenting and sharing domain-specific vocabularies over the WWW. One of the best-known examples of this is the Schema.org project (pronounced *schema dot org*). Schema.org contains lists of common terms for all sorts of domains. Large web companies like Google and Microsoft use Schema.org vocabularies to drive parts of their system.

 Vocabularies aplenty

Along with Schema.org (*http://schem.org*), there are other vocabulary efforts such as the IANA Link Relations registry (*http://g.mamund.com/poysh*), the microformats (*http://microformats.org*) group, and the *Dublin Core Metadata Initiative*, or DCMI (*http://dublincore.org*). A few colleagues and I have also been working on an Internet draft for *Application-Level Profile Semantics*, or ALPS (*http://alps.io*) for short.

I won't have time to go into vocabularies in this book and encourage you to check out these and other similar efforts in order to learn more about how they can be used in your client-side apps.

So what does this all look like? How can you use vocabularies to enable API clients to act on their own safely? Basically, you need to "teach" the API consumer to perform tasks based on some baked-in domain knowledge. For example, I might want to create an API consumer that uses one service to find overdue invoices and then pass that information off to another service for further processing. This means the API consumer needs to "know" about invoices and what it means to be "overdue." If the API I am using has published a vocabulary, I can look there for the data and action element identifiers I need to perform my work.

As just one example, here's what that published vocabulary might look like as expressed in a simplified ALPS XML document:

```
<alps>
  <doc>Invoice Management Vocabluary</doc>
  <link rel="invoice-mgmt" href="api.example.org/profile/invoice-mgmt" />

  <!-- data elements -->
  <descriptor id="invoice-href" />
  <descriptor id="invoice-number" />
  <descriptor id="invoice-status">
    <doc>Valid values are: "active", "closed", "overdue"</doc>
  </descriptor>

  <!-- actions -->
  <descriptor id="invoice-list" type="safe" />
  <descriptor id="invoice-detail" type="safe" />
  <descriptor id="invoice-search" type="safe">
    <descriptor href="#invoice-status" />
  </descriptor>
  <descriptor id="write-invoice" type="unsafe">
  <descriptor href="#invoice-href" />
  <descriptor href="#invoice-number" />
  <descriptor href="#invoice-status">
  </dscriptor>
</alps>
```

 The ALPS specification is just one profile style for capturing and expressing vocabularies. You can learn more about the ALPS specification by visiting alps.io. Two others worth exploring are XMDP (XHTML Metadata Profiles) and Dublin Core's Application Profiles (DCAP).

Now when I build my client application, I know that I can "teach" that app to understand how to deal with an invoice record (invoice-number and invoice-status) and know how to search for overdue invoices (use search-invoice with the invoice-status value set to "overdue"). All I need is the starting address for the service and the ability to recognize and execute the search for overdue invoices. The pseudo-code for that example might look like this:

```
:: DECLARE ::
search-link = "invoice-search"  ❶
search-status = "overdue"
write-invoice = "write-invoice"
invoice-mgmt = "api.example.org/profile/invoice-mgmt"

search-href = "http://api.example.org/invoice-mgmt"
search-accept = "application/vnd.siren+json"
```

```
write-href = "http://third-party.example.org/write-invoices"
write-accept = "application/vnd.hal+json"

:: EXECUTE ::
response = REQUEST(search-href AS search-accept)
IF(response.vocabulary IS invoivce-mgmt) THEN ❷
  FOR-EACH(link IN response)
    IF(link IS search-link) THEN
      invoices = REQUEST(search-link AS search-accept WITH search-status) ❸
      FOR-EACH(link IN invoices)
        REQUEST(write-href AS write-accept
          FOR write-invoice WITH EACH invoice) ❹
      END-FOR
    END-IF
  END-FOR
END-IF

:: EXIT ::
```

Although this is only pseudo-code, you can see the app has been loaded with domain-specific information (❶). Then, after the initial request is made, the response is checked to see if it promises to use the invoice-mgmt vocabluary (❷). If that check passes, the app searches all the links in the response to find the search-link and, if found, executes a search for all invoices with the status of overdue (❸). Finally, if any invoices are returned in that search, they are sent to a new service using the write-invoice action (❹).

Something to note here is that the defensive coding is on display (the if statements) and the code has only initial URLs memorized—the remaining URLs come from the responses themselves.

Leveraging vocabularies for your API means you can focus on the important aspects (the data elements and actions) and not worry about plumbing details such as URL matching, memorizing the exact location of a data element within a document, etc.

React to link relations for workflow

The last client implementation principle I'll cover here is to *react to link relations for workflow*. This means that when working to solve a multistep problem, focus on selected link relation values instead of writing client apps that memorize a fixed set of steps. This is important because memorizing a fixed set of steps is a kind of *tight-binding* of the client to a fixed sequence of events that may not actually happen at runtime due to transient context issues (e.g., part of the service is down for maintenance, the logged-in user no longer has rights to one of the steps, etc.). Or over time, new steps might be introduced or the *order* of events might change within the service. These are all reasons not to bake multistep details into your client app.

You might recognize this principle of not memorizing steps as the difference between path-finders and map-makers from Chapter 5, *The Challenge of Reusable Client Apps*.

Instead, since the service you are using has also followed the API principles of *document link identifiers, publish vocabularies*, and *don't take things away*, you can implement a client that is trained to look for the proper identifiers and use vocabulary information to know which data elements need to be passed for each operation. Now, even if the links are moved within a response (or even moved to a different response) your client will still be able to accomplish your goal well into the future.

One way to approach this *react to links* principle is to isolate all the important actions the client will need to take and simply implement them as standalone, stateless operations. Once that is done, you can write a single routine that (1) makes a request, and (2) inspects that request for one of the known actions, and when found, executes the recognized action.

Following is an example of a Twitter-like quote-bot I created for my 2011 book *Building Hypermedia APIs*:

```
/* these are the things this bot can do */
function processResponse(ajax) {
  var doc = ajax.responseXML;

  if(ajax.status===200) {
    switch(context.status) {
      case 'start':
        findUsersAllLink(doc);
        break;
      case 'get-users-all':
        findMyUserName(doc);
        break;
      case 'get-register-link':
        findRegisterLink(doc);
        break;
      case 'get-register-form':
        findRegisterForm(doc);
        break;
      case 'post-user':
        postUser(doc);
        break;
      case 'get-message-post-link':
        findMessagePostForm(doc);
        break;
      case 'post-message':
        postMessage(doc);
        break;
      case 'completed':
```

```
        handleCompleted(doc);
        break;
      default:
        alert('unknown status: ['+g.status+']');
        return;
    }
  }
  else {
    alert(ajax.status);
  }
}
```

In the preceding example, this routine constantly monitors the app's current internal `context.status` and, as it changes from one state to another, the app knows just what to be looking for within the current response and/or what action to take in order to advance to the next step in the effort to reach the final goal. For this bot, the goal is to post inspirational quotes to the available social media feed. This bot also knows that it *might* need to authenticate in order to access the feed, or possibly even create a new user account. Notice the use of the JavaScript `switch...case` structure here. There is no notion of execution order written into the code—just a set of possible states and related operations to attempt to execute.

Writing clients in this way allows you to create middleware components that can accomplish a set goal without forcing that client to memorize a particular order of events. That means even when the order of things changes over time—as long as the changes are made in a backward-compatible way—this client will still be able to complete its assigned tasks.

So, some valuable principles for implementing clients that support change over time include:

- Code defensively
- Code to the media type
- Leverage the API vocabulary
- React to link relations for workflow

Summary

This chapter focused on dealing with the challenge of change over time for web APIs. We looked at examples of planning for and handling change over the decades in three key web-related fields: TCP/IP and Postel's Law, HTTP and the MUST IGNORE principle, and the backward-compatibility pledge that underpins the design of HTML. We then looked at some general principles we can use when designing APIs, implementing API services, and building client apps that consume those APIs.

The key message of this chapter is that change is inevitable and the way to deal with it is to plan ahead and adopt the point of view that all changes do not require you break the interface. Finally, we learned that successful organizations adopt a *change aesthetic*—a collection of related principles that help guide API design, inform service implementors, and encourage API consumers to all work toward maintaining backward compatibility.

Bob and Carol

 "Hi, Bob. I stopped over to see how you are dealing with all the versioning stuff we talked about a last week."

"Hey, Carol. You know, we found a number of examples similar to the ones we mentioned in our last get-together. Postel's Law for TCP/IP, HTTP's MUST IGNORE principle, even a quote from Tim Berners-Lee about how HTML parsers should ignore things they don't understand."

 "So, that's 25 or more years of dealing with change that never invalidated existing implementations. That's encouraging. But these are all transport and transfer-level specifications. Our challenge is at the application domain level, right? "

"Yep. And that definitely makes things a bit more interesting—but not at all impossible. While the actual *implementation* details for TCP/IP and HTTP might be different, the *principles* behind them apply to all aspects of API design and implementation."

 "Great, so we can just ignore all the versioning stuff then and keep rolling along."

"Not quite. We identified some important guiding principles on how to handle change over time that we will be shared with all our teams. It focuses on making sure all service API changes are backward-compatible."

"That's the key, isn't it, Bob? With backward compatibility as our key principle, teams can add features and enrich data responses without breaking existing apps."

"Exactly. I've emailed you the list of principles already and we'll incorporate them into the guidance docs we share with everyone."

"Sounds great. By the way, what's the story on those new features you promised me in our last meeting?"

"Oh, didn't you hear? We released those into production yesterday. I guess you never noticed since we didn't have to break any existing clients in the process."

"Well played, Bob. Well played."

References

1. Blaise Pascal's Wager has more to do with the nature of uncertainty and probability theory than anything else. A decent place to start reading about his Wager is the Wikipedia entry (*http://g.mamund.com/jfbth*).

2. Alan Kay's 2011 talk on *Programming and Scaling* (*http://g.mamund.com/cxmbf*) contains a commentary on how TCP/IP has been updated and improved over the years without ever having to "stop" the Internet.

3. TCP/IP is documented in two key IETF documents: RFC793 (*http://g.mamund.com/dqgcy*) (TCP) and RFC791 (*http://g.mamund.com/bqgcy*) (IP).

4. The *Client tolerance of bad servers* note can be viewed in the W3C's HTTP protocol (*http://g.mamund.com/pppyd*) archive pages.

5. The IETF specification document for RFC1945 (*http://g.mamund.com/soofi*) contains eight separate examples of the MUST IGNORE principle. The HTTP 1.1 (*http://g.mamund.com/cdzjr*) specification (RFC2616) has more than 30 examples.

6. Dave Orchard's 2003 blog post "Versioning XML Vocabularies" (*http:// g.mamund.com/kpvcu*) does a good job of illustrating a number of valuable "Must Ignore" patterns.

7. Tim Berner-Lee's Markup archive from 1992 (*http://g.mamund.com/xmwxe*) is a great source for those looking into the earliest days of HTML.

8. The 2119 Words can be found in IETF's RFC2119 (*http://g.mamund.com/qqflb*).

9. The book *Software Architecture in Practice* was written by Len Bass, Paul Clements, and Rick Kazman.

10. I learned about GitHub's approach to managing backward compatibility from a Yandex 2013 talk by Jason Rudolph on "API Design at GitHub." As of this writing, the video (*http://g.mamund.com/whhgx*) and slides (*http://g.mamund.com/rutmz*) are still available online.

11. The Schema.org effort includes the website (*http://schema.org*), a W3C community site (*http://g.mamund.com/stqcc*), a GitHub repository (*http:// g.mamund.com/rfvbu*), and an online discussion group (*http://g.mamund.com/ xxxgn*).

12. The book *Building Hypermedia APIs* (O'Reilly) is a kind of companion book to this one. That book focuses on API design with some server-side implementation details.

13. The Dublin Code Application Profile (DCAP) spec "includes guidance for metadata creators and clear specifications for metadata developers." You can read more about it here (*http://dublincore.org/documents/profile-guidelines/*).

14. In 2003, Tantek Çelik defined the XHTML Meta Data Profile (XMDP). It supports defining document profiles that are both human- and machine-readable. The specification can be found online (*http://gmpg.org/xmdp*).

Collection+JSON Clients

"The human animal differs from the lesser primates in his passion for lists."

—H. Allen Smith

Bob and Carol

"You know, Carol, I've been reviewing the Collection +JSON hypermedia format and wondering if it would help us on our quest for a more adaptable API client."

"Interesting that you should mention Cj, Bob. My team tells me it may be promising, too."

"Right. I notice that Cj looks a lot like Siren and HAL but also has some things in the docs about the CRUD pattern similar to your plain JSON client."

"Exactly! And, along with support for CRUD, Cj offers support for templates similar to the action elements in Siren."

"I am a bit skeptical about the way Cj sends data in its Items collection."

"Right, Cj requires additional metadata for each domain object and it will be hard to simply deserialize our domain objects into the response as we do in Siren and HAL."

"Huh, that's more work for the server-side representor and more payload for the client. I wonder if we need all that description."

"As far as we can tell, Cj payload size is not any larger than our typical HTML payloads, Bob."

"Hm. I wonder if that metadata provides something important we can't see yet?"

"Well, some on my team think additional metadata will improve adaptability."

"Well, let's try it out. My team can build a Cj representor pretty quickly. And your group should be able to create a Cj client without too much trouble, right, Carol?"

"Yep. Let's see what our teams come up with and meet back here in another week."

"OK, Carol. Let's do it!"

The last hypermedia format we'll review in this book is the Collection+JSON (Cj) format. It has similarities with both HAL (see Chapter 4) and Siren (see Chapter 6) but also has a rather unique approach. The Cj format is designed, from the very beginning, as a *list-style* format—it is meant to return lists of records. As we'll see when we review the design in the next section, there is more to the format than just that, but lists are what Cj is designed to deal with.

Cj also takes a cue from the classic Create-Read-Update-Delete (CRUD) pattern used by most web API clients today. We covered this style in Chapter 2, and some of the lessons from the client we built in that chapter will apply for the Cj client, too.

In this chapter, we'll take a quick look at the format design, the Cj representor code, and the Cj general client. Then, as we have for other client implementations, we'll introduce changes to see how well the API client holds up as the backend API makes backward-compatible changes.

Finally, we'll be sure to check in on our progress along the path to meeting the OAA Challenge. While HAL excels at handling ADDRESSES and Siren has great support for ACTIONS, Cj was designed to meet the OBJECTS challenge—sharing metadata about the domain objects at runtime. And, as we'll see in the review, Cj meets the OBJECT challenge with a novel solution—by making them inconsequential to the client–server experience.

The Collection+JSON Format

I designed and published the Collection+JSON format in 2011—the same year Mike Kelly released his HAL specification. Collection+JSON (aka Cj) was designed to make it easy to manage lists of data like blog posts, customer records, products, users, and so on. The description that appears on the Cj specification page says:

> [Cj] is similar to the Atom Syndication Format (RFC4287) and the Atom Publishing Protocol (RFC5023). However, Collection+JSON defines both the format and the protocol semantics in a single media type. [Cj] also includes support for Query Templates and expanded write support through the use of a Write Template.

One way to think about Cj is that it is a JSON version of the Atom format with forms added (see Figure 8-1). The good news is that Cj follows Atom's support for the Create-Read-Update-Delete (CRUD) pattern. That means most developers can understand Cj's read/write semantics rather easily. The added bonus for Cj is that it has elements for describing HTML-like forms for filtering data (with Cj's `queries` element) and for updating content on the server (via the `template` element). However, as we'll see in the review that follows, the way the `template` element is used can be a bit of a challenge.

 You can find a more complete description of the Collection+JSON media type by checking out the online Cj documentation. There is also a Cj discussion list and GitHub organization where additional information is shared. See "References" on page 298 at the end of this chapter for details.

Figure 8-1. The Collection+JSON document model

The basic elements of every Cj message are:

Links

A set of one or more `link` elements. These are very similar to HAL and Siren `link` elements.

Items

One or more data items—basically the API domain objects. The `properties` of HAL and Siren are similar to Cj `items`.

Queries

These are basically HTML GET forms. Cj `queries` are like HAL's templated links and Siren's `action` elements (with the `method` set to GET).

Template

In Cj, all *write* operations (HTTP POST and PUT) are done using the `template` element. It contains one or more `data` objects—each one like HTML `input` elements. Again, this is similar to Siren `action` elements. HAL doesn't have anything that matches the Cj `template`.

Cj also has an `error` element for returning error information and a `content` element for returning free-form text and markup. We'll not cover these here today. You can read up on them in the Cj documentation mentioned in the reference section ("References" on page 298).

Here's an example of a simple Collection+JSON message that shows the major sections] of a Cj document, including `links` (❶), `items` (❷), `queries` (❸), and the `template` (❹) element:

```json
{
  "collection": {
    "version": "1.0",
    "href": "http://rwcbook12.herokuapp.com", ❺
    "title": "TPS - Task Processing System",
    "links": [ ❶
      {
        "href": "http://rwcbook12.herokuapp.com/",
        "rel": "collection",
        "prompt": "All task"
      }
    ],
    "items": [ ❷
      {
        "rel": "item",
        "href": "http://rwcbook12.herokuapp.com/1sv697h2yij",
        "data": [
          {"name": "id", "value": "1sv697h2yij", "prompt": "id"},
          {"name": "title", "value": "Marina", "prompt": "title"},
          {"name": "completed", "value": "false", "prompt": "completed"}
        ]
      },
      {
        "rel": "item",
        "href": "http://rwcbook12.herokuapp.com/25ogsjhqtk7",
        "data": [
          {"name": "id", "value": "25ogsjhqtk7", "prompt": "id"},
          {"name": "title", "value": "new stuff", "prompt": "title"},
          {"name": "completed", "value": "true", "prompt": "completed"}
        ]
      }
    ],
    "queries": [ ❸
      {
        "rel": "search",
        "href": "http://rwcbook12.herokuapp.com/",
        "prompt": "Search tasks",
        "data": [
          {"name": "title", "value": "", "prompt": "Title"}
        ]
      }
    ],
```

```
      "template": { ❹
        "prompt": "Add task",
        "rel": "create-form",
        "data": [
          {"name": "title", "value": "", "prompt": "Title"},
          {"name": "completed", "value": "false", "prompt": "Complete"}
        ]
      }
    }
  }
}
```

Another important attribute of a Cj document is the root-level href (see ❺). The value of href is used when adding a new record to the items collection. We'll talk more about this property when we cover the template element (see "Template" on page 255).

Links

The links element in a Cj document is always a valid JSON array which contains one or more link objects. Important link properties include href, rel, and prompt. These work similarly to the way HTML <a>...</a> tags do—static URLs for HTTP GET actions:

```
"links": [
  {
    "href": "http://rwcbook12.herokuapp.com/home/",
    "rel": "home collection",
    "prompt": "Home"
  },
  {
    "href": "http://rwcbook12.herokuapp.com/task/",
    "rel": "self task collection",
    "prompt": "Tasks"
  },
  {
    "href": "http://rwcbook12.herokuapp.com/user/",
    "rel": "user collection",
    "prompt": "Users"
  }
]
```

In Cj, the links section typically holds links that are relevant for the current document or, in a human-centric UI, the current screen or web page. Along with important navigation links for the app (see in the previous example), the links section may include things like page-level navigation (first, previous, next, last) or other similar links.

Another handy property on Cj link objects is the render property. This tells consuming apps how to treat the link. For example, if the render value is set to "none", client apps are not expected to display the link. This is handy when passing `link` elements for things like CSS stylesheets, profile URLs, or other types of information:

```
"links": [
  {
    "href": "http://api.example.org/profiles/task-management",
    "rel": "profile",
    "render" : "none"
  }
]
```

Items

Probably the most unique element in Cj documents is the `item` sections. The `items` section is similar to HAL's root-level `properties` and Siren's `properties` object. Cj `items` contain the domain objects in the response, such as users, customers, products, and so forth. However, unlike the way HAL and Siren express domain objects, Cj has a highly structured approach. HAL and Siren express their domain objects as either simple name–value pairs or, in the case of Siren, as `subentities`. And both HAL and Siren support sending nested JSON objects as properties. But Cj doesn't work like that and this can be a source of both frustration and freedom.

Here is an example of a user object expressed as a Cj `item`:

```
{
  "rel": "item http://api.example.org/rels/user",
  "href": "http://api.example.org/user/alice",  ❶
  "data": [  ❷
    {"name": "id", "value": "alice", "prompt": "ID", "render":"none"},
    {"name": "nick", "value": "alice", "prompt": "Nickname"},
    {"name": "email", "value": "alice-ted@example.org", "prompt": "Email"},
    {"name": "name", "value": "Alice Teddington, Jr.", "prompt": "Full Name"}
  ],
  "links": [  ❸
    {
      "prompt": "Change Password",
      "rel": "edit-form http://api.example.org/rels/changePW",
      "href": "http://api.example.org/user/pass/alice"
    },
    {
      "prompt": "Assigned Tasks",
      "rel": "collection http://api.example.org/rels/filterByUser",
      "href": "http://api.example.org/task/?assignedUser=alice"
    }
  ]
}
```

As you see in this example, a Cj `item` contains the `rel` and `href` (❶), and a list of `data` elements (❷), and may also contain one or more `link` elements for read-only actions (❸) associated with the `item`. The way Cj expresses the item properties (`id`, `nick`, email, and name) is unique among the formats covered in this book. Cj documents return not just the property identifier and value (e.g., `"id":"alice"`) but also a suggested `prompt` property. Cj also supports other attributes, including `render` to help clients decide whether to display the property on screen. This highly structured format makes it possible to send both the domain data and metadata about each property and object. As we'll see when we start working on the Cj client app, this added data comes in handy when creating a human-centric interface.

The `links` collection within each Cj `item` contains one or more static *safe* (read-only) links, like those in the root-level `links` collection. This space can be used to pass item-level links within a Cj response. For example, in the preceding snippet, you can see a link that points to a form for updating the user password and a link that points to a filtered list of tasks related to this `user` object. The item-level `links` section is optional and any link that appears in the collection must be treated as safe (e.g., dereferenced using HTTP `GET`).

Queries

The `queries` element in Collection+JSON is meant to hold safe requests (e.g., HTTP `GET`) that have one or more parameters. These are similar to HTML forms with the `method` attribute set to `GET`. The `queries` section in a Cj document is an array with one or more query objects. They look similar to Cj link objects but can have an associated `data` array, too.

Here's an example:

```
{
  "rel": "search",
  "name" : "usersByEmail",
  "href": "http://api.example.org/user/",
  "prompt": "Search By Email",
  "data": [
    {
      "name": "email",
      "value": "",
      "prompt": "Email",
      "required": "true"
    }
  ]
}
```

As you can see from the preceding example, a Cj query object has `rel`, `name`, `href`, and `prompt` attributes. There also may be one or more `data` elements. The `data` elements are similar to HTML `input` elements. Along with the `name`, `value`, and `prompt` attributes, `data` elements can have `required` and (not shown in the previous example) `readOnly` and `pattern` attributes. These last attributes help services send clients additional metadata about the arguments for a query.

Note that Cj query objects do not have an attribute to indicate which HTTP method to use when executing the query. That is because Cj queries always use the HTTP `GET` method.

There is another Cj element that is similar to HTTP FORM: the `template` element.

Template

Cj's `template` element looks similar to the Cj `queries` element—but it's even *smaller*. It only has a set of one or more `data` elements. These `data` elements represent the input arguments for a write action (e.g., HTTP `POST` or `PUT`). Let's take a look at what a Cj `template` looks like:

```
"template": {
  "prompt": "Add Task",
  "data": [
    {"name": "title", "value": "", "prompt": "Title", "required": "true"},
    {"name": "tags", "value": "", "prompt": "Tags"},
    {"name": "completeFlag", "value": "false", "prompt": "Complete",
      "patttern": "true|false"}
  ]
}
```

The `template` element can have an optional prompt, but the most important part of the `template` is the `data` array that describes the possible input arguments for the write operation. Like the `data` elements that appear in Cj `queries` and `items`, the `template`'s `data` elements include `name` and `value` properties along with a `prompt` property. And, like the `queries` version of `data` elements, they can have additional metadata attributes, including `readOnly`, `required`, and `pattern`. The `pattern` element works the same way as the HTML `pattern` attribute.

There are two important aspects of write operations missing from the Cj `template`: (1) the target URL, and (2) the HTTP method. That's because in Cj, the `template` applies to two different parts of the CRUD model: create and update. Just how the request is executed depends on what the client app wants to do.

Using Cj templates to create new resources

When used to create a new member of the collection, the client app fills out the template and then uses the HTTP `POST` for the method and the value of the Cj document's `href` as the target URL.

For example, using the Cj document represented at the start of this chapter (see "The Collection+JSON Format" on page 249), a client application can collect inputs from a user and send a `POST` request to add a new `task` record.

The HTTP request would look like this:

```
*** REQUEST ***
POST / HTTP/1.1 ❶
Host: http://rwcbook12.herokuapp.com
Content-Type: application/vnd.collection+json
...

"template": {
  "data": [
    {"name": "title", "value": "adding a new record"},
    {"name": "tags", "value": "testing adding"},
    {"name": "completeFlag", "value": "false"}
  ]
}
```

 The Cj specification says that clients can send the `template` block (as seen in the previous example) or just send an array of `data` objects, and servers should accept both. Also, servers should accept payloads with `data` objects that include `prompts` and other properties and just ignore them.

As you can see in the previous example, the URL from the Cj *document* `href` along with the HTTP POST method is used to add a new resource to the Cj collection.

Using Cj templates to update an existing resource

When client apps want to update an existing resource, they use the HTTP PUT method and the `href` property of the `item` to update. Typically, client apps will automatically fill in the `template.data` array with the values of the existing item, allow users to modify that data, and then execute the PUT request to send the update information to the server:

```
*** REQUEST ***
PUT /1sv697h2yij HTTP/1.1 ❶
Host: http://rwcbook12.herokuapp.com
Content-Type: application/vnd.collection+json
...
"template": {
  "data": [
    {"name": "id", "value": "1sv697h2yij"},
    {"name": "title", "value": "Marina Del Ray"},
    {"name": "completed", "value": "true"}
  ]
}
```

Note that (at ❶), the URL from the item's `href` property is used along with the HTTP PUT method. This is how Cj clients use the `template` to update an existing `item`.

So—one template, two ways to use it. That's how Cj describes write operations.

Error

The Collection+JSON design also includes an `error` element. This is used to pass domain-specific error information from server to client. For example, if a resource cannot be found or an attempt to update an existing record failed, the server can use the `error` element to return more than HTTP 404 or 400. It can return a text description of the problem and even include advice on how to fix it.

For example, if someone attempted to assign a TPS task to a nonexistent user, the server might respond like this:

```
{
  "collection": {
    "version": "1.0",
    "href": "//rwcbook12.herokuapp.com/error/",
    "title": "TPS - Task Processing System",
    "error": {
      "code": 400,
      "title": "Error",
      "message": "Assigned user not found (filbert). Please try again.",
      "url": "http://rwcbook12.herokuapp.com/task/assign/1l9fz7bhaho"
    }
  }
}
```

As mentioned earlier, there are some additional elements and properties of Cj documents that I won't cover here. You can check out the full specification at the online site listed in the Reference section at the end of this chapter (see "References" on page 298).

A Quick Summary

By now, we can see that the three featured hypermedia types (HAL, Siren, and Cj) have several things in common. Like HAL and Siren, Cj has an element (`links`) for communicating ADDRESSES. And, like Siren, Cj's `queries` and `template` elements communicate ACTION metadata in responses. And all three have a way to communicate domain-specific OBJECTS (HAL's root-level properties, Siren's `properties` object and Cj's `items` collection). Cj's `items` collection is unique because it includes metadata about each property in the domain object (e.g., `prompt`, `render`, etc.). This elevates Cj's ability to handle the OBJECT aspect of the OAA Challenge. We'll talk about this again when we build the Cj client app.

For now, we have enough background to review the Cj representor and then walk through our Cj client SPA code.

The Collection+JSON Representor

As with other formats, the process of coding a Cj representor is a matter of converting our internal resource representation (in the form of a WeSTL object) into a valid Collection+JSON document. And, like the other representors, it takes only about 300 lines of NodeJS to build up a fully functional module to produce valid Cj responses.

 The source code for the Cj representor can be found in the associated GitHub repo (*https://github.com/RWCBook/cj-client*). A running version of the Cj version of the TPS API described in this section can be found online (*http://rwcbook12.herokuapp.com/task/*).

Following is a quick walk-through of the Cj representor code with highlights.

The Top-Level Processing Loop

The top-level processing loop for my Cj representor is very simple. It starts by initializing an empty `collection` object (to represent a Cj document in JSON) and then populates this object with each of the major Cj elements:

- Links
- Items
- Queries
- Template
- Error (if needed)

```
function cj(wstlObject, root) {
  var rtn;

  rtn = {};
  rtn.collection = {}; ❶
  rtn.collection.version = "1.0";

  for(var segment in wstlObject) {
    rtn.collection.href = root+"/"+segment+"/"; ❷
    rtn.collection.title = getTitle(wstlObject[segment]); ❸
    rtn.collection.links = getLinks(wstlObject[segment].actions);
    rtn.collection.items = getItems(wstlObject[segment],root);
    rtn.collection.queries = getQueries(wstlObject[segment].actions);
    rtn.collection.template = getTemplate(wstlObject[segment].actions);

    // handle any error
    if(wstlObject.error) { ❹
      rtn.collection.error = getError(wstlObject.error);
```

```
    }
  }
  // send results to caller
  return JSON.stringify(rtn, null, 2); ❺
}
```

The code just shown has just a few interesting items. After initializing a collection document (❶) and establishing the document-level href (❷), the code walks through the passed-in WeSTL object tree (❸) and constructs the Cj title, links, items, queries, and template elements. Then, if the current object is an error, the Cj error element is populated (❹). Finally, the completed Cj document is returned (❺) to the caller.

Now, let's take a look at each of the major routines used to build up the Cj document.

Links

The links element in Cj holds all top-level links for the document. The Cj representor code scans the incoming WeSTL object for any action element that qualifies and, if needed, resolves any URI templates before adding the link to the collection.

Here's the code:

```
// get top-level links
function getLinks(segment, root, tvars) {
  var link, rtn, i, x, tpl, url;

  rtn = [];
  if(Array.isArray(segment)!==false) {
    for(i=0,x=segment.length;i<x;i++) { ❶
      link = segment[i];
      if(link.type==="safe" &&
        link.target.indexOf("app")!==-1 &&
        link.target.indexOf("cj")!==-1) ❷
      {
        if(!link.inputs) {
          tpl = urit.parse(link.href);
          url = tpl.expand(tvars); ❸
          rtn.push({ ❹
            href: url,
            rel: link.rel.join(" ")||"",
            prompt: link.prompt||""
          });
        }
      }
    }
  }
  return rtn; ❺
}
```

Here are the high points in the `getLinks` function:

❶ If we have action objects, loop through them.

❷ First, check to see if the current link meets the criteria for top-level links in a Cj document.

❸ If it does, use the passed-in `tvars` collection (template variables) to resolve any URI Template.

❹ Then add the results to the link collection.

❺ Finally, return the populated collection to the caller.

Items

The next interesting function is the one that handles `items`. This is the most involved routine in the Cj representor. That's because Cj does quite a bit to supply both data and metadata about each domain object it passes to the client app.

Here's the code:

```
// get list of items
function getItems(segment, root) {
  var coll, temp, item, data, links, rtn, i, x, j, y;

  rtn = [];
  coll = segment.data;
  if(coll && Array.isArray(coll)!==false) {
    for(i=0,x=coll.length;i<x;i++) {
      temp = coll[i];

      // create item and link
      item = {}; ❶
      link = getItemLink(segment.actions);
      if(link) {
        item.rel = (Array.isArray(link.rel)?link.rel.join(" "):link.rel);
        item.href = link.href;
        if(link.readOnly===true) {
          item.readOnly="true";
        }
      }

      // add item properties
      tvars = {}
      data = [];
      for(var d in temp) { ❷
        data.push(
          {
```

```
            name : d,
            value : temp[d],
            prompt : (g.profile[d].prompt||d),
            render:(g.profile[d].display.toString()||"true")
          }
        );
        tvars[d] = temp[d];
      }
      item.data = data;

      // resolve URL template ❸
      tpl = urit.parse(link.href);
      url = tpl.expand(tvars);
      item.href = url;

      // add any item-level links ❹
      links = getItemLinks(segment.actions, tvars);
      if(Array.isArray(links) && links.length!==0) {
        item.links = links;
      }

      rtn.push(item); ❺
    }
  }
  return rtn; ❻
}
```

The getItems routine is the largest in the Cj representor. It actually handles three key things: the URL for the item, the item's data properties, and any links associated with the item. Here's the breakdown:

❶ For each data item in the list, first set the href property.

❷ Then loop through the properties of the domain object and construct Cj data elements.

❸ After collecting the data values, use that collection to resolve any URL template in the item's href.

❹ Next, go collect up (and resolve) any Cj link objects for this single item.

❺ Once all that is done, add the results to the internal item collection.

❻ Finally, return the completed collection to the calling routine.

The resulting item collection looks like this:

```
"items": [
  {
    "rel": "item",
    "href": "http://rwcbook12.herokuapp.com/task/1l9fz7bhaho",
    "data": [
      {"name":"id","value":"1l9fz7bhaho","prompt":"ID","render":"true"},
      {"name":"title","value":"extensions","prompt":"Title","render":"true"},
      {"name":"tags","value":"forms testing","prompt":"Tags","render":"true"},
      {"name":"completeFlag","value":"true","prompt":"Complete Flag",
        "render":"true"},
      {"name":"assignedUser","value":"carol","prompt":"Asigned User",
        "render":"true"},
      {"name":"dateCreated","value":"2016-02-01T01:08:15.205Z",
        "prompt":"Created","render":"false"}
    ],
    "links": [
      {
        "prompt": "Assign User",
        "rel": "assignUser edit-form",
        "href": "http://rwcbook12.herokuapp.com/task/assign/1l9fz7bhaho"
      },
      {
        "prompt": "Mark Active",
        "rel": "markActive edit-form",
        "href": "http://rwcbook12.herokuapp.com/task/active/1l9fz7bhaho"
      }
    ]
  }
  ... more items here ...
]
```

Queries

The getQueries routine is the one that generates the "safe" parameterized queries—basically HTML GET forms. That means, along with a URL, there is a list of one or more argument descriptions. These would be the input elements of an HTML form. The code that generates Cj queries is very straightforward and looks like this:

```
// get query templates
function getQueries(segment) {
  var data, d, query, q, rtn, i, x, j, y;

  rtn = [];
  if(Array.isArray(segment)!==false) {
    for(i=0,x=segment.length;i<x;i++) {  ❶
      query = segment[i];
      if(query.type==="safe" &&  ❷
        query.target.indexOf("list")!==-1 &&
        query.target.indexOf("cj") !==-1)
```

```
    {
      q = {}; ❸
      q.rel = query.rel.join(" ");
      q.href = query.href||"#";
      q.prompt = query.prompt||"";
      data = [];
      for(j=0,y=query.inputs.length;j<y;j++) { ❹
        d = query.inputs[j];
        data.push(
          {
            name:d.name||"input"+j,
            value:d.value||"",
            prompt:d.prompt||d.name,
            required:d.required||false,
            readOnly:d.readOnly||false,
            patttern:d.pattern||""
          }
        );
      }
      q.data = data;
      rtn.push(q); ❺
    }
  }
}
  return rtn; ❻
}
```

The walk-through is rather simple:

❶ Loop through all the transitions in the WeSTL document.

❷ Find the transitions that are valid for the Cj `queries` collection.

❸ Start an empty query object and set the `href` and `rel` properties.

❹ Loop through the WeSTL `input` elements to create Cj `data` elements for the query.

❺ Add the completed query to the collection.

❻ Finally, return that collection to the calling routine.

Again, there is no HTTP method supplied for each query since the spec says all Cj `queries` should be executed using HTTP `GET`.

That covers the read operations in Cj. Next is the work to handle the write operations —the ones handled by the Cj `template`.

Template

In Cj, write operations are represented in the `template` element. The `getTemplate` routine in our Cj representor handles generating the `template` element, and the code looks like this:

```
// get the add template
function getTemplate(segment) {
  var data, temp, field, rtn, tpl, url, d, i, x, j, y;

  rtn = {};
  data = [];
  if(Array.isArray(segment)!==false) {
    for(i=0,x=segment.length;i<x;i++) {
      if(segment[i].target.indexOf("cj-template")!==-1) { ❶
        temp = segment[i];

        // emit data elements
        data = [];
        for(j=0,y=temp.inputs.length;j<y;j++) { ❷
          d = temp.inputs[j];
          field = { ❸
            name:d.name||"input"+j,
            value:(d.value||"",
            prompt:d.prompt||d.name,
            required:d.required||false,
            readOnly:d.readOnly||false,
            patttern:d.pattern||""
          };
          data.push(field); ❹
        }
      }
    }
  }
  rtn.data = data;
  return rtn; ❺
}
```

There is not much to the `getTemplate` routine, so the highlights are a bit boring:

❶   Loop through the WeSTL transitions and find the one valid for Cj `template`.

❷   Then loop through the transition's `input` collection.

❸   Use that information to build a Cj `data` element.

❹   And add that to the collection of `data` elements for this `template`.

❺   Finally, after adding the completed `data` collection to the `template` object, return the results to the caller.

As a reminder, there is no `href` property or HTTP method for Cj `templates`. The URL and method to use are determined by the client at runtime based on whether the client is attempting a Create or Update action.

That leaves just one small object to review: the Cj `error` element.

Error

Unlike HAL and Siren, Cj has a dedicated `error` element for responses. This makes it easy for clients to recognize and render any domain-specific error information in server responses. There are only four defined fields for the Cj `error` object: `title`, `message`, `code`, and `url`. The `getError` function is small and looks like this:

```
// get any error info
function getError(segment) {
  var rtn = {};

  rtn.title = "Error";
  rtn.message = (segment.message||"");
  rtn.code = (segment.code||"");
  rtn.url = (segment.url||"");

  return rtn;
}
```

There is really nothing to talk about here since the routine is so simple. It is worth pointing out that Cj responses can include both error information *and* content in the `links`, `items`, `queries`, and `template` elements. That makes it possible to return a fully populated Cj document along with some error information to help the user resolve any problems.

With the Cj representor walk-through completed, it's time to review the Cj client SPA.

The Collection+JSON SPA Client

OK, now we can review the Collection+JSON single-page app (SPA). This Cj client supports all the major features of Cj, including `links`, `items`, `queries`, and `template`. It also supports other Cj elements, including `title`, `content`, and `error` elements.

The source code for the Cj SPA client can be found in the associated GitHub repo (*https://github.com/RWCBook/cj-client*). A running version of the app described in this section can be found online (*http://rwcbook12.herokuapp.com/files/cj-client.html*).

As we did for the SPAs described in Chapter 2 (JSON), Chapter 4 (HAL), and Chapter 6 (Siren), we'll start with a review of the HTML container and then move on to review the top-level parsing routine, along with the major functions that parse the key Cj document sections, to build up the rest of the general Cj client.

The HTML Container

All the SPA apps in this book start with an HTML container, and this one is no different. Here is the static HTML that is used to host the Cj documents sent by the server:

```
<!DOCTYPE html>
<html>
  <head>
    <title>Cj</title>
    <link href="./semantic.min.css" rel="stylesheet" />
  </head>
  <body>
    <div id="links"></div> ❶
    <div style="margin: 5em 1em">
      <h1 id="title" class="ui page header"></h1> ❷
      <div id="content" style="margin-bottom: 1em"></div> ❸
      <div class="ui mobile reversed two column stackable grid">
        <div class="column">
          <div id="items" class="ui segments"></div> ❹
        </div>
        <div class="column">
          <div id="edit" class="ui green segment"></div>
          <div id="template" class="ui green segment"></div> ❺
          <div id="error"></div> ❻

          <div id="queries-wrapper">
            <h1 class="ui dividing header">
              Queries
            </h1>
            <div id="queries"></div> ❼
          </div>
        </div>
      </div>

      <div>
        <pre id="dump"></pre>
      </div>

    </div>
  </body>
  <script src="dom-help.js">//na </script>
  <script src="cj-client.js">//na </script> ❽
  <script>
    window.onload = function() {
      var pg = cj();
      pg.init("/", "TPS - Task Processing System"); ❾
```

```
      }
    </script>
  </html>
```

A lot of the HTML shown here supports the layout needs of the CSS library. But you can still find all the major Cj document elements represented by <div> tags in the page. They are:

❶ The links collection

❷ The title element

❸ The content element

❹ The items element

❺ The template element

❻ The error element

❼ The queries element

The Cj parsing script is loaded at ❽ and, after everything loads, the initial request starts at ❾. That line calls into the top-level parse loop for the Cj library.

The Top-Level Parse Loop

In the Cj client, the top-level parse loop gets called each time a user makes a selection in the UI, which follows the Request, Parse, Wait (RPW) pattern I covered in Chapter 5. It turns out the parse loop for Cj is a bit simpler than the ones for the JSON, HAL, and Siren clients:

```
// init library and start
  function init(url) {
    if(!url || url==='') {
      alert('*** ERROR:\n\nMUST pass starting URL to the Cj library');
    }
    else {
      global.url = url;
      req(global.url,"get"); ❶
    }
  }

  // primary loop
  function parseCj() { ❷
    dump();
    title();
    content();
```

```
      links();
      items();
      queries();
      template();
      error();
      cjClearEdit();
    }
```

This code set should look pretty familiar by now. After making the initial request (❶), the parseCj routine (❷) is called and it walks through all the major elements of a Collection+JSON document. The only other interesting elements in this code snippet are the internal routines. First, the call to the dump() method at the start of the loop—this is just for debugging help on screen—and second, the cjClearEdit() call at the end of the routine to handle cleaning up the HTML div used to display the UI's current editing form.

I'll skip talking about the title and content routines here—you can check them out in the source code. We'll now walk through the other major routines to handle Cj responses.

Links

The routine that handles parsing and rendering Cj links is pretty simple. However, it has a bit of a twist. The code checks the domain-specific metadata about the link. For example, some links are not rendered on the screen (e.g., HTML stylesheets, IANA profile identifiers, etc.). Some other links should actually be rendered as embedded images instead of navigational links. The Cj design allows servers to indicate this level of link metadata in the message itself—something the HAL and Siren clients do not support in their current design.

Here's the code for the links() function:

```
// handle link collection
function links() {
  var elm, coll, menu, item, a, img, head, lnk;

  elm = domHelp.find("links");
  domHelp.clear(elm);
  if(global.cj.collection.links) { ❶
    coll = g.cj.collection.links;
    menu = domHelp.node("div");
    menu.className = "ui blue fixed top menu";
    menu.onclick = httpGet;

    for(var link of coll) { ❷
      // stuff render=none Cj link elements in HTML.HEAD ❸
      if(isHiddenLink(link)===true) {
        head = domHelp.tags("head")[0];
        lnk = domHelp.link({rel:link.rel,href:link.href,title:link.prompt});
```

```
      domHelp.push(lnk,head);
      continue;
    }
    // render embedded images, if asked ❹
    if(isImage(link)===true) {
      item = domHelp.node("div");
      item.className = "item";
      img = domHelp.image({href:link.href,className:link.rel});
      domHelp.push(img, item, menu);
    }
    else {
      a = domHelp.anchor({rel:link.rel,href:link.href,text:link.prompt, ❺
        className: "item"});
      v.push(a, menu);
    }
  }
  domHelp.push(menu, elm); ❻
  }
}
```

While there is quite a bit of code here, it's all straightforward. The highlights are:

❶ After making sure there are Cj links to process, set up some layout to hold them.

❷ Now start looping through the links collection.

❸ If the link element should now be rendered, place it in the HTML <head> section of the page.

❹ If the link element should be rendered as an image, process it properly.

❺ Otherwise, treat is as a simple <a> tag and add it to the layout.

❻ Finally, push the results to the viewable screen.

Figure 8-2 shows an example of rendering the Cj links at runtime.

Figure 8-2. Rendering Cj links at runtime

It turns out that the cases where the link element is not displayed (❸) or the link is an image (❹) takes more code than cases where the link element is just a navigational element (❺). We'll see some more of that kind of code when we parse the items collection.

Items

The items() function is the most involved routine in the Cj library. At 125 lines, it is also the longest. That's because (as we saw when reviewing the items handling in the Cj representor) the items element is the most involved of all in the Cj document design. I won't include all the lines of this routine but will show the key processing in the routine. You can find the full set of code in the source code repo associated with this chapter.

I'll break up the code review for the items() routine into three parts:

- Rendering Cj item editing links
- Rendering Cj item links
- Rendering Cj item data properties

First, the code that handles each item's Read-Update-Delete links—the last three elements of the CRUD pattern. Each Cj item has an href property and, optionally, a readOnly property. Using this information as a guide, Cj clients are responsible for rendering appropriate support for the read, update, and delete links. You can see this in the code that follows. At ❶, the read link is created. The update link is created at ❷ and the delete link is created at ❸. Note the checking of both the readOnly status of the client as well as whether the template can be found in the Cj document. These values are used to decide which links (update and delete) are rendered for the item:

```
// item link
a = domHelp.anchor( ❶
  {
    href:item.href,
    rel:item.rel,
    className:"item link ui basic blue button",
    text:item.rel
  }
);
a.onclick = httpGet;
domHelp.push(a1,buttons);

// edit link
if(isReadOnly(item)===false && hasTemplate(g.cj.collection)===true) {
  a = domHelp.anchor( ❷
    {
      href:item.href,
```

```
      rel:"edit",
      className:"item action ui positive button",
      text:"Edit"
    }
  );
  a.onclick = cjEdit;
  domHelp.push(a2, buttons);
}

// delete link
if(isReadOnly(item)===false) {
  a = domHelp.anchor( ❸
    {
      href:item.href,
      className:"item action ui negative button",
      rel:"delete",
      text:"Delete"
    }
  );
  a.onclick = httpDelete;
  domHelp.push(a3,buttons);
}
```

The next important snippet in the items() routine is the one that handles any item-level links. In the code you can see (❶) that, if there are links for this item, each link is checked to see if it should be rendered as an image (❷) and, if not, if it can be rendered as a navigational link (❸). Finally, after the links are processed, the results are added to the item display (❹):

```
if(item.links) { ❶
  for(var link of item.links) {
    // render as images, if asked
    if(isImage(link)===true) { ❷
      p = domHelp.node("p");
      p.className = "ui basic button";
      img = domHelp.image(
        {
          className:"image "+link.rel,
          rel:link.rel,
          href:link.href
        }
      );
      domHelp.push(img, p, buttons);
    }
    else {
      a = domHelp.anchor( ❸
        {
          className:"ui basic blue button",
          href:link.href,
          rel:link.rel,
          text:link.prompt
        }
```

```
      );
      a.onclick = httpGet;
      domHelp.push(a,buttons);
    }
  }
  domHelp.push(buttons,segment); ❹
}
```

The last snippet to review in the items() routine is the one that handles all the actual data properties of the item. In this client, they are rendered one by one as part of a UI table display. As you can see, the code is not very complicated:

```
for(var data of item.data) {
  if(data.display==="true") {
    tr = domHelp.data_row(
      {
        className:"item "+data.name,
        text:data.prompt+" ",
        value:data.value+" "
      }
    );
    domHelp.push(tr,table);
  }
}
```

That's all for the items() routine. Figure 8-3 is an example of the generated UI for Cj items.

Figure 8-3. Generated Cj items

Next up is the routine that handles the queries element of the Cj document.

Queries

The queries() routine processes all the elements in the Cj queries collection and turns them into HTML GET forms. The code is not very complex, but it is a bit verbose. It takes quite a few lines to generate an HTML form! The code our Cj client uses for generating the UI for Cj queries follows:

```
// handle query collection
function queries() {
  var elm, coll;
  var segment;
  var form, fs, header, p, lbl, inp;

  elm = domHelp.find("queries");
  domHelp.clear(elm);
  if(global.cj.collection.queries) { ❶
    coll = global.cj.collection.queries;
    for(var query of coll) { ❷
      segment = domHelp.node("div");
      segment.className = "ui segment";
      form = domHelp.node("form"); ❸
      form.action = query.href;
      form.className = query.rel;
      form.method = "get";
      form.onsubmit = httpQuery;
      fs = domHelp.node("div");
      fs.className = "ui form";
      header = domHelp.node("div");
      header.innerHTML = query.prompt + " ";
      header.className = "ui dividing header";
      domHelp.push(header,fs);
      for(var data of query.data) { ❹
        p = domHelp.input({prompt:data.prompt,name:data.name,value:data.value});
        domHelp.push(p,fs);
      }
      p = domHelp.node("p"); ❺
      inp = domHelp.node("input");
      inp.type = "submit";
      inp.className = "ui mini submit button";
      domHelp.push(inp,p,fs,form,segement,elm); ❻
    }
  }
}
```

The queries routine has just a few interesting points to cover:

❶ First, see if there are any queries in this response to process.

❷ If so, loop through each of them to build up a query form.

❸ Create the HTML <form> element and populate it with the proper details.

❹ Walk through each data element to create the HTML <inputs> that are needed.

❺ Then add the submit button to the form.

❻ Finally, add the resulting markup to the UI for rendering on the page.

That's how the Cj client handles generating all the safe query forms (e.g., HTTP GET). There are a few parts that deal with the HTML layout that are left out here, but you can see the important aspects of the queries() routine. Figure 8-4 shows an example of the generated query forms in our Cj client app.

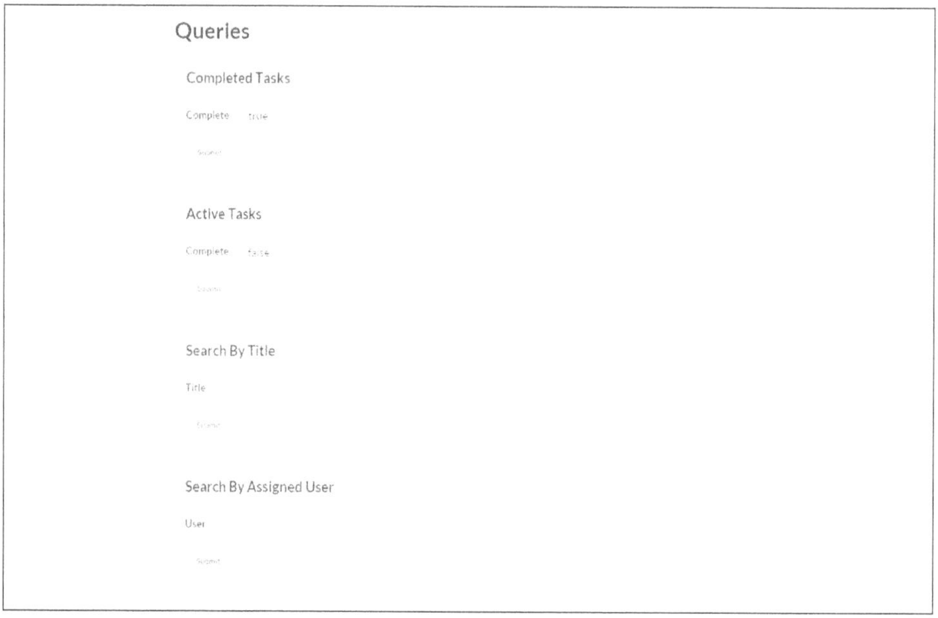

Figure 8-4. The generated Cj query forms

Template

Just as Cj queries describe safe actions (e.g., HTTP GET), the Cj template describes the unsafe actions (e.g., HTTP POST and PUT). The code looks very similar to the code for generating Cj queries:

```
// handle template object
function template() {
  var elm, coll;
  var form, fs, header, p, lbl, inp;

  elm = domHelp.find("template");
  domHelp.clear(elm);
  if(hasTemplate(global.cj.collection)===true) { ❶
    coll = global.cj.collection.template.data;
    form = domHelp.node("form"); ❷
    form.action = global.cj.collection.href;
    form.method = "post";
    form.className = "add";
    form.onsubmit = httpPost;
    fs = domHelp.node("div");
```

```
      fs.className = "ui form";
      header = domHelp.node("div");
      header.className = "ui dividing header";
      header.innerHTML = global.cj.collection.template.prompt||"Add";
      domHelp.push(header,fs);
      for(var data of coll) { ❸
        p = domHelp.input(
          {
            prompt:data.prompt+" ",
            name:data.name,
            value:data.value,
            required:data.required,
            readOnly:data.readOnly,
            pattern:data.pattern
          }
        );
        domHelp.push(p,fs);
      }
      p = domHelp.node("p"); ❹
      inp = domHelp.node("input");
      inp.className = "ui positive mini submit button";
      inp.type = "submit";
      d.push(inp,p,fs,form,elm); ❺
    }
  }
```

Here are the highlights for the template routine:

❶ Confirm there is a template element in the loaded Cj document.

❷ If there is, start building and populating an HTML <form>.

❸ Using the template's data properties, create one or more HTML <input> elements.

❹ After all the inputs are created, add an HTML submit button.

❺ Finally, add the completed HTML form to the UI.

You will also notice in the preceding code that the HTML <form> element is set to use the POST method. This takes care of the create use case for Cj template. For the update use case, there is a *shadow* routine in the Cj client called cjEdit(). This is invoked when the user presses the Edit button generated for each item. I won't review the code for cjEdit() here (you can check out the source yourself) but will just mention that it looks almost identical except for a few changes related to the HTTP PUT use case.

Figure 8-5 is an example of the Cj template rendered for the create use case.

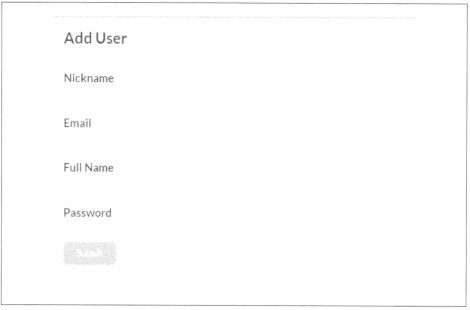

Figure 8-5. Generating the Cj create UI

The only code left to review for the Cj client is the code that handles any error elements in the response.

Error

Cj is the only hypermedia design featured in this book that has built-in support for sending domain-specific error information. The Cj error element is very simple. It has only four properties: title, message, code, and url. So the client routine for rendering errors is simple, too.

The following code shows that the Cj client app just echoes the properties of the error element in Cj responses directly to the screen:

```
// handle error object
function error() {
  var elm, obj;

  elm = domHelp.find("error");
  domHelp.clear(elm);
  if(global.cj.collection.error) {
    obj = global.cj.collection.error;

    p = d.para({className:"title",text:obj.title});
    domHelp.push(p,elm);

    p = d.para({className:"message",text:obj.message});
```

```
      domHelp.push(p,elm);

      p = d.para({className:"code",text:obj.code});
      domHelp.push(p,elm);

      p = d.para({className:"url",text:obj.url});
      domHelp.push(p,elm);
    }
  }
```

Quick Summary

The Cj client differs from the HAL and Siren clients reviewed earlier in the book in a number of respects, most significantly in the way domain objects are handled in Cj. Instead of just echoing a set of name–value pairs or even a nested JSON object graph, Collection+JSON only supports returning flat lists of items. Each item represents more than just a domain object's properties. It also includes metadata about the domain object (prompt and render information) and a collection of one or more link elements associated with the domain object.

The way safe and unsafe actions are expressed in Cj is also unique. Instead of leaving it up to source code (as in HAL) or relying on a general model for all actions (as in Siren), the Cj design supports two different action elements: the queries and template elements. Cj queries are for safe actions (e.g., HTML GET) and the template is for unafe actions (e.g., HTTP POST and PUT).

The other main element in Cj documents is the links collection, which is very similar to the way both HAL and Siren express links, too.

Now that we have a fully functional Cj general client, let's introduce some modifications to the backend TPS API and see how it deals with backward-compatible changes.

Dealing with Change

In previous chapters covering the JSON (Chapter 2), HAL (Chapter 4), and Siren (Chapter 6) SPA clients, I introduced various backward-compatible changes to the TPS API in order to explore the runtime adaptability of the client. The changes all dealt with one or more changes that the three key aspects web API clients need to deal with: OBJECTS, ADDRESSES, and ACTIONS. How the client apps reacted to the changes gave us an indication of their adaptability using our OAA Challenge.

The source code for the updated Cj representor with Note support can be found in the associated GitHub repo (*https://github.com/ RWCBook/cj-client-note*). A running version of the app described in this section can be found online (*http://rwcbook13.herokuapp.com/ files/cj-client.html*).

For the Cj client, I'll introduce an entirely new OBJECT (Notes) along with a full set of ACTIONS and ADDRESSES. This level of change represents examples of all the kinds of changes we've introduced to the other SPA clients before. This will test the Cj client's ability to recognize and deal with domain objects and operations that were introduced long after the initial production release of the API and client implementations.

Adding the Note Object to the TPS API

Let's assume that the TPS team decides to add support for attaching comments or Notes to Task records in the TPS API. That means defining a Note object's fields and adding support for the basic CRUD operations on Note objects along with some other NOTE-specific actions like filters, etc.

In this section, I'll review the API design elements (internal Note object and public API) and the resulting WeSTL document, and take a look at a bit of the server code. Then, after completing the backend changes, we'll fire up the Cj client and see what happens.

The note API design

Our Note object will have a small set of fields, support the basic CRUD operations, a couple of filters, and a custom `NoteAssignTask` operation. Table 8-1 shows the Note object properties.

Table 8-1. Note Object Properties

Property	Type	Status	Default
id	string	required	none
title	string	required	none
text	string	optional	none
assignedTask	taskID	required	none

Along with the Create-Read-Update-Delete (CRUD) actions, we'll need a couple of filters (`NoteListByTitle` and `NoteListByText`) that allow users to enter partial strings and find all the Note records that contain that string. We'll also add a special operation to assign a Note to a Task (`NoteAssignTask`) that takes id values (a Note id and a Task id). Table 8-2 lists all the operations, arguments, and HTTP protocol details.

Table 8-2. TPS Note Object API

Operation	URL	Method	Returns	Inputs
NoteList	/note/	GET	NoteList	none
NoteAdd	/note/	POST	NoteList	id, title, text, asssignedTask
NoteItem	/note/{id}	GET	NoteItem	none
NoteUpdate	/note/{id}	PUT	NoteList	id, title, text, assignedTask
NoteRemove	/note/{id}	DELETE	NoteList	none
NoteAssignTask	/note/assign/{id}	POST	NoteList	id, assignedTask
NoteListByTitle	/note/	GET	NoteList	title
NoteListByText	/note/	GET	NoteList	text

That's all we need on the design side. Let's look at how we'll turn this design into a working API in our TPS service.

The note API service implementation

I won't go into the details of the internal server-side code (data and object manipulation) for implementing the Notes object support in the TPS API. However, it is worth pointing out a few things on the interface side since they affect how we'll set up the Cj responses sent to the existing client.

The first thing to add is the component code that defines the object described in Table 8-1. This code also validates inputs and enforces relationship rules (e.g., making sure users don't assign Note records to nonexistent Task records). In the TPS API service, the Note object definition looks like this:

```
props = ["id","title","text","assignedTask","dateCreated","dateUpdated"]; ❶
elm = 'note';

// shared profile info for this object ❷
profile = {
  "id" : {"prompt" : "ID", "display" : true},
  "title" : {"prompt" : "Title", "display" : true},
  "text" : {"prompt" : "Text", "display" : true},
  "assignedTask" : {"prompt" : "Assigned Task", "display" : true},
  "dateCreated" :  {"prompt" : "Created", "display" : false},
  "dateUpdated" :  {"prompt" : "Updated", "display" : false}
};
```

Notice that the props array (❶) defines valid fields for a NOTE and the profile object (❷) contains the rules for displaying objects to users (e.g., the prompt and display flags).

Following is the addTask routine for the note-component.js server-side code. It shows how the component builds up a new Note record to store (❶) and validates the inputs (❷), including checking for the existence of the supplied assignedTask ID (❸). Then, as long as there are no errors found, the code sends the new Note record off for storage (❹):

```
function addNote(elm, note, props) {
  var rtn, item, error;

  error = "";

  item = {} ❶
  item.title = (note.title||"");
  item.text = (note.text||"");
  item.assignedTask = (note.assignedTask||"");

  if(item.title === "") { ❷
    error += "Missing Title ";
  }
  if(item.assignedTask==="") {
    error += "Missing Assigned Task ";
  }
  if(component.task('exists', item.assignedTask)===false) { ❸
    error += "Task ID not found. ";
  }

  if(error.length!==0) {
    rtn = utils.exception(error);
  }
  else {
    storage(elm, 'add', utils.setProps(item,props)); ❹
  }

  return rtn;
}
```

That's enough of the internals. Now let's look at the interface code—the WeSTL entries that define the transitions for manipulating Note objects, and the resource code that handles the HTTP protocol requests exposed via the API.

Here are some of the transition descriptions for Note objects. I've included the note FormAdd transition that will populate the Cj template (❶) and the two transitions for the "Assign Task" action: the one that offers a link to the form (❷) and the template for making the assignment (❸):

```
// add task ❶
trans.push({
  name : "noteFormAdd",
  type : "unsafe",
  action : "append",
  kind : "note",
  target : "list add hal siren cj-template",
  prompt : "Add Note",
  inputs : [
    {name : "title", prompt : "Title", required : true},
    {name : "assignedTask", prompt : "Assigned Task", required : true},
    {name : "text", prompt : "Text"}
  ]
});

...

trans.push({ ❷
  name : "noteAssignLink",
  type : "safe",
  action : "read",
  kind : "note",
  target : "item cj read",
  prompt : "Assign Task",
});
trans.push({ ❸
  name : "noteAssignForm",
  type : "unsafe",
  action : "append",
  kind : "note",
  target : "item assign edit post form hal siren cj-template",
  prompt : "Assign Task",
  inputs : [
    {name: "id", prompt:"ID", readOnly:true, required:true},
    {name: "assignedTask", prompt:"Task ID", value:"", required : true}
  ]
});
```

Because the Cj media type design relies heavily on the CRUD pattern, unsafe operations that don't easily fall into the CRUD model (in this case, the noteAssignForm operation) need to be handled differently. In Cj, these nonstandard CRUD actions are offered as templates and executed with an HTTP POST—the way you'd create a new object in a standard CRUD pattern.

To support this, I need *two* transitions: one that returns the "assign template" (noteAssignLink) and the other that accepts the POST call to commit the assign arguments to storage (noteAssignForm). Since WeSTL doesn't supply URLs, the source code (in the /connectors/note.js file on the server) does that at runtime.

Here's what that snippet of code looks like:

```
// add the item-level link
wstl.append({name:"noteAssignLink",href:"/note/assign/{id}",
  rel:["edit-form","/rels/noteAssignTask"],root:root},coll);

// add the assign-page template
wstl.append({name:"noteFormAdd",href:"/note/",
  rel:["create-form","/rels/noteAdd"],root:root},coll);
```

Finally, I'll need to account for this when handling HTTP requests, too. Here is the code that responds to the HTTP GET for the "assign page" (e.g., /note/assign/1qw2w3e):

```
case 'GET':
  if(flag===false && parts[1]==="assign" && parts[2]) {
    flag=true;
    sendAssignPage(req, res, respond, parts[2]);
  }
```

And here's the snippet of code that responds to the HTTP POST request that commits the assignment:

```
case 'POST':
  if(parts[1] && parts[1].indexOf('?')===-1) {
    switch(parts[1].toLowerCase()) {
      case "assign":
        assignTask(req, res, respond, parts[2]);
      break;
    }
  }
```

There is more in the server-side code (e.g., adding the page-level link to the new Notes API, etc.) that you can check out yourself. The point here is that Cj forces API designers to explicitly account for the non-CRUD unsafe actions (via POST) right up front. This is a bit more work for API designers (well, you'd have to do it eventually anyway) but it makes support in the Cj client much easier. In fact, that support is *already there*.

So let's see what happens when we fire up our existing, unchanged, Cj client against this updated TPS API.

Testing the note API with the existing Cj client

In a real-life scenario, the TPS API would be updated into production without prior warning to all the existing Cj clients. Then at some point, one of the clients might make an initial request to the TPS API, just as in previous days, and automatically see the new Notes option at the top of the page (see Figure 8-6).

Figure 8-6. *New Notes option in the Cj client*

When the user clicks on the Notes link, the fully populated interface comes up with all the display and input constraints enforced. Along with the expected Read, Edit, and Delete buttons for each item plus the Add Note form, users will also see (in Figure 8-7) the special Assign Task link that appears for each Note in the list.

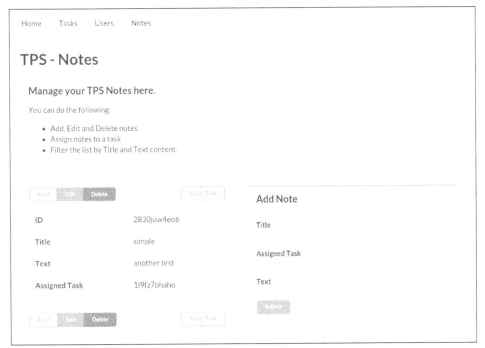

Figure 8-7. *The Notes page in the Cj client*

Finally, clicking the Assign Task button will bring up the screen that prompts users to enter the id value of the Task to which this note should be attached (see Figure 8-8).

Figure 8-8. Assigning a Note to a Task

So, the existing Cj client was able to support all the new API functionality (the new OBJECT, ADDRESSES, and ACTIONS) without any new coding or configuration. At this point, the TPS web API team has quite a bit of freedom to modify the existing production API. As long as the changes are backward-compatible, not only will the Cj client not *break* when new changes appear, but the new changes will be fully supported (not just safely ignored) for now and into the future.

Cj and the OAA Challenge

The OAA Challenge tests whether the format was designed to support dynamically changing the API's OBJECTS, ADDRESSES, and ACTIONS *and* have a standard client application automatically adapt to those changes at run time without the need for any custom coding. The Collection+JSON format is the only format we've covered in this book that was *designed* to meet the OAA Challenge without the need for private extensions or customization of the format.

That means that web APIs that can output responses in Cj can assume that there is a client that is able to adapt to changes in things like:

- Adding new links and forms
- Changing the URLs of existing links and forms
- Changing the input rules for forms
- Adding new resource objects
- Changing the rules on whether users can edit or delete resource objects

This gives API providers a wide range of choices for updating existing APIs without breaking any client apps using that same API. And that means client app developers do not have to constantly monitor the change notices from a service provider in order to head off a fatal crash or unexpected loss of functionality.

There are trade-offs for this ability to adapt, too. The standard Cj client applications lose some aspect of control—they end up showing the UI that the API wants them to see, they follow the workflow provided by the API, and they show the links and forms the API thinks are important. The layout is even controlled, to some extent, by the API provider. These can be hard things to accept for those who spend most of their time crafting pixel-perfect bespoke user interfaces for web APIs.

However, there is room here for both API provider and client developer to each take control of the things that matter. If client-side developers decide they want full control of the user experience, Cj client apps can be crafted to continue to *ignore* new functionality. Some of the techniques for making this possible were covered in "Client Implementors" on page 235. And, as long as API providers follow the rules outlined in "Server Implementors" on page 229, client apps will not experience unexpected breakage even if they ignore the providers' new features.

Quick Summary

So, working with Cj is pretty nice. But things are not perfect with our Cj client. As you might have noticed on those last couple screens, entering the text of a note is a problem—the text box is too small. It should be rendered as an HTML <textarea> control to support longer text entry and even scroll bars. Even more problematic is the Assign Task data entry. There, users are expected to supply two rather opaque record identifiers (NoteID and TaskID) in order to complete the Assign Task action. That's not very user-friendly and it is likely to be rejected by any team responsible for building quality user experiences.

To fix this shortcoming, we'll need to extend the Cj design to do a better job of describing (and supporting) user-friendly input experiences. There are lots of options for improvement and I'll just focus on two of them for now: (1) improving client-side support for input types, and (2) supporting a drop-down or suggested list of possible values for input.

Extending Collection+JSON

Cj has powerful support for passing metadata on links (ADDRESSES), forms (ACTIONS), and domain objects (OBJECTS). However, it has relatively weak support for passing metadata about user-supplied inputs. The ability to indicate input properties such as required, readOnly, and pattern (all directly from HTML5) is a start, but more is needed. For example, Swiber's Siren (see Chapter 6) has much stronger support for input metadata.

The good news is that Cj has a clear option for creating extensions to fill in gaps in the design. And that's what I'll do here. This section outlines an extension for supporting a `type` attribute for Cj `data` elements (*à la* HTML5's `type` attribute) and a `suggest` attribute to provide input metadata similar to that of the HTML `<select>` input control.

 The source code for the updated Cj representor with Note support can be found in the associated GitHub repo (*https://github.com/ RWCBook/cj-client-types*). A running version of the app described in this section can be found online (*http://rwcbook14.hero kuapp.com/files/cj.client.html*).

These extensions will improve the ability of Cj client apps to provide a solid user experience.

Supporting Improved Input with Cj-Types

Adding support for HTML5-style input types (e.g., `email`, `number`, `url`, etc.) is a pretty simple extension for Cj. It's just a matter of adding the `type` property to the Cj output and honoring it on the client side. There are also a series of associated properties like `min`, `max`, `size`, `maxlength`, etc. that should also be supported.

The Cj media type has an option for adding backward-compatible extensions to allow new features to emerge without the need for advanced approval and modification of the media type specification itself.

Extending Cj with cj-types

Here is an example of an extension I'll call `cj-types` to add support for improved client-side input validation. First, let's see what that would look like in the Cj representation. Note the use of the `pattern` (❶ and ❸) and `"type":"email"` (❷):

```
"template": {
  "prompt": "Add User",
  "rel": "create-form userAdd create-form",00
  "data": [
    {"name": "nick","value": "","prompt": "Nickname","type": "text",
      "required": "true","pattern": "[a-zA-Z0-9]+"}, ❶
    {"name": "email","value": "","prompt": "Email","type": "email"}, ❷
    {"name": "name","value": "","prompt": "Full Name","type": "text",
        "required": "true"},
    {"name": "password","value": "","prompt": "Password","type":"text",
        "required": "true","pattern": "[a-zA-Z0-9!@#$%^&*-]+"} ❸
  ]
}
```

The specification for the cj-types extension can be found in the associated GitHub repo (*https://github.com/RWCBook/cj-types-spec*). You can also view the completed spec online (*http://rwcbook.github.io/cj-types-spec/*).

Another handy HTML UI element is the <textarea> element. Adding support for textarea in Cj is also pretty simple. The Cj template would look like this (see ❶):

```
"template": {
  "prompt": "Add Note",
  "rel": "create-form //localhost:8181/rels/noteAdd",
  "data": [
    {"name": "title","value": "","prompt": "Title",
      "type": "text","required": "true"},
    {"name": "assignedTask","value": "","prompt": "Assigned Task",
      "type": "text","required": "true"},
    {"name": "text","value": "","prompt": "Text",
      "type": "area","cols": 40,"rows": 5} ❶
  ]
}
```

Updating the representor

Updating our Cj representor (see "The Collection+JSON Representor" on page 258) module to support the new types extension happens in two places:

- The getQueries() routine
- The getTemplate() routine

To save space, I'll just include a snippet from the getTemplate() implementation of our Cj representor here:

```
// emit data elements
data = [];
for(j=0,y=temp.inputs.length;j<y;j++) {
  d = temp.inputs[j];
  field = {
    name:d.name||"input"+j,
    value:(isAdd===true?d.value:g.tvars[d.name])||"",
    prompt:d.prompt||d.name,
    type:d.type||"text" ❶
  };
  if(d.required){field.required=d.required.toString();} ❷
  if(d.readOnly){field.readOnly=d.readOnly.toString();}
  if(d.pattern){field.pattern=d.pattern;}
  if(d.min){field.min=d.min;}
  if(d.max){field.max=d.max;}
  if(d.maxlength){field.maxlength=d.maxlength;}
  if(d.size){field.size=d.size;}
```

```
    if(d.step){field.step=d.step;}
    if(d.cols){field.cols=d.cols;}
    if(d.rows){field.rows=d.rows;}
    data.push(field);
  }
```

This is really just a set of added property checks against the internal WeSTL document (see "The WeSTL Format" on page 101) to see if any of the new type values exist and, if they do, they are passed along in the Cj representation. The highlights are:

❶ If the type property exists in the WeSTL document, add that to the representation; otherwise, use the default "text" type then…

❷ Go through the list of all the other possible cj-type properites and, if they are in the WeSTL, add them to the Cj representation.

Note that, if the new properties don't exist, they are not sent at all. This keeps the representor from emitting confusing properties with some kind of default value for *every* Cj template or query element.

Next we can take a look at the client-side implementation of the cj-types extension.

Updating the Cj client library

Like the code for the Cj representor, the update for the Cj client library is pretty simple. We just need to check for the existence of the new cj-types properties on the data elements and, if they are there, emit them as valid HTML DOM elements.

Here's a code snippet from the template() function in the cj-client.js library:

```
for(var data of coll) {
  p = domHelp.input(
    {
      prompt:data.prompt+" ",
      name:data.name,
      value:data.value,
      required:data.required,
      readOnly:data.readOnly,
      pattern:data.pattern,
      type:data.type,
      max:data.max,
      min:data.min,
      maxlength:data.maxlength,
      size:data.size,
      step:data.step,
      cols:data.cols,
      rows:data.rows,
      suggest:data.suggest
```

```
    }
);
```

You can see that all this code does is pass the properties from the Cj representation on to the domHelp library for conversion into value HTML DOM elements. The real magic happens in my dom-help.js library and that looks like this:

```
inp.name = args.name||"";
inp.className = inp.className + "value "+ (args.className||"");
inp.required = (args.required||false);
inp.readOnly = (args.readOnly||false);
if(args.pattern) {inp.pattern = args.pattern;}
if(args.max) {inp.max = args.max;}
if(args.min) {inp.min = args.min;}
if(args.maxlength) {inp.maxlength = args.maxlength;}
if(args.size) {inp.size = args.size;}
if(args.step) {inp.step = args.step;}
if(args.cols) {inp.cols = args.cols;}
if(args.rows) {inp.rows = args.rows;}
```

In the preceding code, the args collection was passed in from the call to dom Help.input() and the inp variable holds an instance of an HTML <input … /> control. There are a few minor details for handling the <area>…</area> but I'll skip those for now.

Once it's all put together and in place, Figure 8-9 shows how the CJ client screen looks with support for the area input type added.

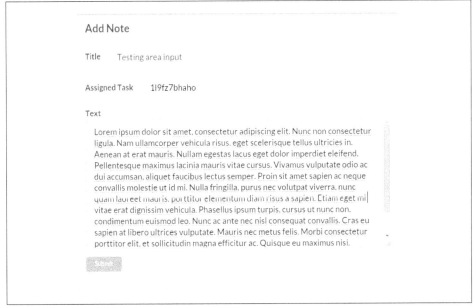

Figure 8-9. Adding Cj support for textarea input

So, adding support for most HTML5-style inputs was rather easy. But there are a couple of HTML5-style inputs that take a bit more effort, and one of them is badly needed for the TPS user experience—the <select> or drop-down list.

The Cj-Suggest Extension

Supporting HTML-style drop-down lists takes a bit of planning. I'll need to make modifications to the Cj document design, representor, and client library. I won't go through a lot of detail here—just the highlights.

 Check out the cj-suggest extension specification in the associated GitHub repo (*https://github.com/RWCBook/cj-suggest-spec*) and completed spec document online (*http://rwcbook.github.io/cj-suggest-spec/*).

Extending Cj with cj-suggest

First, we'll need a way to communicate the drop-down input within the Cj data elements. The design I chose allows for two types of implementation: direct content and related content. I'll explain the differences as we go along.

Here is a sample suggest element that uses the direct content approach:

```
data :
  [
    {
    "name": "completeFlag",
    "value": "false",
    "prompt": "Complete",
    "type": "select", ❶
    "suggest": [ ❷
      {"value": "false", "text": "No"},
      {"value": "true", "text": "Yes"}
    ]
    }
  ]
```

At ❶, the new type attribute is set to "select" and, at ❷, the suggest element is an array with an object that holds both the value and the text for HTML <select> elements.

The other type of suggest implementation I want to support is what I call the *related* model. It uses related data in the response as content for the drop-down list. That means I need to add a new element to the Cj document's root: related. This Cj root element is a named object with one or more named JSON arrays that hold content for a drop-down list. Here's what that looks like (see ❶):

```
{
  "collection": {
    "version": "1.0",
    "href": "//localhost:8181/task/assign/1l9fz7bhaho",
    "links": [...],
    "items": [...],
    "queries": [...],
    "template": {...},
    "related": { ❶
      "userlist": [
        {"nick": "alice"},
        {"nick": "bob"},
        {"nick": "carol"},
        {"nick": "fred"},
        {"nick": "mamund"},
        {"nick": "mook"},
        {"nick": "ted"}
      ]
    }
  }
}
```

And here's the matching implementation for the suggest attribute (❶) for Cj data elements:

```
data: [
  {
    "name": "assignedUser",
    "value": "mamund",
    "prompt": "User Nickname",
    "type": "select",
    "required": "true",
    "suggest": {"related": "userlist","value": "nick","text": "nick"} ❶
  }
]
```

Now, Cj client applications can find the related data in the response (by the value of related) and use the property names listed in the suggest element to populate the drop-down list.

Updating the Cj representor

We need to include the related property in the output of the Cj representor. That's pretty easy. We just create a small function to pull any related content into the response (❶) and add that to the top-level routine that builds up the Cj response document (❷):

```
// handle any related content in the response
function getRelated(obj) {
  var rtn;

  if(obj.related) {
```

```
    rtn = obj.related; ❶
  }
  else {
    rtn = {};
  }
  return rtn;
}

...

// building the Cj response document
rtn.collection.title = getTitle(wstlObject[segment]);
rtn.collection.content = getContent(wstlObject[segment]);
rtn.collection.links = getLinks(wstlObject[segment].actions);
rtn.collection.items = getItems(wstlObject[segment],root);
rtn.collection.queries = getQueries(wstlObject[segment].actions);
rtn.collection.template = getTemplate(wstlObject[segment].actions);
rtn.collection.related = getRelated(wstlObject[segment]); ❷
```

Updating the Cj client library

The Cj client library has a handful of things to deal with now, including:

- Recognizing the new suggest attribute in responses

- Locating any possible related content in the responses

- Parsing the suggest element into a valid <select> element in the UI

- Processing the value of the <select> element and including it in the POST and PUT actions

Most of this work will happen in my dom-help.js routine—that's where the request to create an input element in the UI takes place. Here is a snippet of code I added to the input(args,related) routine:

```
....
if(args.type==="select" || args.suggest) { ❶
  inp = node("select");
  inp.value = args.value.toString()||"";
  inp.className = "ui drop-down ";
  if(Array.isArray(args.suggest)) { ❷
    for(var ch of args.suggest) {
      opt = option(ch);
      push(opt,inp);
    }
  }
}
if(related) { ❸
  lst = related[args.suggest.related];
  if(Array.isArray(lst)) { ❹
    val = args.suggest.value;
    txt = args.suggest.text;
```

```
      for(var ch of lst) { ❺
        opt = option({text:ch[txt],value:ch[val]});
        push(opt,inp);
      }
    }
  }
}
....
```

In the preceding code:

❶ See if this is a suggest control.

❷ If there is an array of values, use that to build the <option> elements for the
    HTML <select> control.

❸ Check to see if a pointer to the related content in the response was passed.

❹ If it was, and it returns a valid array of data...

❺ Use that content to build up the <option> elements.

There are some additional client-side library changes to manage the details and collect and send selected values back to the service. You can check out the source code
for details.

Once all this is in place, the UI for screens like Assign Task look much more inviting
(Figure 8-10).

Figure 8-10. Adding drop-down support to Cj

Now, with the `suggest` extension and added support for improved input metadata, Cj offers not only fully functional support for adding new OBJECTS to the backend API, but it also has better user interface support. It is worth pointing out that most of the input support I added to Cj as extensions already exists as part of the design for Siren (see "Actions" on page 181).

Reader Challenge

My `suggest` implementation has two modes: direct and related. There is at least one more mode I didn't implement that I'd really like to see: web mode. In web mode, the `suggest.related` value is a valid URL pointing to an API response that returns the list of choices. It could be used to create a simple drop-down or it could be used to implement a key-stroke experience that performs a search on each key press and returns suggested results. I'll leave the details to my intrepid readers to work out on their own—and submit as an update to the online GitHub repo.

Quick Summary

In this section, I added two Cj extensions:

cj-types
  For enriching the way client-side inputs are displayed and validated

cj-suggest
  To add support for drop-down list inputs

The good news is that adding these kinds of extensions to Cj is pretty straightforward. It is also worth noting that these were backward-compatible extensions. If a standard Cj client that doesn't have support for `cj-types` and `cj-suggest` gets an API response that contains these values, that client can safely ignore them and continue to work without breaking. This approach is actually clearly outlined in the Collection+JSON spec:

> Any extensions to the Collection+JSON vocabulary MUST not redefine any objects (or their properties), arrays, properties, link relations, or data types defined in this document. Clients that do not recognize extensions to the Collection+JSON vocabulary SHOULD ignore them.

Now that we've explored the Cj format, implemented the server-side representor, and the extensible Cj client, it's time to wrap this up and move on to our last challenge.

Summary

In previous chapters covering the JSON (Chapter 2), HAL (Chapter 4), and Siren (Chapter 6) SPA clients, I introduced various backward-compatible changes to the

TPS API in order to explore the runtime adaptability of the client. The changes all dealt with one or more changes that the three key aspects web API clients need to deal with: OBJECTS, ADDRESSES, and ACTIONS. How the client apps reacted to the changes gave us an indication of their adaptability using our OAA Challenge.

Here's a quick summary of our experience so far:

JSON client
> Changes to URLs, adding fields, or actions all were ignored by the client app. That gave us no "wins" on the OAA Challenge.

HAL client
> Changes to URLs did not adversely affect the client. However, changes to domain objects and actions were ignored. That's one "win" for HAL: ADDRESSES.

Siren client
> Changes to URLs and actions were all recognized and supported in the Siren client. However, changes to domain objects were not picked up by the client. That's two "wins" for Siren: ADDRESSES and ACTIONS.

Cj client
> As we saw in this chapter, adding an entirely new domain object (NOTES) was automatically picked up by the Cj client. All the URLs, fields, and operations appeared in the UI without the need to make any changes to the client code. That gives Cj all three "wins" in the OAA Challenge (OBJECTS, ADDRESSES, and ACTIONS).

Of course, along the way, each client was enhanced through the application of extensions such as HAL-FORMS (see "The HAL-FORMS Extension" on page 144), POD documents (see "The POD Specification" on page 211), and `cj-types` and `cj-suggest` (from this chapter). And there are other possible ways in which to improve both the adaptability and the user experience of all of the client implementations reviewed in the book. But the Collection+JSON design offers clients the widest possible range of adaptability for the kinds of API changes that are most commonly experienced by API client apps.

Metadata and Adaptability

An important pattern that has run throughout the client examples in the book: the relationship between metadata and adaptability. As you scan the message models used for our client examples, you'll find that each one, in order, has provided increased levels of metadata in the API responses. From the plain JSON responses that contain no metadata on up to the Cj responses which (sometimes) contain more metadata than data. And with each increase in metadata, the client libraries gain more ability to adapt to changes in the backend API. It follows that if you want to improve the adaptability of your client applications, you need to focus on the *metadata* shared in responses.

Of course, not all production implementations need to support adaptability on all three of the axes featured here (OBJECTS, ADDRESSES, ACTIONS). The application of HAL, Siren, Cj (or other media types) makes sense when they help solve real problems. It is also not likely that just one format is appropriate for all API implementations and it is up to API designers and implementors (both server and client) to select the formats that provide the best feature match for the expected use cases.

While the Cj format seems to solve most of our problems, there is one more challenge worth exploring: the challenge of implementing a single SPA application that supports more than one hypermedia format—and can automatically switch between formats at runtime based on the service response.

And that's the challenge we'll take up in the next—and final—chapter of the book.

Bob and Carol

"Well, Bob, Collection+JSON turned out to be a very interesting hypermedia type."

"Yes, it did, Carol. My team tells me they had no trouble putting together the representor for it, too. Even with the added metadata in the responses."

"Right, and that added metadata helped our client team build a very adaptable general client app. The Cj app seems much more adaptable to backend API changes than any of the others we've tried so far."

"Yep, it seems the Cj format was designed to meet the OAA Challenge we've been talking about."

"Exactly, Cj allows API providers to supply all the metadata needed to support dynamic changes in the OBJECTS, ADDRESSES, and ACTIONS."

"I will admit that I heard some on the API design side saying they were finding API operations were a bit more challenging to implement due to Cj's reliance on CRUD."

"Yes. It turns out that operations like "Assign user" in our TPS API don't map easily to the simple CRUD pattern."

"But our API team was able to provide item-level links that point to responses with POST templates to make it all work."

"And by doing that, our client app was able to support the new Notes functionality without any client-side updates. That was great."

"Yep. The API team was really pleased when they realized that Cj gives them the ability to introduce that level of new functionality and have it automatically appear in the client app."

"Of course, we needed to add some extensions to improve the human-driven UI. The good news is that adding UI extensions seems really easy in Cj."

"Well, Carol. I think this was the most successful general hypermedia client app we've built so far."

"I agree, Bob. Kind of makes me wonder if there are any more challenges we need to address."

"Actually, I think there is. My server-side team has been thinking about implementing a microservice-style backend and that might cause us some trouble for these hypermedia clients."

"You think so?"

"Well, I need to check back with my team. Let's meet again tomorrow to discuss it, OK?"

"OK, Bob. See you tomorrow."

References

1. The Atom Syndication Format is documented in RFC4287 (*http://g.mamund.com/wnqmf*) and the Atom Publishing Protocol is covered in RFC5023 (*http://g.mamund.com/jjbcj*).

2. The most up-to-date specification docs for Cj can be found here (*http://g.mamund.com/aycij*).

3. You'll find various Cj examples and extensions in the online GitHub repository (*https://github.com/collection-json*).

4. The Google discussion group for Cj is archived here (*http://g.mamund.com/qiqed*).

5. The HTML <input> element has quite a few options. Check out the docs (*http://g.mamund.com/ddbgh*) online at the W3C website.

6. The specification for the HTML <textarea> element can be found at the W3C website (*http://g.mamund.com/yctfc*).

Image Credits

- Diogo Lucas: Figure 8-1

Hypermedia and Microservices

"Tricks? Gadzooks, Madam, these are not tricks! I do magic. I create, I transpose, I transubstantiate, I break up, I recombine—but I never trick!"

—Merlin, *The Seven Faces of Dr. Lao*

Bob and Carol

 "OK, let's get right to it, Carol."

"Right, Bob. So far, we continue to have good success using the hypermedia formats for the client apps. However, I notice that some of your server-side teams want to make their own choices about which media types they support."

 "Yep. As we've adopted more of a microservice style on the backend, each product team is starting to make their own decisions on these things."

"Well, if everyone gets to pick any format they want, things can get out of hand. We can't keep rewriting client apps each time a team changes their mind."

 "Agreed. Hm... Isn't there something we can do to provide some level of freedom, but limit the range of options?"

"How about we give teams a list of approved media types? If we can limit the set options, then we can engineer the clients accordingly."

"You mean build a client for each approved format? What happens if a single client needs more than one service and each service uses different media types?"

"Well, I think we can build a single client that can support more than one format."

"Really? These formats are each pretty unique and it is not clear we can treat them all the same within a single client's codebase."

"Bob, even though each format has unique strengths and weaknesses, we've found common parts in all of them. I think we've identified a common structure to all our client apps no matter what message format is used."

"You think there's enough commonality between these formats that you can build a single API consumer app?"

"Right. All three formats end up requiring the same basic processing code—(1) make a request, (2) parse the response, and (3) then wait for user input—the RPW loop we talked about last month."

"So, what are you saying, Carol?"

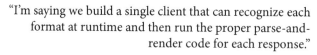

"I'm saying we build a single client that can recognize each format at runtime and then run the proper parse-and-render code for each response."

"OK, Carol. I'll talk to my team and as long as we can all agree on the list of formats, this could work."

"Great, Bob. I'll get my team started on mapping out a single client that can handle multiple formats and you can work with your backend teams to establish the fixed set of supported media types."

Microservices began to surface as a discussion topic in late 2013. The first extensive writing about it appeared in March 2014 on Martin Fowler's blog. At that time, Fowler offered this definition of microservices:

> The microservice architectural style is an approach to developing a single application as a suite of small services, each running in its own process and communicating with lightweight mechanisms, often an HTTP resource API.

This definition touches many of the hot buttons people have in mind when they think of APIs on the Web:

- "A suite of small services" describes the collection of one or more single-capability components.
- "Each running in its own process" points out that each capability is a standalone service.
- "Often with an HTTP resource API" identifies the implementation details directly.

While there is some disagreement on the fine points of this definition (must microservices only communicate over HTTP?, what constitutes "small"?, etc.) there is wide agreement on the general pattern: a set of services loosely connected using common application-level protocols.

In fact, another definition of microservices that I think is helpful sounds a bit like my description and it is the one offered by Adrian Cockcroft:

> Loosely-coupled service-oriented architecture with bounded contexts.

Cockcroft's definition side-steps the "small" and "HTTP API" aspects of microservices and focuses on something else—*bounded context*. This phrase comes from Eric Evans' work on domain-driven design (DDD). Evans' notion of focusing on the problem domain and making that the design canvas is very powerful. It follows rather closely the kinds of things I covered in Chapter 5, *The Challenge of Reusable Client Apps*, too. So, as you might imagine, Cockcroft's ideas have influenced the way I designed and implemented the simple microservice examples in this book.

Finally, in the book *Microservice Architecture* (O'Reilly), my API Academy colleagues and I came up with what I think is a very handy definition:

> A *microservice* is an independently deployable component of bounded scope that supports interoperability through message-based communication. *Microservice architecture* is a style of engineering highly automated, evolvable software systems made up of capability-aligned microservices.

Two big points to notice in this latest attempt:

- Each microservice is independently deployable and has a bounded scope (*à la* Evans's DDD) that passes messages.
- A collection of capability-aligned and evolvable components makes up a microservice architecture.

We know from previous work in this book that messages are what hypermedia APIs are all about. Messages carry the API data and the *metadata* needed to describe the OBJECTS, ADDRESSES, and ACTIONS of the service. And in this chapter, we'll see that a single client app that understands one or more message models is able to knit together a set of seemingly unrelated capabilities (in the forms of one or more deployed microservices) and create a unique application that is more than the sum of its (microservice) parts. Even better, this application can continue to work without breaking as the various microservices evolve over time.

The Unix Philosophy

There is a parallel between the new microservice pattern of the 2010s and the UNIX operating system from the 1970s. In the foreword for the 1978 edition of Bell Labs' "UNIX Timesharing System" documentation, McIroy, Pinson, and Tague offer the following four points as a set of "maxims that have gained currency among the builders and users of the UNIX system."

1. Make each program do one thing well. To do a new job, build afresh rather than complicate old programs by adding new features.

2. Expect the output of every program to become the input to another, as yet unknown, program. Don't clutter output with extraneous information. Avoid stringently columnar or binary input formats. Don't insist on interactive input.

3. Design and build software, even operating systems, to be tried early, ideally within weeks. Don't hesitate to throw away the clumsy parts and rebuild them.

4. Use tools in preference to unskilled help to lighten a programming task, even if you have to detour to build the tools and expect to throw some of them out after you've finished using them.

These maxims have made their way into the microservice world to varying degrees. The first one ("do one thing well") is commonly seen in microservices. That's why we see lots of small components, loosely connected over HTTP (although other protocols are used for microservices, too).

The second maxim ("Expect the output … to become the input…") is also an important element—especially when you consider that the output of hypermedia APIs uses a structured format like HAL, Siren, Cj, etc. that can be reliably read by other service consumers on the Web. This is one of the reasons these formats offer so much promise in the microservice environment—they make it easy for services that have *never before met* to successfully share inputs and outputs.

The other two maxims talk more about developer/designer behavior ("Design … to be tried early" and "build the tools.") than about any specific pattern or implementation detail, but they are still valuable points.

So, with these two perspectives as a backdrop, let's see what happens when we turn our TPS web API into a set of loosely coupled microservices.

The TPS Microservices at BigCo

Since our example API is so simple, it is easy to recognize some viable context boundaries for re-engineering it as set of standalone microservices. A more rich and complex API might offer a bit more challenge when trying to locate "bounded contexts," but ours does not—and that's just fine.

Here is the set of microservices I'll implement for this chapter:

Task Service
    This provides all the capabilities to manage task objects.

User Service
    This will be our standalone user object manager.

Note Service
    This is where we'll manage all the content notes.

In addition to these three services, I'll create one more: the *Home Service*. The Home Service will act as the system root and provide connections to all the other services as needed. The Home Service will host the client-side app that will act as the consumer of the other three services.

To keep things interesting, I'll make sure each of the three primary services support only one hypermedia format. The *Task Service* will reply in Collection+JSON. The *User Service* will only speak Siren. And the *Note Service* will converse in HAL messages. That means our *Home Service* will need to be able to talk in multiple languages in order to successfully interact with all the other components. This one-to-one linking between services and formats is a bit of a contrived example, but the general problem (that services speak varying languages at runtime) is a very real one.

In the next few sections, I'll do a quick review of the APIs for each microservice and then spend a bit more time on the *Home Service* that consumes the others. It's in that final API consumer that we'll see how we can leverage all the client libraries we've built up so far and bring them together into a single multilingual API client.

The Tasks Service with Collection+JSON

The *Task Service* implementation has the same functionality as the one that exists in the TPS web API. The only substantial difference is that I've stripped out support for all the other objects (Users and Notes). Most all the code is the same as what you've seen in the previous chapters and I won't review that here. I will, however, show some snippets from the initial API server router (app.js) to highlight changes to make this a single-capability service.

 The source code for the standalone Task Service client can be found in the associated GitHub repo (*https://github.com/RWCBook/ ms-tasks*). A running version of the app described in this section can be found online (*http://rwcbook16.herokuapp.com/task/*).

Following is a snippet from the ms-tasks project's app.js file—the root file of the Task Service:

```
var port = (process.env.PORT || 8182); ❶
var cjType = "application/vnd.collection+json"; ❷

var reRoot = new RegExp('^\/$','i'); ❸
var reFile = new RegExp('^\/files\/.*','i');
var reTask = new RegExp('^\/task\/.*','i');

// request handler
function handler(req, res) {
  var segments, i, x, parts, rtn, flg, doc, url;

  // set local vars
  root = '//'+req.headers.host;
  contentType = contentType;
  flg = false;
  file = false;
  doc = null;

  // default to Cj ❹
  contentAccept = req.headers["accept"];
  if(!contentAccept || contentAccept.indexOf(cjType)!==-1) {
    contentType = contentType;
  }
}
```

```
  else {
    contentType = cjType;
  }
  ...
}
```

The highlights of this snippet are:

❶ Set the listener port for this service. I used 8184 for my local running instances.

❷ Set the media type for this service to be `application/vnd.collection+json`.

❸ Set up the routing rules for root, task, and general file requests.

❹ Force the incoming accept header to result in `application/vnd.collection +json`.

A more robust way to handle content negotiation might be to simply return "415 - Unsupported media type" if a client makes a call that does not resolve to `application/vnd.collection+json`, but it is common (and well within the HTTP specifications) for services to ignore incoming accept headers and just blurt out the only format they know. The client needs to account for that, too.

The other `app.js` snippet worth seeing here is the one that handles the routing of requests:

```
...
// parse incoming request URL ❶
parts = [];
segments = req.url.split('/');
for(i=0, x=segments.length; i<x; i++) {
  if(segments[i]!=='') {
    parts.push(segments[i]);
  }
}

// re-direct / to /task/ ❷
try {
  if(flg===false && reRoot.test(req.url)) {
    handleResponse(req, res,
      {code:302, doc:"", headers:{'location'.'//'+req.headers.host'"/task/"}]});
  }
}
catch (ex) {}

// task handler ❸
try {
  if(flg===false && reTask.test(req.url)) {
    flg = true;
    doc = task(req, res, parts, handleResponse);
```

```
  }
}
catch(ex) {}

// file handler ❹
try {
  if(flg===false && reFile.test(req.url)) {
    flg = true;
    utils.file(req, res, parts, handleResponse);
  }
}
catch(ex) {}

// final error ❺
if(flg===false) {
  handleResponse(req, res, utils.errorResponse(req, res, 'Not Found', 404));
}
...
```

And the key points are:

❶ Parse the incoming URL into a collection of parts for everyone to deal with.

❷ If the call is to the root, redirect the client to the /task/ URL.

❸ Handle any /task/ requests.

❹ Handle by /file/ requests.

❺ Emit a 404 error for any other requests.

What is not shown here is the Task connector and component code as well as the Cj representor code. We've seen that already and you can check out the source code (*https://github.com/RWCBook/ms-tasks*) for details.

Now, with this service up and running, the response you get when you send a direct request to the /task/ URL looks like this:

```
{
  "collection": {
    "version": "1.0",
    "href": "//localhost:8182/task/",
    "title": "TPS - Tasks",
    "content": "<div>...</div>",
    "links": [
      {
        "href": "http://localhost:8182/task/",
        "rel": "self task collection","prompt": "Tasks"
      }
    ],
    "items": [
```

```
    {
      "rel": "item","href": "//localhost:8182/1l9fz7bhaho",
      "data": [
        {"name":"id","value":"1l9fz7bhaho","prompt":"ID","display":"true"},
        {"name":"title","value":"extensions","prompt":"Title",
          "display":"true"},
        {"name":"tags","value":"forms testing","prompt":"Tags",
          "display":"true"},
        {"name":"completeFlag","value":"true","prompt":"Complete Flag",
          "display":"true"},
        {"name":"assignedUser","value":"carol","prompt":"Asigned User",
          "display":"true"},
      ],
      "links": [
        {
          "prompt": "Assign User","rel": "assignUser edit-form",
          "href": "//localhost:8182/task/assign/1l9fz7bhaho"
        },
        {
          "prompt": "Mark Completed","rel": "markCompleted edit-form",
          "href": "/localhost:8182/task/completed/1l9fz7bhaho"
        },
        {
          "prompt": "Mark Active","rel": "markActive edit-form",
          "href": "//localhost:8182/task/active/1l9fz7bhaho"
        }
      ]
    }
    ...
  ],
  "queries": [...],
  "template": {
    "prompt": "Add Task","rel": "create-form //localhost:8182/rels/taskAdd",
    "data": [
      {"name": "title","value": "","prompt": "Title","required": true},
      {"name": "tags","value": "","prompt": "Tags"},
      {"name": "completeFlag","value": "false","prompt": "Complete"}
    ]
  }
 }
}
```

So, we have a Task Service up and running. Let's move on to the User Service next.

The User Service with Siren

Just like the Task Service, the User Service I created is a single-capability microservice that allows consumers to manipulate User objects via the web API. This time, I rigged the User Service to only speak Siren. So all consumers will get Siren responses.

The source code for the standalone User Service client can be found in the associated GitHub repo (*https://github.com/RWCBook/ms-users*). A running version of the app described in this section can be found online (*http://rwcbook17.herokuapp.com/user/*).

And the top app.js file looks like this:

```
var port       = (process.env.PORT || 8183); ❶
var sirenType  = "application/vnd.siren+json"; ❷

var csType     = '';
var csAccept   = '';

// routing rules
var reRoot = new RegExp('^\/$','i');
var reFile = new RegExp('^\/files\/.*','i');
var reUser = new RegExp('^\/user\/.*','i');

// request handler
function handler(req, res) {
  var segments, i, x, parts, rtn, flg, doc, url;

  // set local vars
  root = '//'+req.headers.host;
  contentType = sirenType;
  flg = false;
  file = false;
  doc = null;

  // we handle siren here ❸
  contentAccept = req.headers["accept"];
  if(!contentAccept || contentAccept.indexOf(sirenType)!==-1) {
    contentType = contentType;
  }
  else {
    contentType = sirenType;
  }
  ...
}
```

Note the use of a new local port (❶) of 8183, the setting of the default media type to application/vnd.siren+json (❷), and the forcing of the accept header to the siren media type (at ❸).

The other User Service snippet (shown next) is the routing code which includes:

❶ Parsing the URL.

❷ Redirecting root requests to /user/.

❸ Handling User calls.

❹ Handling any calls to the '/files/ URL space.

❺ Emitting 404 - Not Found for everything else.

```
// parse incoming request URL ❶
parts = [];
segments = req.url.split('/');
for(i=0, x=segments.length; i<x; i++) {
  if(segments[i]!=='') {
    parts.push(segments[i]);
  }
}

// re-direct / to /user/ ❷
try {
  if(flg===false && reRoot.test(req.url)) {
    handleResponse(req, res,
      {code:302, doc:"", headers:{'location':'//'+req.headers.host+"/user/"}});
  }
}
catch (ex) {}

// user handler ❸
try {
  if(flg===false && reUser.test(req.url)) {
    flg = true;
    doc = user(req, res, parts, handleResponse);
  }
}
catch(ex) {}

// file handler ❹
try {
  if(flg===false && reFile.test(req.url)) {
    flg = true;
    utils.file(req, res, parts, handleResponse);
  }
}
catch(ex) {}

// final error ❺
if(flg===false) {
  handleResponse(req, res, utils.errorResponse(req, res, 'Not Found', 404));
}
}
```

As you would expect, the responses from the User Service look like this:

```
{
  "class": ["user"],
  "properties": {
    "content": "
...
"
  },
  "entities": [
    {
      "class": ["user"],
      "href": "//localhost:8183/user/alice",
      "rel": ["item"],
      "type": "application/vnd.siren+json",
      "id": "alice",
      "nick": "alice",
      "email": "alice@example.org",
      "password": "a1!c#",
      "name": "Alice Teddington, Sr.",
      "dateCreated": "2016-01-18T02:12:55.747Z",
      "dateUpdated": "2016-02-07T04:43:44.500Z"
    }
    ...
  ],
  "actions": [
    {
      "name": "userFormAdd","title": "Add User",
      "href": "http://rwcbook11.herokuapp.com/user/",
      "type": "application/x-www-form-urlencoded",
      "method": "POST",
      "fields": [
        {"name": "nick","type": "text","value": "","title": "Nickname",
          "required": true, "pattern": "[a-zA-Z0-9]+"},
        {"name": "email","type": "email","value": "","title": "Email"},
        {"name": "name","type": "text","value": "","title": "Full Name",
          "required": true},
        {"name": "password","type": "text","value": "","title": "Password",
          "required": true,"pattern": "[a-zA-Z0-9!@#$%^&*-]+"
        }
      ]
    }
    ...
  ],
  "links": [
    {
      "rel": ["self","user","collection"],
      "href": "http://localhost:8183/user/",
      "class": ["user"],"title": "Users",
      "type": "application/vnd.siren+json"
    },
    {
      "rel": ["profile"],
```

```
      "href": "http://rwcbook17.herokuapp.com/user/", ❶
      "class": ["user"],"title": "Profile",
      "type": "application/vnd.siren+json"
    }
  ]
}
```

Note the appearance of the profile link in the response (❶). This is a reference to the POD extension we created in Chapter 6, *Siren Clients* to make it easier to pass domain object information to Siren responses.

Now we need one more base-level service—the Notes Service.

The Notes Service with HAL

I implemented the Notes Service as a standalone single-capability component that speaks HAL. Like the others, the only thing I needed to do to create the service is to strip down the app.js file to only respond to /note/ calls and only return HAL-formatted responses.

> The source code for the standalone Note Service client can be found in the associated GitHub repo (*https://github.com/RWCBook/ms-notes*). A running version of the app described in this section can be found online (*http://rwcbook18.herokuapp.com/note/*).

Here's the top of the app.js file with the new port (8184 at ❶), default media type (❷), and accept processing (at ❸).

```
// shared vars
var port       = (process.env.PORT || 8184); ❶
var halType    = "application/vnd.hal+json"; ❷

var csType     = '';
var csAccept   = '';

// routing rules
var reRoot = new RegExp('^\/$','i');
var reFile = new RegExp('^\/files\/.*','i');
var reNote = new RegExp('^\/note\/.*','i');

// request handler
function handler(req, res) {
  var segments, i, x, parts, rtn, flg, doc, url;

  // set local vars
  root = '//'+req.headers.host;
  contentType = halType;
  flg = false;
  file = false;
```

```
  doc = null;

  // it's a HAL world ❸
  contentAccept = req.headers["accept"];
  if(!contentAccept || contentAccept.indexOf(htmlType)!==-1) {
    contentType = contentAccept;
  }
  else {
    contentType = halType;
  }
```

The routing code also should look very familiar now:

```
  ...
  // parse incoming request URL
  parts = [];
  segments = req.url.split('/');
  for(i=0, x=segments.length; i<x; i++) {
    if(segments[i]!=='') {
      parts.push(segments[i]);
    }
  }

  // handle options call
  if(req.method==="OPTIONS") {
    sendResponse(req, res, "", 200);
    return;
  }

  // handle root call (route to /note/)
  try {
    if(flg===false && reRoot.test(req.url)) {
      handleResponse(req, res,
        {code:302, doc:"", headers:{'location':'//'+req.headers.host+"/note/"}}
      );
    }
  }
  catch (ex) {}

  try {
    if(flg===false && reNote.test(req.url)) {
      flg = true;
      doc = note(req, res, parts, handleResponse);
    }
  }
  catch(ex) {}

  // file handler
  try {
    if(flg===false && reFile.test(req.url)) {
      flg = true;
      utils.file(req, res, parts, handleResponse);
    }
```

```
  }
  catch(ex) {}

  // final error
  if(flg===false) {
    handleResponse(req, res, utils.errorResponse(req, res, 'Not Found', 404));
  }
}
```

And the Note Service responds in HAL, as expected (this is an abbreviated display):

```
{
  "_links": {
    "collection": {
      "href": "http://localhost:8184/note/",
      "title": "Notes","templated": false},
    "note": {"href" : "http://localhost:8184/:note-note"},
    "profile": {"href": "http://localhost:8184/note.pod"},
  },
  "content": "<div>...</div>",
  "related": {"tasklist": [ ... ]},
  "id": "aao9c8ascvk",
  "title": "Sample",
  "text": "this note was created using the Note microservice for the TPS API.",
  "assignedTask": "1l9fz7bhaho",
  "dateCreated": "2016-02-13T19:26:25.686Z",
  "dateUpdated": "2016-02-13T19:26:25.686Z"
}
```

Notice the profile link that appears in the response. This is a reference to the same POD extension that was added to the Siren representation (see "The POD Specification" on page 211) and the collection and note links that can be used to make HAL-FORMS calls (see "The HAL-FORMS Extension" on page 144). Now, this service's HAL response is providing OBJECT metadata (via POD), ACTION metadata (via HAL-FORMS), and the ADDRESSES (via the native HAL _link array).

So, that's all the base-level microservices. The real work is in the next section. That's when we'll modify the Home Service to serve up the TPS client that is able to talk in multiple languages.

One Client to Rule Them All

So, when considering the challenge of creating a single client that can properly interact with multiple microservices, with each service selecting their own representation format, the real question is:

"How hard is it to create a single client that can successfully 'speak' multiple formats?"

It turns out that it is not all that difficult. Especially since we've already done the important work of creating standalone libraries for parsing HAL, Siren, and Cj. All that is needed now is a bit of rearranging, a few snips here and there, and the client libraries we've been working on individually can fit together nicely in a single package.

First, we'll look at the Home Service to see just what role that server-side component plays in all this, and then we'll drill down in the new multilingual client that brings everything together.

The Home Service

The Home Service I created has two important jobs:

- Act as a *gateway* for all the other microservices (Tasks, Users, Notes).
- Serve up the standalone multiformat client that is capable of consuming the APIs of those microservices.

First, when dealing with loosely coupled microservices, it is hard for any one component to know the details about all the others. Instead, most microservice implementations rely on a proxy or gateway to resolve requests at runtime and make sure they end up at the right place.

I didn't want to build a standalone API gateway and I didn't want you to have to select and install one for this book. Instead I wrote a tiny bit of "proxy code" into the Home Service. And here's how I did it.

The source code for the standalone Home Service client can be found in the associated GitHub repo (*https://github.com/RWCBook/ms-home*). A running version of the client app described in this section can be found online (*http://rwcbook15.herokuapp.com/files/home.html*).

First, I hardcoded some addresses for both a local version of the microservices and a remote running version of them:

```
// services
var addr = {};
addr.local = {};
addr.remote = {};
addr.selected = {};
addr.local.taskURL = "//localhost:8182/task/";
addr.local.userURL = "//localhost:8183/user/";
addr.local.noteURL = "//localhost:8184/note/";
addr.remote.taskURL = "//rwcbook16.herokuapp.com/task/";
addr.remote.userURL = "//rwcbook17.herokuapp.com/user/";
addr.remote.noteURL = "//rwcbook18.herokuapp.com/note/";
```

Next, near the top of the app.js for the Home Service, I added a bit of code that inspects the incoming request's host header to see where that request is heading and use that to select a set of addresses:

```
// fix up redirects
if(root.indexOf("localhost")!==-1) {
  addr.selected = addr.local;
}
else {
  addr.selected = addr.remote;
}
```

Finally, whenever a consumer of the Home Service makes a call to one of the related services, I redirect that call to the proper standalone service component:

```
// task handler (send to external service)
try {
  if(flg===false && reTask.test(req.url)) {
    handleResponse(req, res, {code:302, doc:"",
      headers:{'location':addr.selected.taskURL}});
  }
}
catch(ex) {}

// user handler (send to external service)
try {
  if(flg===false && reUser.test(req.url)) {
    handleResponse(req, res, {code:302, doc:"",
      headers:{'location':addr.selected.userURL}});
  }
}
catch(ex) {}

// note handler (send to external service)
try {
  if(flg===false && reNote.test(req.url)) {
    flg = true;
    handleResponse(req, res, {code:302, doc:"",
      headers:{'location':addr.selected.noteURL}});
  }
}
catch(ex) {}
```

Now the client hosted by the Home service doesn't need to know anything about *where* these other services are located. It just makes a call back to the Home service (e.g., /task/). Upon receiving the client request, the Home service selects the proper URL and passes that URL back to the client (via a 302 Redirect request). The client then uses this new URL to make a direct call to the running microservice.

In this way, the Home service does not handle the microservice requests, just the ones specific to the Home service. The remainder of the Home service is dedicated to serving up the HTML SPA container and associated JavaScript files for the client. We'll look at that next.

The Multiformat Client SPA Container

The first thing to review is the HTML SPA container for our multiformat client. It looks similar to previous containers except for one thing. This container has bits of markup from the three previous containers all in one.

I'll review the SPA container in a few key snippets. The first one is the top of the HTML `<body>` section. It contains a fixed menu area (❶) that holds a set of relative URLs—one for each service. There is also a "shared layout" area (❷) that holds the `title`, `content`, and `error` elements. The fixed elements are new for our clients, but the other sections should look familar.

```
<!DOCTYPE html>
<html>
  <body>
    <!-- fixed menu -->
    <div id="menu"> ❶
      <div class="ui blue fixed top menu">
        <a href="/home/" rel="home" class="item" title="Home">Home</a>
        <a href="/task/" rel="task" class="item ext" title="Tasks">Tasks</a>
        <a href="/user/" rel="user" class="item ext" title="Users">Users</a>
        <a href="/note/" rel="note" class="item ext" title="Notes">Notes</a>
      </div>

      <!-- shared layout --> ❷
      <h1 id="title" class="ui page header"></h1>
      <div id="content" style="margin: 1em"></div>
      <div id="error"></div>
    </div>
    ...
```

The next three markup blocks in the HTML container match up to the three media type formats this client understands. For example, here is the markup for handling Collection+JSON responses:

```
<!-- cj layout -->
<div id="cj" style="display:none;">
  <div id="c-links" style="display:none;"></div> ❶
  <div style="margin: 5em 1em">
    <div class="ui mobile reversed two column stackable grid">
      <div class="column">
        <div id="c-items" class="ui segments"></div> ❷
      </div>
      <div class="column">
        <div id="c-edit" class="ui green segment"></div> ❸
        <div id="c-template" class="ui green segment"></div> ❹
        <div id="queries-wrapper">
```

```
      <h1 class="ui dividing header">
        Queries
      </h1>
      <div id="c-queries"></div> ❺
    </div>
   </div>
  </div>
 </div>
</div>
```

Note the callouts show Cj-specific elements for links (❶), items (❷), an edit block (❸), the template (❹), and queries (❺).

The next markup block in the client is for rendering Siren responses where the callouts identify the siren links (❶), properties (❷), entities (❸), and actions (❹):

```
<!-- siren layout -->
<div id="siren" style="display:none;">
  <div id="s-links"></div> ❶
  <div style="margin: 5em 1em">
    <div class="ui mobile reversed two column stackable grid">
      <div class="column">
        <div id="s-properties" class="ui segment"></div> ❷
        <div id="s-entities" class="ui segments"></div> ❸
      </div>
      <div class="column">
        <div id="s-actions"></div> ❹
      </div>
    </div>
  </div>
</div>
```

Then there is the HAL section of markup which holds the links, embedded, and properties (❶, ❷ and ❸, respectively). There is also an element to hold all the input forms (❹) for HAL interactions:

```
<!-- hal layout -->
<div id="hal" style="display:none;">
  <div style="margin: 5em 1em">
    <div id="h-links" style="margin-bottom: 1em"></div> ❶
    <div class="ui mobile reversed two column stackable grid">
      <div class="column">
        <div id="h-embedded" class="ui segments"></div> ❷
        <div id="h-properties"></div> ❸
      </div>
      <div class="column">
        <div id="h-form"></div> ❹
      </div>
    </div>
  </div>
</div>
```

I actually could have created a single standardized SPA block of elements that all three of the message formats could use. But, for this sample, I wanted to make it easy to see how each message model maps to HTML blocks. In a robust production app, I'd probably use just one set of container elements—and even those might be dynamically generated at runtime based on the media type of the response.

Finally, at the bottom of the HTML page is a series of references to JavaScript files (❶) —one for each format (cj-lib.js, siren-lib.js, and hal-lib.js) along with the local client files (❷, dom-help.js and home.js). At ❸, you can see the home client firing up and waiting for the next human interaction:

```
<script src="cj-lib.js">//na </script> ❶
<script src="siren-lib.js">//na </script>
<script src="hal-lib.js"?>//na </script>
<script src="dom-help.js">//na </script>
<script src="home.js">//na </script> ❷
<script>
  window.onload = function() { ❸
    var pg = home();
    pg.init();
  }
</script>
```

The Format-Switching Client UI

As you might be able to guess from the way the HTML looks for the client, this app is designed to handle three different media type responses: HAL, Siren, and Cj. The way this works is that libraries for each of them are loaded at runtime and then, as each request comes in, it is routed to the proper library and rendered in the appropriate HTML block. That functionality is contained in the home.js script.

The home.js script is not very big, and there are two parts worth reviewing here. First, at the start of the home.js script, all the other format libraries are initialized and the static page is filled in.

Here's what that code looks like:

```
function home() {

  var d = domHelp();
  var cj = cjLib(); ❶
  var siren = sirenLib();
  var hal = halLib();

  var global = {};
  global.accept = "application/vnd.hal+json," ❷
    + "application/vnd.siren+json,"
```

```
      + "application/vnd.collection+json";

  // init library and start
  function init() {
    cj.init(this.req, this.rsp, "TPS - Tasks"); ❸
    siren.init(this.req, this.rsp, "TPS - Users");
    hal.init(this.req, this.rsp, "TPS - Notes");

    hideAll();
    setTitle();
    setHome();
    setLinks();
    setContent();
  }
```

In the preceding snippet you see where each library is loaded (❶) and then intitial-
ized (at ❸). Note that pointers to this module's Ajax object (`this.req` and `this.rsp`)
are passed to each format library. That makes sure all requests originate from *this*
module where they can be further inspected and then properly routed. You can also
see (at ❷) that the client's HTTP `ACCEPT` variable is initialized to include all three of
the formats this client understands when talking to services.

When up and running, the client code renders this menu and a bit of static content,
then waits for user clicks (see Figure 9-1).

Figure 9-1. Rendering the home screen in the multiclient

Another important element in this snippet is at ❷. This line of code sets the default
accept header for our multiformat client by loading it with all three formats this client understands. Now, each initial request to any of the services will have the following value for the `accept` header:

```
Accept: application/vnd.hal+json, application/vnd.siren+json,
    application/vnd.collection+json
```

This is the HTTP way for a client to tell a server:

"Hey service, I understand these three formats. Please send your responses as either a HAL, Siren, or Cj message. kthxbye."

It is up to the server to read and honor this request.

The other part of this default request is handling the response and routing it to the right library. In the home.js client code, the routing between libraries happens in the HTTP request handler. There, the library inspects the content-type header and routes the incoming response accordingly:

```
function rsp(ajax) {
  var ctype

  if(ajax.readyState===4) {
    hideAll();
    try {
      ctype = ajax.getResponseHeader("content-type").toLowerCase();
      switch(ctype) {
        case "application/vnd.collection+json":
          cj.parse(JSON.parse(ajax.responseText));
          break;
        case "application/vnd.siren+json":
          siren.parse(JSON.parse(ajax.responseText));
          break;
        case "application/vnd.hal+json":
          hal.parse(JSON.parse(ajax.responseText));
          break;
        default:
          dump(ajax.responseText);
          break;
      }
    }
    catch(ex) {
      alert(ex);
    }
  }
}
```

The code just shown looks very similar to the representor.js code we've seen in the server-side implementations used throughout the book (see "Implementing the Message Translator Pattern" on page 100). This client code is actually the *mirror* to that server code. That's because this code is an implementation of a client-side representor. It takes the public representation (in HAL, Siren, or Cj) and converts that into the client's base object graph, which is, for human-centric web browsers, the HTML DOM. The important difference is that the server-side representor uses the client's accept header to route the internal object graph to the proper representor. And the client-side representor (seen previously) uses the server's content-type header to route the external representation to the proper library to convert that message into a local HTML DOM for display.

This is an important design pattern for implementing loosely coupled interactions between components on a network. They share a common structured message model (HAL, Siren, Cj) and send them back and forth using a clear metadata tag to help receivers identify the message model. It is up to each party (providers and consumers) to do the work of translating between their own internal object models and the format-based shared message models.

Once the routing is decided, the entire response is passed to that library's parsing routine to handle all the translating and rendering. So, let's take a quick look at the media-type libraries for this client.

The Cj Render Library

In the following Collection+JSON render library (cj-lib.js) snippet, you can see the init() and parse() routines. At ❶ the init routine accepts the pointers to the shared ajax handlers. Once the rsp handler in home.js receives the server response and routes it back here (via the parse method), the incoming Cj message is stored (❷) and the response is rendered (❸) just as in the dedicated Cj client. After all the rendering is done, the <div id="cj">…</div> block is revealed (❹) to wait for human interaction. It's the classic Request, Parse, Wait (RPW) interaction pattern from Chapter 5 in action:

```
// init library and start
function init(req,rsp) { ❶
  global.req = req;
  global.rsp = rsp;
}

// primary loop
function parse(collection) {
  var elm;

  // store response
  global.cj = collection; ❷

  //render ❸
  dump();
  title();
  content();
  items();
  queries();
  template();
  error();
  cjClearEdit();
```

```
// show
elm = domHelp.find("cj"); ❹
if(elm) {
  elm.style.display="block";
}
}
```

Figure 9-2 shows what the actual HTML UI looks like when handling Cj responses from the Task Service.

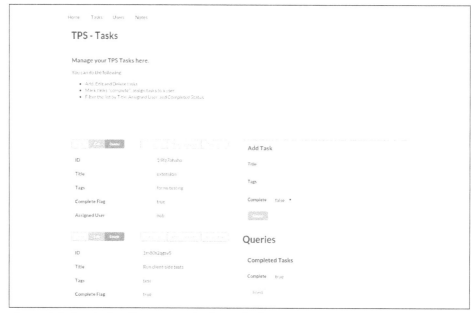

Figure 9-2. Rendering Cj responses in the multiclient

The Siren render library

The Siren `parse` routine looks similar (including the "reveal" code at ❶). You'll notice the `title` is passed in from the `home.js` routine. This is an optional item that covers the lack of a built-in `title` element in Siren. When using differing response formats in the same UI, there will naturally be some variances in the UI details, so adding these optional elements helps:

```
// init library and start
function init(req, rsp, title) {
  global.req = req;
  global.rsp = rsp;
  global.title = title||"Siren Client";
}

// primary loop
```

```
function parse(sirenMsg) {
  var elm;

  global.sirenMsg = sirenMsg;

  sirenClear();
  title(),
  getContent();
  dump();
  links();
  entities();
  properties();
  actions();

  elm = domHelp.find("siren"); ❶
  if(elm) {
    elm.style.display="block";
  }
}
```

Figure 9-3 shows the same client rendering Siren responses from the User Service.

Figure 9-3. Rendering Siren responses in the multiclient

The HAL render library

And finally, the HAL `parse` routine (see the following code). By now, it should all seem rather straightforward. The pattern is simple: initialize the library with request and response pointers; when a request is routed into the library, render it as you usually do and then reveal the results for the human to deal with.

Here's what the HAL initial code looks like:

```
// HAL init library and start
function init(req, rsp, title) {
  global.title = title||"HAL Client";
  global.req = req;
  global.rsp = rsp;
}

// primary loop
function parse(hal) {

  global.hal = hal;

  halClear();
  title();
  setContext();
  if(g.context!=="") {
    selectLinks("list", "h-links");
    content();
    embedded();
    properties();
  }
  else {
    alert("Unknown Context, can't continue");
  }
  dump();

  elm = domHelp.find("hal");
  if(elm) {
    elm.style.display="block";
  }
}
```

Figure 9-4 shows the rendering of HAL responses from the Note Service.

Again, the exact details of the UI vary depending on which response format is returned. This is natural. Just as we get varying UI displays when moving from one website to another with our default client (the web browser), we'll likely experience the same varying UI experience when we move from one microservice to another while using our multilingual client.

An Experiment for the Reader

The microservices I implemented are actually able to deliver their functionality in more than one representation format. For example, the Task Service can speak HAL and Siren just as well as Cj. What do you think would happen to the multiformat client if you simply change the response formats of the microservices at runtime? If the client and microservers are coded properly, the apps would function just fine (although there'd be minor UI experience differences).

Figure 9-4. Rendering HAL responses in the multiclient

Let's wrap this up with a short summary of what we learned in this chapter.

Summary

After all the work creating dedicated UI clients for each of three selected hypermedia formats (Chapter 4, *HAL Clients*, Chapter 6, *Siren Clients*, Chapter 8, *Collection+JSON Clients*), this chapter brought that all together in a single user interface experience. We now have a single API client application that can talk to services in one of three message formats. And to make it all possible, we decomposed our TPS web API into three standalone, single-capability microservices, each making their own decision on which format to use for responses. We saw that—with just minor changes in our standalone media type libraries—we were able to use previous code libraries as plug-ins for our single multilingual client app:

Handling multiple formats

It should be clear that adding support for another media type (e.g., Atom, UBER, Mason, etc.) is not at all that daunting. For clients, we just need to do the same work of building up a working client-side rendering library and add it as another plug-in for this client. For servers, we need to implement the patterns covered in Chapter 3, *The Representor Pattern*. Then both client and server can use HTTP metadata (`accept` and `content-type` headers) to trigger translations from shared messages to internal object models.

Adapting to changes via metadata

One of the things we were able to learn from these experiments is that, in order for clients to successfully adapt to changes on the server, two things must be present. First, servers must promise to only introduce backward-compatible changes—ones that will not invalidate existing implementations. Second, clients must be able to acquire their knowledge of OBJECTS, ADDRESSES, and ACTIONS from metadata in messages—not from source code. It is the power of recognizing and processing metadata in responses that provides clients with the ability to adapt.

Supporting backward compatibility

We also saw that both service providers and API consumers were coded to encourage backward-compatibility and reduce the occurrence of breaking changes by applying the rules we covered in Chapter 7, *Versioning and the Web*.

Leveraging interaction design

The examples in the book all focused on implementing the RPW loop for human-centric client applications. As mentioned in Chapter 5, *The Challenge of Reusable Client Apps*, our hypermedia clients were designed to implement a version of Verplank's DO-FEEL-KNOW loop. They rely on humans to handle the FEEL (sense) and KNOW (decide) elements while the machine (the client app) handles the DO step. Building clients that can also handle FEEL and KNOW steps will require implementing some level of additional understanding into the client app—something that is certainly possible but outside the scope of this book.

In some ways, we've come full circle. We pointed out in Chapter 1, *Our HTML Roots and Simple Web APIs* that the initial power of the web browser was that it was able to connect to any web server, anywhere with any additional editing or alteration. That's because the web browser relied on the HTML hypermedia format to understand the interaction design of the web server. The HTML browser does very well on the OAA Challenge.

However, as web-based APIs became commonplace, developers ended up creating an interaction design that weakened the ability of clients to adapt to changes in OBJECTS, ADDRESSES, and ACTIONS resulting in a reliance on the kinds of JSON-only clients we saw at the start of the book. These clients soundly failed the OAA Challenge!

But, as we saw over the last several chapters, there are now a handful of powerful structured message formats (HAL, Siren, Cj, and others) that allow developers to re-capture the ability to build adaptable clients—ones that do well on the OAA Challenge. And that can lead to more freedom and innovation for services, too.

Hopefully, this last chapter has given you some ideas of your own on how you can use media-type libraries as plug-ins to improve the flexibility of your own API clients and how you can use hypermedia to improve their adaptability over time. Finally, you may now have some ideas on how you can start creating machine-to-machine clients that can create their own specifications for solving a problem and interpreting responses at a more meaningful level. Then, you'd have API consumers that can go further and last longer without the need for direct human interaction at every click and turn along the way.

But that's an adventure for another time.

Bob and Carol

 "Well, Bob. It's been an interesting week."

"Yes, Carol, it has. We learned quite a bit when we decom-posed our single TPS web API into a set of standalone microservices."

 "I was surprised at how easily we could turn our standalone client libraries into plug-in components for a single univer-sal client."

"Yes, and as I look at your team's client code, it seems that it wouldn't be too hard to add support for another hyperme-dia format in the future, right?"

 "That's right. We really have a new kind of client platform now—one that can be safely extended over time."

"Hm... that's a good point. Now our service teams are also free to build components at their own pace without endangering existing clients, too."

Interesting. We've both learned to build more loosely coupled components but have come to the same conclusion by doing almost the opposite of each other."

"Really? How do you mean?"

"Well, while your server-side team was busy breaking up your web API into separate microservices, my client-side team was working to bring all our separate client implementations into a single multiformat deliverable."

"Huh, that's right. Using hypermedia formats lets *my* team limit the scope of each service and allows *your* team to expand the reach of a single client."

"And we were able to reduce overall client code by increasing the amount of metadata in the message. That's been an important lesson."

"You know, Carol, I wonder if we can apply these same lessons to some of our machine-to-machine applications. They take a lot of non-reusable custom code right now."

"Well, Bob, maybe we should go visit with the M2M teams and talk to them about it."

"Not a bad idea, Carol. I'll try to set something up sometime soon. In the meantime, my server team has a whole bunch of new microservices they'd like to start building."

"And there are lots of improvements we can make to our client plug-in platform. See you next week to talk about progress, Bob?"

"Sure, Carol. See you again next week."

References

1. Fowler maintains a landing page (*http://g.mamund.com/qscaj*) for the microservices topic at his public blog.

2. Adrian Cockcroft's slides and a video of his "State of the Art in Microservices" (*http://g.mamund.com/ycuob*) is a great presentation worth checking out.

3. Read more about Eric Evans and DDD on the Domain Language website (*http://g.mamund.com/nnvgn*). Fowler also has a page about Bounded Context (*http://g.mamund.com/ysqgo*).

4. You can read a PDF scan of the original foreword to the 1978 *UNIX Timesharing System* online (*http://g.mamund.com/zumsf*).

5. The book *Microservice Architecture* (O'Reilly) is a solid introduction to the general topic of microservices in an organizational context.

Epilogue: Welcome to Your Future

"The best way to predict the future is to invent it."

—Alan Kay

Bob and Carol

"Nice party, eh? My name is Bob."

"Hi Bob. I'm Carol. So, you're the guest of honor, right? Congrats on the acquisition and welcome to BigCo."

"Thanks. It was just a small startup—nothing ground-breaking. We just had good timing, I think."

"Well, everyone here is talking about your API provider skills and looking forward to seeing it in action."

"And I've heard lots of great things about you, too, Carol. You've been involved in quite a few high-impact client-side projects here."

"Yep. I, too, have had good timing!"

"Well, I'm anxious to get started on something new here. Maybe we'll be able to work together on a project soon."

"I'd like that, Bob. We've been working on our TPS HTML app for a while and I think it's time to take it to the next level."

 "Hm. Sounds interesting. Maybe we both have another high-impact project in our future."

"You never know what the future holds, Bob."

 "No, Carol, you never know."

Project List

This appendix contains the list of projects in the *RESTful Web Clients* GitHub repository (*https://github.com/rwcbook*). You can use this as a cross-reference back to the code examples in the book. This is accurate as of the release date of the book.

You can also use this as a standalone guide to the repository itself. However, over time, this list might become outdated and the best source will be the repository itself. So it will be a good idea to keep an eye on the repository for any additions/updates.

Chapter 1, *Our HTML Roots and Simple Web APIs*

- *https://github.com/RWCBook/html-only* (simple declarative implementation of the TPS website/app)
- *http://rwcbook01.herokuapp.com* (running instance of the HTML-only implementation)
- *https://github.com/RWCBook/json-crud* (initial JSON-CRUD [RPC] implementation of the TPS web API)
- *http://rwcbook02.herokuapp.com/* (running instance of the JSON-CRUD web API implementation)
- *https://github.com/RWCBook/json-crud-docs* (human-readable documentation for the JSON-CRUD web API implementation)

Chapter 2, *JSON Clients*

- *https://github.com/RWCBook/json-client* (JSON client source code)

- *http://rwcbook03.herokuapp.com/files/json-client.html* (running instance of the JSON client web app)
- *https://github.com/RWCBook/json-crud-v2* (updated JSON-CRUD [RPC] implementation of the TPS web API with tag support)
- *http://rwcbook04.herokuapp.com/* (running instance of the updated JSON-CRUD [RPC] web API implementation with tag support)
- *https://github.com/RWCBook/json-client-v2* (updated JSON client source code (V2) with tag support)
- *http://rwcbook05.herokuapp.com/files/json-client.html* (running instance of the updated JSON client [V2] with tag support)

Chapter 3, *The Representor Pattern*

- *http://github.com/RWCBook/wstl-spec* (Web Service Transition Language [WeSTL] Specification)
- *https://rwcbook.github.io/wstl-spec* (WeSTL Specification web page)

Chapter 4, *HAL Clients*

- *https://github.com/RWCBook/hal-client* (HAL client source code)
- *https://rwcbook06.herokuapp.com/files/hal-client.html* (running instance of the HAL client web app)
- *https://github.com/RWCBook/hal-client-active* (HAL client source code with MarkActive support)
- *http://rwcbook07.herokuapp.com/files/hal-client.html* (running instance of HAL client with MarkActive support)
- *https://github.com/RWCBook/hal-client-forms* (HAL client source code with HAL-FORMS support)
- *http://rwcbook08.herokuapp.com/files/hal-client.html* (running instance of HAL client with HAL-FORMS support)
- *https://github.com/RWCBook/hal-forms* (HAL-FORMS specification repo)
- *http://rwcbook.github.io/hal-forms/* (POD specification web page)

Chapter 5, *The Challenge of Reusable Client Apps*

No repositories for this chapter.

Chapter 6, *Siren Clients*

- *https://github.com/RWCBook/siren-client* (TPS API that outputs Siren-formatted responses; Baseline Siren client source code)
- *http://rwcbook09.herokuapp.com/home/* (running instance of the TPS API returning Siren messages)
- *http://rwcbook09.herokuapp.com/files/siren-client.html/* (running instance of the Siren client web app)
- *https://github.com/RWCBook/siren-client-email* (Siren client source code with email feature)
- *http://rwcbook10.herokuapp.com/files/siren-client.html* (running instance of the Siren client with Email feature)
- *https://github.com/RWCBook/siren-client-pod* (Siren client source code with POD support)
- *http://rwcbook11.herokuapp.com/files/siren-client.html* (running instance of the Siren client with POD support)
- *https://github.com/RWCBook/pod-spec* (Profile Object Display [POD] specification repo)
- *http://rwcbook.github.io/pod-spec/* (POD specification web page)

Chapter 7, *Versioning and the Web*

No repositories for this chapter.

Chapter 8, *Collection+JSON Clients*

- *https://github.com/RWCBook/cj-client* (TPS API that outputs Cj-formatted responses; Baseline Cj client source code)
- *http://rwcbook12.herokuapp.com/task/* (running instance of the TPS API returning Cj messages)
- *http://rwcbook12.herokuapp.com/files/cj-client.html* (running instance of the baseline Cj client)
- *https://github.com/RWCBook/cj-client-note* (Cj client source code with Note object support)
- *http://rwcbook13.herokuapp.com/files/cj-client.html* (running instance of Cj client with Note object support)

- *https://github.com/RWCBook/cj-client-types* (TPS API and client with types extension)

- *http://rwcbook14.herokuapp.com/files/cj-client.html* (running instance of Cj client with types support)

- *https://github.com/RWCBook/cj-types-spec* (`cj-types` extension specification repo)

- *http://rwcbook.github.io/cj-types-spec/* (`cj-types` extension specifications web page)

- *https://github.com/RWCBook/cj-suggest-spec* (`cj-suggest` extension specification repo)

- *http://rwcbook.github.io/cj-suggest-spec/* (`cj-suggest` extension specification web page)

Chapter 9, *Hypermedia and Microservices*

- *https://github.com/RWCBook/ms-home* (TPS home service that hosts the multilingual client app)

- *http://rwcbook15.herokuapp.com/files/home.html* (running instance of the multilingual client app)

- *https://github.com/RWCBook/ms-tasks* (TPS Tasks microservice API)

- *http://rwcbook16.herokuapp.com/task/* (running instance of the Tasks microservice)

- *https://github.com/RWCBook/ms-users* (TPS Users microservice API)

- *http://rwcbook17.herokuapp.com/user/* (running instance of the Users microservice)

- *https://github.com/RWCBook/ms-notes* (TPS Note microservice API)

- *http://rwcbook18.herokuapp.com/note/* (running instance of the Notes microservice)

Tools and Resources

This is a list of the hardware, software, and services I used when assembling this book. I found all these tools useful and encourage you to check them out.

Hardware

Shuttle Cube PC
My home-office workstation is a Shuttle Cube PC (*http://g.mamund.com/ekmpm*) with Intel Core i5 Processor, 8 GB RAM, 1 TB disk space, and a dual monitor (Dell Ultrasharp 21") setup running XUbuntu 14.4.

Lenovo Carbon Laptop
When I was on the road, I usually brought along a Lenovo X1 Carbon (*http://g.mamund.com/qwdkz*) with Intel Core i5 processor, 4 GB RAM, 128 GB SSD, and a 14" monitor running Windows 8.1 OS.

Google Pixel
Occasionally I carry a Google Chromebook Pixel (*http://g.mamund.com/xacdb*) Netbook with me. It has Intel Core i5, 8 GB RAM, 32 GB storage, and a 13" touchscreen.

Drawing tools
For this book project, I made a habit of drawing diagrams and flow charts to help me better visualize the ideas in the book. Most of the time I used a simple setup of 3" × 5" unlined note cards and Sharpie-brand Fine Point and Ultra Fine Point pens and then scanned those into the computer. I also occasionally used the Live-Scribe3 (*http://g.mamund.com/ljrfx*) Smartpen and paper to sketch out my ideas and automatically transfer them to the computer for editing and sharing.

Software

gedit

I edited most of this book using a locally installed copy of gedit (*http://g.mamund.com/vdden*). I like gedit because it is a very simple editor and is available on a wide range of OS platforms. I used it both to write the code and the text for the book.

Caret and Caret-T

Thomas Wilburn's Caret (*http://thomaswilburn.net/caret/*) and the related fork Caret-T (*http://g.mamund.com/qpcfo*) editors for Chrome browser and Chrome OS came in handy when I was away from my workstation and needed an easy way to quickly update pages and commit them to the repo.

AsciiDoc

My "go to" format for writing is AsciiDoc (*http://asciidoc.org/*). It's my favorite flavor of the Markdown family of languages and—lucky for me—is one of the supported formats for O'Reilly's Atlas publishing system (see "Services" on page 339).

Node.js

I used Node.js (*https://nodejs.org/*) as the runtime platform for most all the code in this book. It's fast, simple, reliable, and was available on every OS I used when working on the book.

node-inspector

I usually just rely on *alert-debugging* by writing `console.log()` all over any of my source code that happens to be "not working" at the moment. But when I get really serious about debugging, I use `node-inspector` (*http://g.mamund.com/nlzah*).

Tidy

I use Tidy (*http://www.html-tidy.org/*) to review and format my HTML output. This is especially handy when generating HTML from code. When I am not using my own workstation or laptop, I use an online version of Tidy.

sirenlint

I used Kevin Swiber's `sirenlint` (*http://g.mamund.com/amytn*) CLI tool for validating Siren documents. Swiber designed the Siren media type and his tool is very helpful.

curl

I used the `curl` (*http://curl.haxx.se/*) CLI utility to poke at my running API servers. It is especially handy for APIs that don't return structured formats like HAL, Cj, or Siren.

Libraries

I tried to use as *few* external libraries as possible with this book. Even though it meant I needed to write a bit more code and, in some cases, the functionality of some apps is less than production-ready, I think the lack of dependencies makes the code easier to read, install, and support over time.

URI Template JS

I used the URI Template JS (*https://github.com/fxa/uritemplate-js*) to handle RFC6570 URI templates. There are several good libraries out there and I like this one because it works easily as both a server-side NodeJS library and a client-side JavaScript component.

Semantic UI

I really like the Semantic UI (*http://semantic-ui.com/*) CSS libraries. "Semantic is a development framework that helps create beautiful, responsive layouts using human-friendly HTML." The libraries are easy to use and have a minimal impact on plain HTML layout while still offering consistently pleasing interface options. All the client-side examples rely on Semantic UI and I encourage you to look into using it.

Services

Atlas

The book was composed and built using O'Reilly Media's Atlas platform (*https://atlas.oreilly.com/*). This Git-based, AWS-hosted service allowed me to edit, check in, and build my manuscript from anywhere I had an Internet connection—and I did that quite often!

GitHub

I used GitHub (*http://github.com*) to host and manage the source code (*https://github.com/RWCBook*) for this book.

Heroku

All the demo apps from this book were tested (and some are actively hosted) on Heroku's Cloud Platform (*https://www.heroku.com/home*). I used Heroku Toolbelt for deployment.

Tidy

I used John Hendley's HTML Tidy (*http://infohound.net/tidy/*) page to quickly check my generated HTML. While I have a command-line version of Tidy, sometimes I am not on my own machine and Hendley's implementation is clean and easy to use.

Amazon Player

As you will notice if you check the header comments in my source code, I tend to write and code with music as my background. I relied upon Amazon's Music Player (*http://g.mamund.com/enern*) to deliver my cloud-based media from a handful of devices as long as I had an Internet connection.

Index

objects, 59-62
   testing after updating, 77
JSON-serialized objects, 46-47

K

Kelly, Mike, 117
KNOW step (hypermedia interaction loop),
   167-170

L

linked SubEntities (Siren), 183
links
   Cj, 252, 259, 268-270
   HAL, 118, 119, 120, 123, 131
   HTML support for, 39
   lack of in WEB API responses, 54
   react to links principle, 241-243
   Siren, 181, 190, 196
list form URLs, 42

M

Maldonado (Ulm) Model of human-machine
   interaction, 159-161
map-style (hypermedia) clients, 155
Masse, Mark, 56
media type messages, 236-238
message format selection, 227 (see output format selection)
Message Translator pattern, 98
metadata
   adaptability and, 295
   POD extension and, 211
microservices, 301-327
   client that handles multiple formats,
      313-325
   definition, 301
   format-switching client UI, 318-325
   Home Service, 314-316
   multiformat client SPA container, 316
   Notes Service, 311-313
   Tasks Service, 304-307
   TPS web API and, 303-313
   UNIX philosophy and, 302
   User Service, 307-311
modularity, 94
multiformat client SPA container, 316
MUST IGNORE, 223-225

N

non-breaking changes, guidelines for, 226-243
   API designers, 227-229
   client implementors, 235-243
   server implementors, 229-235
non-hypermedia (path-style) clients, 155
Norman, Donald, 155
Note object
   API design, 278
   API service implementation, 279-282
   testing the Note API with existing Cj client,
      282
   TPS API and, 278-284
Notes Service, 311-313

O

OAA Challenge, 59
   Cj, 284
   HAL, 119
   JSON clients, 81
   Siren, 217
OBJECT metadata, 211
objects (see OAA Challenge) (see specific
   objects, e.g.: JSON objects)
Ohno, Taiichi, 155
open-solution apps, 156-159
Orchard, David, 224
output format selection, 85-110
   adapting and translating, 96-99
   assumptions favoring a single format, 91
   Atom Syndication Format, 87
   decision-making process, 86-93
   fallacy of the Right One, 89
   new hypermedia formats, 87-89
   reframing the problem, 90-93
   representor pattern, 93-110
   requirements for supporting multiple for-
      mats, 92
   selection algorithm, 95
   separating format from functionality, 94
   XML vs. JSON, 86, 89
   XMLHttpRequest object and, 86

P

Parkinson, C. Northcote, 56
Parkinsons Law of Triviality, 41
Parnas, David, 94
Pascal's Wager, 221

as websites, 32-33
conversion to web API, 33
web browser, as client, 38
Web Service Transition Language (WeSTL), 98,
    101-109
    and state transitions, 103
    runtime, 105

website, web application as, 32-33

X

XML, output format selection and, 86, 89
XMLHttpRequest object, 86, 161

About the Author

An internationally known author and speaker, **Mike Amundsen** travels the world consulting and talking about network architecture, web development, and other subjects. As Director of Architecture for the API Academy at CA Technologies, he works with companies to provide insight on how best to capitalize on the opportunities web APIs present to both consumers and the enterprise.

Amundsen has authored numerous books and papers. His 2013 collaboration with Leonard Richardson, *RESTful Web APIs* (O'Reilly) and his 2011 book, *Building Hypermedia APIs with HTML5 and Node* (O'Reilly), are common references for building adaptable web applications. Amundsen is also coauthor of *Microservice Architecture* (O'Reilly) with Irakli Nadareishvili, Ronnie Mitra, and Matt McLarty.

Colophon

The animal on the cover of *RESTful Web Clients* is the Asian badger (*Meles leucurus*). These animals are widespread throughout central and northern Asia, where they occupy a range of habitats, including forests, mountain regions, semi-deserts, tundra, and the occasional suburban neighborhood.

Also known as the sand badger, these creatures tend to be smaller and lighter in color than their European counterparts, with coarse, brownish-gray fur covering their stocky bodies. Their faces are white, with dark facial stripes that taper over each eye. They also possess short limbs equipped with strong claws for digging.

The Asian badger's size varies according to region. The Siberian subspecies *Meles leucurus sibiricus* is considered the largest; boars can grow up to 28 inches long and weigh up to 29 pounds.

Sand badgers are sociable animals, hibernating in family groups and living in communal burrows. Mating occurs primarily in the springtime. Sows typically give birth between mid-January and mid-March.

Many of the animals on O'Reilly covers are endangered; all of them are important to the world. To learn more about how you can help, go to *animals.oreilly.com*.

The cover image is from *Shaw's Zoology*. The cover fonts are URW Typewriter and Guardian Sans. The text font is Adobe Minion Pro; the heading font is Adobe Myriad Condensed; and the code font is Dalton Maag's Ubuntu Mono.

Learn from experts.
Find the answers you need.

Sign up for a **10-day free trial** to get **unlimited access** to all of the content on Safari, including Learning Paths, interactive tutorials, and curated playlists that draw from thousands of ebooks and training videos on a wide range of topics, including data, design, DevOps, management, business—and much more.

Start your free trial at:

oreilly.com/safari

(No credit card required.)

www.ingramcontent.com/pod-product-compliance
Ingram Content Group UK Ltd.
Pitfield, Milton Keynes, MK11 3LW, UK
UKHW052357270125
454293UK00007B/130